Reordering Theological Reflection

Reordering Theological Reflection

Starting with Scripture

Helen Collins

scm press

© Helen Collins 2020

Published in 2020 by SCM Press
Editorial office
3rd Floor, Invicta House,
108–114 Golden Lane,
London EC1Y 0TG, UK
www.scmpress.co.uk

SCM Press is an imprint of Hymns Ancient & Modern Ltd
(a registered charity)

Ancient
&Modern

Hymns Ancient & Modern® is a registered trademark of
Hymns Ancient & Modern Ltd
13A Hellesdon Park Road, Norwich,
Norfolk NR6 5DR, UK

British Library Cataloguing in Publication data

A catalogue record for this book is available
from the British Library

978-0-334-05856-4

Typeset by Regent Typesetting
Printed and bound by
CPI Group (UK) Ltd

Acknowledgements

I wish to express thanks to a number of people who have contributed in significant ways to the completion of this book. My colleagues at Trinity College, Bristol have been an enormous source of support, encouragement and challenge through the many ups and downs of the writing process. Particular thanks go to Justin Stratis, Jamie Davis and Jon Coutts for their expertise, humour and willingness to read and comment on draft chapters. Their enduring commitment to rigorous scholarship as worship in service of the Church has taught me how to be a Christian theologian.

The students of Trinity College have been gracious and enthusiastic guinea pigs for my project. Having the classroom as a regular forum to test out concepts and ideas is an immense privilege and I am so grateful to the students for their generous contributions in discussions and through their assignments. I am particularly indebted to the students in my pastoral groups over the years for their questions, prayers and insights, which have continually informed my thinking. The postgraduate community at Trinity has been a vibrant and creative place for working through definitions and concepts of Practical Theology and this is where the idea for this book was first sparked.

As testified to in the Introduction, my growing interest in theological reflection is intertwined with my own vocational journey, to which there are too many contributors to name them all personally. However, particular thanks go to my Christ the Servant colleagues for teaching me how, regularly and faithfully, to pray and read the Bible in church as the only foundation for that which we call Christian ministry.

Finally, my family has made significant sacrifices to give me the time and space that writing needs. Their constant love, support and lack of interest in the details of my research have been vital sources of sanity and joy. Simon, Phoebe, Lydia and Archie will particularly want to see their names in print, even though they will, almost certainly, not read beyond this page.

Contents

List of Figures

Envisaging the Project: An Introduction

My Theological Reflection 'Journey'

The first time I ever remember hearing the phrase 'theological reflection' was when I attended a Bishop's Advisory Panel to discern whether I was being called to ordained ministry in the Church of England. There was an exercise called the Pastoral Letter that candidates had to complete, and one of the criteria for a successful letter was that it 'reflected theologically' on the situation. By this time, I had a BA in Theology and an MA in the Social Anthropology of Religion, but I had never encountered this concept of 'theological reflection' before. In the absence of any guidance, my evangelical instincts assumed that it must mean that I should quote as many Bible verses as possible to back up my pastoral response. Needless to say, the advisors did not think too much of my less-than-pastoral letter!

Upon recommendation, I trained for ordination on a full-time, residential course where I was soon immersed into the world of Corporate Theological Reflections (CTRs). Pattison's significant article 'Some Straw for the Bricks' notes that 'students undertaking placements on pastoral studies courses are bidden with monotonous regularity to indulge in theological reflection' (1989, p. 2), and this was certainly my experience. Every few weeks, my pastoral group would engage in a theological reflection together. Most of the time seemed to be spent selecting the 'best critical incident' to discuss – without much clarity about the criteria for 'best'. Once identified, we had a fairly enjoyable time dissecting the motives, agendas and emotions of the people involved, thinking about relationships and power dynamics and seeking to 'get under the skin' of the incident. At some point, the facilitator would remind us that time was running away and that we needed a theological resource to bring into the conversation. What then followed was usually a confused smorgasbord of biblical references and stories, with varying degrees of justification for their relevance. Again, we would select the 'best' one to discuss, and would try, half-heartedly, to use the skills of exegesis that we were learning in our lectures. It was always a confusing moment for me when someone would start to say, 'I think I can see how this might be a bit like the situation …', and someone else would say, 'Don't start to make any links, we're not at that bit of the process yet!' Invariably, we would have only five minutes remaining before it was lunchtime to try and make the connections between the situation and the biblical passage and we hardly ever had time to identify any actions that should result. Its most valuable contribution seemed to me to be the opportunity to engage in reflective practice, exploring a situation in depth from different perspectives and gaining some insights into other people and ourselves.

Alongside this, I was embarking upon PhD research into the experience of motherhood within charismatic churches and was learning about the field of practical theology in which the research would be situated. My reading led me deeply into practical theology epistemologies and methodologies, theories of application and correlation, hermeneutics, praxis and methods. Within this context, theological reflection came to be mostly associated with theory, model and method as I worked out my own model for reflecting upon and interpreting the data I collected (see Collins 2018). However, these insights in my academic work never seemed able to infiltrate our pastoral group CTRs in any meaningful or helpful way.

Once ordained, I had the privilege to work with other colleagues, and our weekly team prayer meetings became the focus of our theological reflection (although we did not call it that). Each week we would read the lectionary Bible readings for the day and discuss the passages, asking questions of the text and one another, trying to relate it to our ministry situations and then collecting up our reflections in intercession. Our main concern was, 'What does God seem to be saying to us today through this passage and how should we respond?' Sometimes we stumbled upon profound insights, other times we struggled to find any meaning or relevance. In this context, theological reflection became more of a spiritual discipline, a habitual way of thinking and being, as we wrestled with our callings and contexts within the wider Christian story.

Now, I find myself a tutor in practical theology in a theological college that particularly trains students for ministry, and I am responsible for students' practical training and Anglican formation. My main engagement with theological reflection is twofold. First, it is focused on teaching students how to engage with this practice for the purposes of ministerial/Christian formation. Therefore, my interest has evolved to include the pedagogy of how students learn to use the models and methods of theological reflection and how they are formed by them. Second, within our multi-disciplinary faculty, my role seems to have become chief advocate for the theological basis for and legitimacy of practical theology in response to their puzzlement about the discipline. It is in this stimulating environment that this book was conceived.

The Purpose of this Book

This book is an attempt to bring together the various experiences of theological reflection narrated above and to suggest a renewed method and model for theological reflection specifically for theology students and ministerial practitioners who wish to be formed for participation in Christ's ongoing ministry. Its subsidiary purpose is to address the field of practical theology and colleagues in other theological disciplines with a renewed vision for practical theology. Before I introduce this renewed model and method, I outline the issues with which this book seeks to engage.

As a tutor, I regularly encounter students' frustrations with theological reflection, as I described for myself above. This frustration is well documented in the literature. Graham, Walton and Ward observe that theological reflection 'asks the student to perform feats of intellectual and practical integration that no one on the faculty seems prepared to demonstrate' (2007, p. 5). Likewise, Thompson notes that 'people cannot really see what they are being invited to do and how this really can add value to their lives, thought and faith' (2019, p. 7). Research into the effectiveness of training in theological reflection revealed that:

> Concepts and methods of [theological reflection] as understood and taught in training are, at best, irrelevant to the ministry of newly ordained clergy. At worst, they seem to be a diminishing, humiliating, anxiety-provoking academically inspired irrelevance that helps to devalue and 'strip' people of their own reflective skills and identity. (Pattison, Thompson and Green 2003, p. 123)

I do not think that the force of that statement quite reflects my present context, and one might hope that the work that has been done to improve theological reflection teaching in the years since that article was published has had an impact.[1] However, I am still met with groans from students when they are asked to do a written or group theological reflection. In some contexts, reflectors can become frustrated with theological reflection because they feel ill-equipped to draw on the resources of the Christian tradition. Cameron, Reader, Slater and Rowland (2012) observe the success of the 'description' stage of the reflection among their participants but encountered a reticence when attempting to get the group to turn to the Christian tradition for insight. They suggest three reasons for this reticence: (1) seeing the Bible as 'for experts'; (2) doubting the Bible's relevance in their secular contexts; and (3) a hesitancy about sharing the Christian faith with others. However, in my context of training predominantly ministerial students, I find that they (usually) already have an instinct for weaving together their experiences with their beliefs and Scripture because this is how they have been discipled to be Christians in the world. They may do this with varying degrees of exegetical precision or doctrinal orthodoxy, but they are certainly not strangers to the process of desiring to live in a belief-shaped way. Therefore, in my context, theological reflection can often seem as if it is giving students a solution to a problem they do not have. This book attempts to offer a model that coheres with their already familiar processes of theological reflection.

As a tutor, I also regularly encounter colleagues' frustrations with theological reflection for different reasons. The concerns of my biblical studies colleagues in relation to practical theology include its use of Scripture, the place of exegesis, the practice of hermeneutics, the role of history, and the authority of revelation. My systematic theologian colleagues express frustration with practical theology's lack of engagement with the role and work of the Holy Spirit, the activity of God, the place of tradition, the understanding of the Church, and the meaning of 'experience'. Our relatively small faculty means that it is not possible for me as a practical theologian to avoid these questions and concerns by reading and writing only within my sub-discipline. Furthermore, as my students are the same students that sit in their classes, it seems that we are placing the burden upon the students to somehow bring together these differing questions and perspectives. Therefore, this book seeks to reframe theological reflection in a way that will enable students to engage well with the inter-disciplinary nature of theology.

Focusing on the concerns of students and theological educators, as I have done so far, should not be seen as masking the centrality of the Church in the practical theology task. While this book has a particular focus on students of theology, it assumes that these ministerial students are embedded in church communities and are studying theology in order to serve God's mission. I use the term 'ministerial' to refer primarily to God's ministry in Christ. Therefore, 'ministerial students' incorporates both those training for authorized ministry roles and also all those Christians ministering in the world through participating in Christ's ministry. This book is aimed at life-long learners who are engaging in theological study in order to be equipped for worship, mission and holiness, whatever their intended role. The goal of this book is to serve the Church in enabling Christian 'ministers' better to fulfil their vocation to be the body and bride of Christ. I intend this book to facilitate church practitioners, lay and ordained, faithfully and creatively to discern the work and will of God in their contexts, through using a model I have called the 'scriptural cycle'.

The Need for a New Model

So why yet another book on theological reflection methods in the hope of inspiring more animated and informed engagement? Pattison, Thompson and Green's research suggests that for students, 'assessing and evaluating the process, thinking about method and so on is, bluntly, flogging a dead horse' (2003, p. 129). However, theological reflection methods are not neutral processes and it is essential for students to learn the skills of evaluating methods. The epistemologies and paradigms underlying the methods are deeply theological, making implicit claims about God, creation and humanity. *How* we think about the relationship between God, God's Word, and our lives is as important as *what* we think, and the two shape one another. It is the task of theological educators to inspire interest in the *how* as well as the *what*, *why* and *when* of theology, in order to enable students critically and theologically to assess their own worldviews and so be formed as Christians. The proposed 'how' in this book is a method of theological reflection that starts from Scripture.

Already, such a method might be rejected by practical theologians as impossible because beginning with experience has come to define and characterize the discipline. Ward however, problematizes this:

> [Beginning with experience] is asserted as the very basis for the discipline; as such, liberal theology is imposed by force or inserted into the minds of students by stealth. I think students need to be introduced to a range of approaches and

methods, and then they should be allowed to make up their own minds. Doctrinal ways of doing practical theology need to be considered alongside those that start from experience, and both should be regarded as possible ways of approaching the discipline. (2017, p. 5)

It is the 'insertion by stealth' that this book seeks to challenge by making explicit the theological assumptions that underpin the prevailing approaches to theological reflection beginning with experience and by arguing instead for an alternative way of approaching the discipline, through Scripture.

Furthermore, Cartledge carries out an assessment of practical theology from a charismatic perspective and identifies the following problems within the discipline: 'Scripture is used in a limited manner; experience is addressed in a general sense or via specific incidents rather than being placed within spirituality; and pneumatology is largely absent' (2015, p. 58). Therefore, Christians of an evangelical and/or charismatic tradition are likely to find that prevailing practical theology methods do not align with their theological convictions. The context within which I teach would support this assessment and therefore a new model is needed particularly to enable evangelical and charismatic Christians to engage fruitfully with theological reflection.

There are a number of works that describe their practical theology as beginning from a doctrinal and/or charismatic perspective, and this book is aligned to those approaches.[2] However, these works are not particularly accessible to undergraduate students trying to learn the discipline. Furthermore, they do not propose a pedagogical model that helps students easily implement their advocated method. Therefore, the texts most frequently populating undergraduate reading lists are those that offer diagrammatic pedagogic models such as the pastoral cycle or critical correlation methods.[3] I argue in Chapter 2 that these models are problematic for Christian ministry practitioners, particularly those wishing to reflect on their practice from within their evangelical, charismatic convictions.

To summarize, this book argues that existing methods of theological reflection frequently taught to theology students are not neutral. Due to the fact that they begin from experience, the methods contain theological and epistemological assumptions that particularly conflict with the theological assumptions of charismatic, evangelical Christians and are, I argue, in tension with a desire to form all disciples of Jesus for Christian ministry. This is because the frequently used theological reflection methods do not understand the Bible as Scripture, do not attend explicitly to the agency of the Holy Spirit, and do not adequately account for Christian experience. Therefore, there is an urgent need for a new method of theological reflection that foregrounds the authority of Scripture, the agency of the Holy Spirit, and experience defined as testimonies of encounters with Christ. I argue that theological reflection that starts from Scripture is a better way to ensure that these convictions are foregrounded and nurtured. The purpose of such a 'starting from Scripture' method is twofold: first, to give charismatic evangelicals a method and a model that better aligns with their theological convictions; second, to advocate for a method of theological reflection that is more appropriate for the formation of all Christians for ministry than the methods currently employed in theological education. Therefore, this book proposes a method for theological reflection for formation that is a spiritual discipline for discerning the presence of Christ in our contemporary lives in order that we know how to participate in his ongoing work of ministry to the world. A comparable method is evident in the works of some practical theologians, but these works do not offer a model that enables students and practitioners easily to make use of the method. This book proposes a theological reflection method better suited to forming Christians for ministry and also a model to aid in the teaching and use of the method. The proposed five-stage model is called the scriptural cycle and it employs a narrative theology and charismatic epistemology to implement the stated method.

Definitions

It is necessary now to define the various terms that I have used thus far, in order to bring clarity to the unfolding discussion. Readers should be aware that defining terms is always a contested enterprise and it is beyond the scope of this book to go deeply into the discussions and debates that underlie each definition. My intention here is to be explicit about how I am using each term so that the reader is informed about how to understand what follows.

Theological Reflection

Graham, Walton and Ward (2005) show how different methods for theological reflection have been part of the life of the Church from the beginning. However, the phrase is most often associated with the theological sub-discipline of practical theology and is understood particularly to refer to the processes or methods for doing practical theology that have emerged in the twentieth century. Ward defines practical theology as 'any way of thinking that takes both practice and theology seriously' (2017, p. 5). While perhaps true, I do not consider that such a broad definition is very helpful in the context of this book. Ethics is deeply interested in practice, and biblical studies is interested in the historical practices of the early Church. Therefore, both ethics and biblical studies could be considered practical theology according to Ward's definition. In this book, I am particularly interested in how practical theology and its methods of theological reflection relate to Christian ministerial formation. Therefore, I must clarify the different ways in which practical theology has taken 'both practice and theology seriously' in order to focus my argument. There are many attempts to tell the story of the historical development of practical theology and theological reflection and readers may want to refer to those books for a fuller discussion.[4] Here, taking a similar approach to Ballard and Pritchard (2006), I divide this history heuristically, into four related but distinct strands, which I have termed application, correlation, liberation and formation. These different strands are relevant to my argument because of the ways in which the context and concerns of each strand shaped the theological reflection methods and models that emerged from them.

1 Application

Farley (1983) interprets the history of theology through the lens of fragmentation. In the early Christian centuries, Farley argues, theology was always bound up with the life of faith and was rooted in the Church. During the middle ages, the locus of theology moved more towards the universities, but the sense of theological study as piety and faith remained. However, with the Enlightenment came the classification of different theological sub-disciplines. Schleiermacher is famous for categorizing theology into different sub-disciplines in order to professionalize clergy training in a university setting increasingly characterized by specialization. Schleiermacher saw practical theology as the goal and proper outworking of the other theological sub-disciplines. However, for Farley, this differentiation marked the separation of the study of theology from the practice of holy living. Studying theology became a means of clergy achieving professional competence rather than itself 'a salvation-disposed wisdom' (1983, p. 39). This fragmentation created a situation where 'theology' as worked out in the academy needed to be applied to the life of faith in the Church. Thus, practical theology developed as the sub-discipline that sought to reunite the fragmentation between theological theory and Christian practice that developed with the Enlightenment. Therefore, within this strand of practical theology, theological reflection focuses on applying insights from the different theological sub-disciplines to ministerial practice.

2 Correlation

Tracy has been one of the most significant contributors to developing a correlationist approach to practical theology because of his concern to engage in public theology. He is interested in the ways in which theology engages with the public sphere and he sees the task of theology as a form of apologetics, engaging with questions of ultimate reality in the context of pluralism. For Tracy (1983, 1989, 1996), theologians who are committed both to the Christian tradition and to the insights of rational inquiry into the world must find a way to make these two accounts of reality cohere. He argues that this can only be done with a revisionist, critical correlation method where both perspectives interrogate and inform each other. He defines practical theology as 'The discipline that articulates the mutually critical correlation of the interpreted theory and praxis of the Christian fact and the interpreted theory and praxis of the contemporary situation' (1983, p. 62). Therefore, a dialectic is created between 'the Christian fact' and 'the contemporary situation' where both are understood to be equally interpretative realities, constructed from their own theory-praxis dialectic. For Tracy, this should be a mutual correlation where either side of the dialectic critically challenges and interprets the other side.[5] Therefore, within this strand of practical theology, theological reflection focuses on correlating theology with the insights of other academic disciplines.

3 Liberation

Liberation theology arose in the context of 1960s Latin America and has significantly shaped practical theology. Liberation theologians such as Freire (1970), Segundo (1982) and Gutierrez (1988) understood that conditions of poverty, exclusion and oppression were caused by social and institutional injustice. They were influenced by Marxism, arguing that the greatest need of the oppressed is to become aware of the circumstances of their oppression so that they can work together to bring about change. These liberation theologians developed methods of theology that prioritized the perspectives of the oppressed and focused on sociological and economic analysis of their oppressed situation. Freire's pedagogical theory, which is most clearly articulated in his book *Pedagogy of the Oppressed*, focuses on the '*conscientização*' or 'conscientization' of the marginalized, which he describes as 'the deepening of the attitude of awareness' (2017, p. 82), where the oppressed become aware of the social, political and economic realities of their lives, and engage in action to transform these realities for their liberation. He saw education as the means for conscientizing the poor to the realities of their oppressive situation in order to bring about the just transformation of society. Such an approach to education, developed by Freire and other liberation theologians, emerged into what is now commonly known as the pastoral cycle within practical theology. This method of theology-in-action (cf. Graham, Walton and Ward 2005) is focused upon ensuring faithful and just action and has as its goal the implementation of actions that promote human liberation from oppression. Therefore, within this strand of practical theology, theological reflection focuses on analysing situations for the sake of transforming injustice.

4 Formation

Ballard describes how until the 1960s, pastoral theology in Britain was focused upon giving 'hints and tips' (2000, p. 62) to aspiring clergy as to how to conduct the pastoral parts of their role. This type of skills-based training did not engage with wider theoretical questions and assumed a Christendom context. Graham similarly charts this pragmatic approach to pastoral theology and argues that through the twentieth century pastoral care became 'shaped by a paradigm of individual counselling' (2002, p. 56). She argues that in more recent decades the greater focus upon the laity and upon feminist perspectives has challenged this clergy-centred, skills-focused approach to pastoral theology. However, while there may have been a shift away from skills-based training for clergy, this has been replaced by a focus on formation as reflective practice. Frances Ward (2005) examines how this focus on reflective practice and life-long learning has become central to theological education in the Church of England. Ward argues for the importance of supervision within this understanding of formation and draws on Kolb's (1984) action-reflection cycle as the model for supervision. Therefore, within this strand of practical theology, theological reflection focuses on acquiring skills for ministry and reflecting on ministerial practice.

This categorization of four strands of practical theology demonstrates the pluriformity of 'theological reflection' and the fact that any simple definition risks masking the related but distinct histories, methodologies and aims of the diverse sub-discipline. One of the central arguments of this book is that the theological reflection methods arising out of the first three strands have been co-opted for use in the fourth strand of formation and that this has been to the detriment of theological education for Christian formation, especially for charismatic evangelicals but also for all Christians engaging in ministerial training. All of these four approaches – applying theological truths, correlating with other disciplines, liberating the oppressed and reflective practice – are valuable and necessary contributions to theology. However, methods from the first three strands have frequently been employed uncritically in the task of the fourth strand of formation for the purpose of reflective practice.

This book is situated particularly in the fourth strand of practical theology for formation, but it seeks to redefine this strand of the sub-discipline as that which is concerned with discerning encounters with Christ and participating in his ministry, rather than with skills acquisition or reflective practice. Mudge and Poling define 'formation' as 'the total process by which a given expression of Christian faith – as a company of persons in community in a given setting – comes to be and perdures in *endures* the world' (2009, p. xvii). Similarly, I am concerned with the way Christians in community, in a particular context, emerge, endure and mature as disciples of Jesus Christ and participate with Christ's ministry in, to and for the world. I see theological reflection as the central process or spiritual discipline by which this is achieved. As I have stated, by 'ministry' I am not concerned with only authorized ministers or pastors, but primarily with Christ's ministry. Therefore, a focus on 'ministry' includes all Christians who are called to encounter God in their lives and participate in Christ's ongoing ministry. Ministerial formation is therefore concerned, in its broadest sense, with the processes that enable Christians, individually and corporately, to grow in encountering and participating in Christ's ongoing ministry in the world.

Evangelical, Charismatic

Labels are always contentious and contested but, in my view, also helpful for locating people and their work within a particular discourse. The term 'evangelical' may describe a theological, historical or cultural phenomenon. My primary concern is with a theological understanding, in which 'evangelical' means those 'who affirm Scripture as the authoritative Word of God and accept the creeds of the early church as accurate reflections of the gospel' (Webber 2002, p. 14). In addition to a strong emphasis upon the 'intrinsic authority and trustworthiness of the Bible' (Kings 2003, p. 171), Bebbington (1989) identifies three additional key traits that are still regularly used to define an evangelical worldview, these being (1) 'crucicentrism' – the centrality of Jesus' death on the cross for understanding salvation and redemption; (2) 'conversionism' – the importance of personally encountering and accepting God's salvation offered through Jesus' redemptive death; and (3) 'activism' – a focus upon sharing the good news of Jesus' salvation with other people, through proclamation and deed. Chapter 3 explores further how I understand this evangelical focus on Scripture as the authoritative word of God.

The word 'charismatic' comes from the Greek word *charismata*, meaning 'grace gift', and relates to the gifts of the Holy Spirit, first given to the early Church on the day of Pentecost. A charismatic/pentecostal spirituality emphasizes the contemporary working of the Holy Spirit with particular reference to these identified gifts.[6] I therefore use charismatic/pentecostal to mean a spirituality and theology of expectation, that God can be encountered in the world through the mediation of the Holy Spirit and which is evidenced by the gifts of the Spirit. I prefer to use 'charismatic' instead of 'pentecostal' in defining my approach, even though I draw heavily on pentecostal scholarship. This is due to my location outside of the Pentecostal denomination and in recognition of the differences that ethnicity and social class have had upon the development and practice of charismatic and pentecostal spiritualities.[7] Hocken (2002) identifies nine constant characteristics of a charismatic spirituality: a focus on Jesus; praise; love of the Bible; a belief that God speaks today; commitment to evangelism; an awareness of evil; spiritual gifts; an eschatological expectation; and spiritual power.[8] Chapter 4 explores further the theological basis for assuming a pentecostal/charismatic approach to theological reflection.

It is my conviction that the method for practical theology proposed in this book is applicable across denominations and church traditions. Labelling it 'charismatic, evangelical' is descriptive not prescriptive and is intended to locate it within a discourse rather than in any way to further tribal traditions. I anticipate that those who are already familiar with an evangelical, charismatic spirituality and theology will find it more comfortable to inhabit the proposed method, at least initially. However, such students are cautioned not to make too many assumptions that their own understandings of the labels are consistent with my usage in this book. Such readers may need to work hard to ensure that they use the model with the necessary humility, discernment and critical rigour to overcome their preconceptions. Readers who are less familiar with 'charismatic, evangelical' spirituality, I invite you to persevere. If you possess some conviction that the Bible is important and that Christ is somehow at work in the world by the Holy Spirit in ways we can discern and encounter, then I trust in God's grace that you will find at least some meaning and transformative life in this model, even if you are passionately committed to the priority of experience. It is my conviction that the proposed scriptural cycle model is more appropriate for use in the formation of women and men as Christians for participating in Christ's ministry, whatever their spiritual tradition, in comparison with the models and methods currently used within theological reflection. This is because the other methods are primarily oriented not towards relationship with Christ for the purposes of participating in Christ's ongoing ministry (see Chapter 2) but towards other goals informed by the particular strand of practical theology within which they developed. I argue that all vocational theological education, whatever tradition it is shaped by, should focus primarily on discerning Christ's ongoing ministry for our participation, and the scriptural cycle model is one way of nurturing and forming this discernment.

For now, it is sufficient to state that my charismatic, evangelical approach to theological reflection is not about applying the Christian tradition to experience, or correlating theology with other disciplines, or primarily liberating humans for their flourishing, or a means to form clergy into competent reflective practitioners. Rather:

Theological reflection is the spiritual discipline of corporately studying the Scriptures to discern and testify to the Holy Spirit's initiation and mediation of our contemporary encounters with Christ for our participation in Christ's ongoing ministry in the world.

The remainder of this book attempts to expound and justify this description.

Method and Model

Finally, definitions are required to differentiate the terms 'model' and 'method', which can often be used interchangeably in theological reflection textbooks. Whitehead and Whitehead helpfully distinguish model and method so that, for them, 'a *model* of theological reflection provides an image of the elements that are involved' and the '*method* describes the dynamic or movement of the reflection' (1995, p. x). Their model is a triangle diagram which represents how three elements – the religious tradition, experience and the surrounding culture – are to be brought together in conversation. Their method has three stages – attending, asserting and pastoral response – which guide how the conversation unfolds. O'Neill and Shercliff (2018) note the confusion that exists in the literature on theological reflection with terms such as models, methods, processes, styles and approaches, often used without clarification or differentiation. They build on Whitehead and Whitehead in using 'model' to refer to 'the sources that are to be used' and 'method' to refer to 'the steps by which correlation or conversation is established between the sources' (2018, p. 11). They illustrate this differentiation by saying that the pastoral cycle is a model and Laurie Green's (2012) *Let's Do Theology* is a method based upon the pastoral cycle model.

However, I have found that despite these attempts to clarify the differences between model and method in theological reflection, students remain confused. Therefore, for clarity, I will be using the terms in the following way throughout this book. Method relates to the stated methodological assumptions: the epistemologies, paradigms and theological convictions of the proposed evangelical, charismatic approach to theological reflection focused on encounter and participation. My method is therefore to start theological reflection from Scripture and foreground the agency of the Holy Spirit. Model refers to the particular suggested 'how to' process for implementing the method. My model is therefore the scriptural cycle discussed in Chapter 6. Undoubtedly, there will be other models ('how to's') for achieving the stated method (starting from Scripture/ Holy Spirit) but this book proposes one such example, in the hope that through its use, readers might be able to cultivate the stated methodological instincts and develop their own models.

Chapter Outline

Having given some of the vision and context for the proposed project, I now use a building metaphor to describe the contents of each chapter. This metaphor of building has become integral to the self-understanding of theological reflection, following Pattison's (1989) article entitled 'Some Straw for the Bricks', in which theological reflectors were likened to the slaves in Egypt trying to build without the materials they needed. In this book, I take on this building metaphor to highlight my concern for methodology. Building is much more than having straw and bricks – it requires an architect, a location, permission, foundations and a framework before any bricks are made or laid. The building imagery in these chapters therefore shows how I see each chapter relating to the others and to the whole. Time-poor students may be tempted to skip ahead to the chapter that outlines the model (Chapter 6) and examples of its use (Chapter 7) in order to get their 'straw' to write an assignment or use the model. However, the building metaphor makes explicit that the model does not exist in isolation from its methodological convictions and that ignorance of the preceding steps will likely consign students to being theological labourers rather than co-constructors.

Chapter 2, 'Clearing the Ground', prepares for building by examining the dominant methods and models of theological reflection described in key undergraduate textbooks. I describe and assess popular versions of the critical correlation method (from strand 2 of practical theology) and the pastoral cycle model (from strand 3 of practical theology). I then outline eight critiques of these approaches to show that they are not neutral tools but rather are informed by a host of methodological and theological assumptions, which I show to be in tension with charismatic, evangelical convictions. I assess an alternative method to practical theology that may seem potentially analogous to my work (Killen and de Beer 2002) but which I argue is not. I then outline the method called Canonical Narrative Theology by Graham, Walton and Ward (2005) as this is the theological reflection tradition within which my 'starting from Scripture' method is situated. Finally, I conclude Chapter 2 with a discussion of whether starting points should matter in theological reflection.

Chapter 3, 'Laying the Foundations', recognizes that before a building can be constructed it requires firm and appropriate foundations for the task. I contend that for any theology wishing to be considered Christian, it is Scripture that is the authoritative, foundational basis, the starting point from which any theological project must begin and against which it must be assessed. I assume that some readers will find this position problematic, and potentially incompatible with practical theology, and so therefore, I give an explanation of and justification for this evangelical faith conviction. The chapter explores why the Bible should be considered authoritative, and explains this in terms of the Bible as realistic, unifying narrative, following Frei (1974) and Lindbeck (2002, 2009). I draw on Wright (1992), Brueggemann (1978, 1993) and Loughlin (1996) to nuance and illustrate further this approach, particularly as it relates to formation for ministry. I then assess a number of critiques that have been made of this understanding of Scripture and seek to address the objections raised. The chapter concludes with outlining five principles for how theological reflectors can read the Bible as unified narrative.

Chapter 4, 'Consulting the Architect', continues the methodological discussions by arguing for a pneumatology for theological reflection. This chapter examines the influential works of Browning (1996) and Graham (2002) to show how the agency of the Holy Spirit has often been ignored within practical theology. I analyse three pentecostal/charismatic practical theologians: Anderson (2001), Root (2014) and Cartledge (2015), who each develop a pentecostal approach to practical theology that gives account of God's agency through the Holy Spirit. These works have been significant in informing the focus on encounter and participation in Christ's ministry in my own method. Finally, I discuss the work of Johns (1998) and her advocacy of a pentecostal pedagogic model for formation, which I have drawn on in the formulation of my scriptural cycle model.

Chapter 5, 'Selecting the Materials', focuses on theological reflection by analysing the role of experience in theology. I expound an understanding of testimony as a necessary source for theological reflection, in an asymmetrical interrelationship with Scripture, and I briefly discuss some of the methods needed to access testimony as source. I then examine three specific roles that experience, as reflected upon in other academic disciplines, plays within theological reflection: complexifying our testimonies; diversifying our reading of Scripture; and interrogating our church practices. This is in order to enable accountability and reflexivity so that our participations in Christ's ministry are for the world. I make some brief comments about the role of tradition and reason within my method, and finally I examine the story of the road to Emmaus in Luke 24 to illustrate how the interrelationship between Scripture and testimony works in theological reflection.

Chapter 6, 'Building the Structure', describes the proposed scriptural cycle model for implementing the method. The chapter begins with a discussion of four characteristics for my theological reflection method, drawn from the discussions of Chapters 3, 4 and 5. I then describe the step-by-step process that is designed to fulfil the identified methodological aims. In summary, the model begins with a worshipful, community-centred engagement with Scripture to see what the passage reveals about God, God's interactions with the world, and God's story of who we are. In the second phase the Holy Spirit is invited to bring to our attention a Testimony of a particular life situation to which the passage speaks and which warrants further reflection. This leads into the third phase, a deeper Discernment of the encounter with Christ through the interaction of the Scripture passage and the identified testimony, drawing in insights from other disciplines as appropriate, to complexify, diversify and interrogate the discernment process. The fourth phase is called Encounter and focuses on weaving the threads together, discerning the specific encounter with Christ's ministry which the Holy Spirit has illuminated through the passage and the testimony. The fifth phase is Participation and focuses on discerning how we participate with Christ's ministry now that we have encountered it. The cycle returns to Scripture to enable the ongoing process of reading the Bible to discern the faithfulness of our participation and potentially to examine the interpretation of Scripture that has been used.

Chapter 7, 'Moving In', describes four detailed examples of the model in action in different contexts: a pastoral group reflection on the experience of exile through Isaiah 40—41; a ministry team reflection on a food bank ministry through the Good Samaritan in Luke 10; a personal, devotional reflection on Psalm 23 and the use of social media; and a faith explorers' group examining the body of Christ from 1 Corinthians 12. The chapter concludes with a step-by-step guide as to how a facilitator might lead a group in using the model, with specific questions to focus each stage of the process.

The chapters in this book are not intended to offer the definitive perspective on the issues, but rather to establish the conversations that practical theology urgently needs to be having within the sub-discipline. Having outlined the key questions, this book is an attempt to offer perspectives particularly in relation to an evangelical, charismatic spirituality and theology and an attempt to highlight concerns for theological education for ministerial formation. As I have said, the primary audience for this book is students of theology, but not for the sake of enabling them simply to gain a qualification. My interest in theology students is an outworking of my deep commitment to and love for the Church, which many students of practical theology will give, and already have given, their lives to serving. The Church is desperately in need of truly *theological* reflectors who are confident in discerning how they encounter Christ in order to participate in his ministry and who can enable others to engage in that process of discernment with intelligence, passion, humility, academic rigour and faithfulness. If this book can in any way contribute to that vision, then to God's name be the glory.

Notes

1 For examples, see: Graham, Walton and Ward (2005), Cameron, Bhatti, Duce, Sweeney and Watkins (2010), Cameron, Reader, Slater with Rowland (2012), Miller-McLemore (2014), Ward (2017), O'Neill and Shercliff (2018) and Thompson (2019).

2 For example, see: Anderson (2001), Cartledge (2003), Purves (2004) and Root (2014).

3 For example: Whitehead and Whitehead (1995), Killen and de Beer (2002), Ballard and Pritchard (2006), Green (2012) and Thompson (2019).

4 For example: Woodward and Pattison (2000), Part 1, Graham, Walton and Ward (2005), Ballard and Pritchard (2006), Chapter 3, Miller-McLemore (2014), Part IV Section 3.

5 See Heyer (2004) for a discussion of how Tracy's correlational method has developed in his writings from this earlier articulation.

6 I only capitalize 'pentecostal' when I am referring specifically to the Pentecostal denomination. On most occasions, I use the term

'pentecostal' to describe a theology, spirituality, epistemology and/or Christian tradition that sees the work of the Holy Spirit at Pentecost as its central hermeneutical lens (cf. Yong 2017).

7 Hocken (2002, p. 477) defines the Charismatic Movement as 'the manifestation of pentecostal-type Christianity outside of the Pentecostal denomination'. The impact of race and class upon the practices of pentecostal and charismatic spiritualities is discussed in: Land (2010), Suurmond (1994), Cox (1995) and Hudson (1998).

8 Key texts for understanding the Charismatic Movement in Britain include: Buchanan (1977), Church of England (1981), Smail, Walker and Wright (1995), Goldingay (1996), Scotland (2000), Steven (2002), Ward (2005), Cartledge (2006), Bonnington (2007) and Drake (2014).

2

Clearing the Ground: An Appraisal of Theological Reflection Education

Introduction

On many undergraduate practical theology courses, students are frequently required to make use of different models/ methods of theological reflection and to analyse and evaluate their strengths and weaknesses. This chapter argues that these methods are not neutral but contain implicit theological and epistemological assumptions. I assess what these are in order to show that they are often incompatible with a commitment to the authority of the Bible and the agency of God's Holy Spirit. Graham, Walton and Ward's (2005) book *Theological Reflection: Methods* has become a classic in the field, tracing seven different methods of theological reflection through the history of the Church and into the present time. For each method, the chapter includes an outline, a critical evaluation, questions for reflection and an annotated bibliography, and it is a useful resource for students learning the discipline. However, I consider that the diversity of methods presented in this book is actually rather limited. All but one of the seven methods are united by an overarching methodology of excavating human experience for theological insight. Each method begins with a different source for accessing that experience – personal writing, stories, corporate reflection, public life, praxis, and local culture – but the movement of each reflection is from experience to theological reflection for an outcome. The exception to this would seem to be Canonical Narrative Theology (2005, ch. 3), which uses a similar methodology to that which

I am proposing in this book and so it will be discussed in more detail later in this chapter. Thus, while the initial sources for theological reflection might seem diverse, their methods are quite similar. Therefore, reflectors do not have sufficient opportunity to engage critically with different methodological approaches, and students wishing to reflect from different theological assumptions have a limited range of options.

In this chapter, I assess two popular 'beginning from experience' methods of theological reflection to make explicit the theological assumptions they contain. These two methods are (1) critical correlation (Graham, Walton and Ward call this Speaking of God in Public), which is an example of the correlation strand of practical theology, and (2) the pastoral cycle (which Graham, Walton and Ward call Theology-in-Action), which is an example of the liberation strand of practical theology. I have chosen to focus my analysis on these methods for two reasons. First, these methods both have simple diagram models to illustrate how the reflection takes place, for example, Whitehead and Whitehead (1995) for critical correlation and Green (2012) for the pastoral cycle. I suspect that these methods have become so dominant within practical theology because they offer models for students newly learning the discipline of theological reflection that are simple to teach and to use. Models can be formulaic and rigid, but they can also act as stabilizers or scaffolding, giving a step-by-step approach that students can easily replicate in their own work when they are learning. The aim of this book is to provide a model informed by different methodological convictions to expose and critique the unchallenged assumptions of the dominant methods.

Second, these methods have been selected for analysis because the assessment criteria in my higher education institution assume a critical correlation or pastoral cycle method for written theological reflections. I recognize that reader interest in the details of higher education assessment administration may be fairly limited, but this is an important occasion where institutional processes seem to be influencing theological reflection in a particular direction. Assessment guidelines and criteria for theological reflection on the courses that I teach assume certain things about the assignment that relate very closely to the two methods discussed in this chapter. For example, they assume that the student begins with a description and analysis of a 'significant experience'. While the guidelines point out that the order is not mandatory, the logic of the assessment criteria heavily influences students to begin with experience. There is then the assumption of engagement with and analysis of a theological resource followed by an assessment of their 'correlation' (a term that implies a particular methodology, discussed below). The final area for assessment is the strength of the proposed new actions resulting from the reflection. Therefore, it seems assumed that students will be using some form of the critical correlation or pastoral cycle method in their written assignments. Given that good teaching practice encourages constructive alignment of learning outcomes with teaching and assessment (Biggs and Tang 2011), it is not surprising that these models come to dominate theological reflection teaching in higher education.

In this chapter, I begin by describing and analysing these two dominant methods of theological reflection – critical correlation and the pastoral cycle – and highlight some issues associated with the teaching and application of them. I then outline eight critiques of the methods to show the theological assumptions implicit within them and to make the case that they are in tension with a charismatic, evangelical spirituality. I highlight an alternative theological reflection method – Canonical Narrative Theology – in order to situate my work within that tradition and show why the scriptural cycle model is a necessary addition. This leads on to a final discussion which focuses on the importance of starting points in theological reflection.

Critical Correlation Method

Chapter 1 gave a very brief overview of this method as developed particularly by Tracy. Graham, Walton and Ward (2005) chart the development of this method from St Paul in Athens

(Acts 17) through Justin and Aquinas to Schleiermacher, and they associate the works of Rahner, Tillich, Tracy, and Whitehead and Whitehead with its contemporary usage. Critical correlation particularly involves engaging with insights from other academic disciplines to analyse and interpret the contemporary context. Tillich was one of the first to advocate such a correlationist method. He did this by finding ways to correlate the 'theory' of the theological disciplines to the practice of the Church. For Tillich, systematic theology's method of correlation 'makes an analysis of the human situation out of which the existential questions arise, and it demonstrates that the symbols used in the Christian message are the answers to these questions' (1953, p. 70). In other words, experience raises questions that theology answers, which then raises new questions. Tillich described this method as a circle, but it is a circle that moves in one direction. Tracy critiqued Tillich's approach because he advocated that rational, critical reflection on experience brought its own 'answers', which needed to be compared with the Christian 'answers' 'to determine their significant similarities and differences and their truth-value' (1996, p. 53). Therefore, there was a need for a mutual critical correlation so that both 'common human experience' and the Christian tradition could be critiqued and revised. Browning (1996) developed this further in arguing that, rather than correlating two distinct poles of 'theory' (tradition) and 'praxis' (experience), praxis is theory-laden. Therefore, there is no Christian tradition apart from that which emerged in the context of praxis. For Browning, all theology is a movement from praxis to theory and back to praxis and so he saw practical theology as fundamental to all theological enquiry.

Fowler (1985) reflects on the works of Tracy and Browning, and on his own chapter in Browning's book (Fowler 1983), to identify four characteristics of their shared critical correlation method. Fowler identifies these four characteristics as: (1) dialectical – the method does not privilege theory over practice, so that practice can critique and challenge theory; (2) revelatory – the truths that emerge from the correlation are implicitly understood as a form of revelation; (3) critical – the method has a clear concern with critical hermeneutics and employs a hermeneutic of suspicion; (4) transformational – critical correlation is aimed towards individual and social change. The critical correlation method is therefore understood to be a critical dialectic between the distinct poles of theory and practice in a way that is considered revelatory and transformational.

This literature on critical correlation is helpful for establishing the theoretical basis for the method but is often too abstract to enable students to put the method to use in their theological reflection practice. Therefore, students' introduction to this method often comes through more accessible versions such as Pattison (1989) and Whitehead and Whitehead (1995), and hence I focus particularly on these approaches. Pattison is concerned that students were being asked to reflect theologically on their courses without being given the resources to do so. He therefore proposes the model of a *critical conversation* to conceptualize and order the process of critical correlation. He envisages theological reflection as a three-way conversation between the self, the Christian tradition and the contemporary situation. Pattison suggests personifying each of these sources as individuals engaged in a dynamic conversation of questioning and learning. He lists a number of benefits of this model, including its living, evolving nature; the possibility for mutual attentiveness and insight; the maintaining of difference and distinction; and its accessibility at different levels of engagement. Pattison also acknowledges the problems with this approach, which include its provisionality, its potential to raise more questions than answers, and the possibility for superficial engagement.

Whitehead and Whitehead's *Method in Ministry* (1995) is a significant example of critical correlation for our discussions, because the authors propose the method for use in the context of pastoral ministry. They therefore take a method concerned with Christian philosophical reflection on meaning and truth (strand 2) and recommend its usage for Christians reflecting on their pastoral ministry (strand 4). Influenced by Pattison's conversation metaphor, Whitehead and Whitehead propose a model of a three-way conversation, with their sources being named as experience, the religious tradition, and the surrounding culture (see Figure 1). Their model is represented by a triangle, with a source at each corner and 'the pastoral challenge' in the centre. They highlight that both the religious tradition and the surrounding culture are diverse and situate the believer/community experience within that pluriformity. Whitehead and Whitehead's model assumes that experience initiates the conversation due to an 'urgent concern, a pressing issue' (1995, p. 9) arising in the context. The authors assert that the religious tradition 'enjoys a privileged position' in their method, but it is not clear how this is achieved in their seemingly mutual triad model.

Figure 1: Theological Reflection in Ministry
(Whitehead and Whitehead 1995, p. 6)

In these versions of the critical correlation/conversation method, there is a focus on identifying and establishing the different conversation partners before bringing them together. In some teaching contexts, I have heard this referred to as the 'stool' or 'chair' model in that each conversation partner represents a 'leg' of the chair, and so they are discussed in isolation before the correlation forms the 'seat'. Simplifying the Religious Tradition and Experience as individuals, or triangle corners or stool legs, implies and perpetuates a dichotomy between 'theory' and 'practice' that Browning's praxis-theory-praxis approach sought to disrupt. Any reading, study or interpretation of Scripture is a Christian 'practice' just as any giving or receiving of pastoral care is deeply 'theoretical'. Moreover, although Whitehead and Whitehead acknowledge the pluriform nature of the religious tradition and the surrounding culture, their representation as different points on a triangle gives a false sense of their singular identity. Unsure which religious tradition to choose, students can end up selecting aspects of the tradition with which the points of connection are either already assumed, or alternatively rather obscure.

Furthermore, the terms 'correlation' and 'conversation' are not always clearly understood and can lead students into difficulties. To correlate something means to make an ordered connection or to establish a relation between distinct entities. It is not always clear on what basis students are able to say 'this is like that' or even 'this is that' in correlating experience or culture to the Christian tradition. Tracy insists that correlation does not mean convergence but 'only the notion that *some* relationship is involved' (1989, p. 563). Thus, Tracy highlights a spectrum of relationship from similarity-in-difference between the Christian tradition and the contemporary situation to non-identity between the two. However, the word 'correlate' places the focus on identification and can cause students to focus on making positive connections (which may or may not be appropriate) and therefore overlook the areas of tension and inconsistency between the tradition and the experience.

The term 'conversation' enables the reflector to envisage a more dynamic process of potential disagreement and difficulty than a correlation. However, it remains a problematic metaphor. People can carry on a conversation at cross-purposes without recognizing the misunderstandings. Also, conversations are complex art forms that take significant work and study to understand the unspoken rules of interaction and this is also true for theological reflection. Many students begin to engage in theological reflection without the necessary theological or sociological grammar and nuance. Pattison (1989) recognizes this and argues that theological reflection should not be restricted only to the theologically trained. He suggests that students should start at their own level and seek to develop more nuanced skills as they learn. However, to ask students to carry out a complex conversation when they are just learning a language may explain why many can find it frustrating or unhelpful. Furthermore, many licensed ministry trainees receive only two years of theological training, maybe throughout their whole ministry, and are not given the opportunity to develop the more nuanced skills. I am concerned that we do them and their churches a disservice by initiating superficial conversations and not continuing formally to equip their deeper engagement.

Another danger with this model of critical conversation comes from Fowler's (1985) characteristics outlined above. The critical dialectic between experience and tradition is understood to be revelatory and transforming. However, this presumably only refers to 'good' critical correlations/conversations (whatever they may be) rather than superficial ones. It is not the case that every critical conversation in which the reflector engages will achieve revelation and transformation just because it is a 'critical conversation'. A claim to revelation and transformation assumes that the reflection will achieve significant outcomes, but how are students to know the difference between a 'good' reflection and a superficial one? On what basis are they to differentiate between revelatory and non-revelatory outcomes? Pattison (1989) notes the need for the outcomes of these reflections to be considered provisional and disposable and recognizes that the revelations and transformations will more often be within the reflectors themselves rather than for the Church or society. Pattison's account potentially limits the possibility for theological reflection to aspire towards a biblical vision of a renewed cosmos by focusing instead on personal reflective practice. It also relativizes all our knowledge of the Creator to that which is true 'in the moment' and limits the possibility for us to acknowledge the enduring reality of God's self-revelation, however imperfectly we may access that (this will be discussed further in the chapters that follow).

In teaching this method to students, I have observed mixed results. Occasionally, useful insights can come from exploring an incident and its surrounding culture in isolation from an aspect of the religious tradition and then correlating the two to reveal transforming future actions. However, as with Pattison, I have frequently noted that these insights are usually more in the realm of successful reflective practice on individual performance rather than new, enduring *theologically* inspired insights for the Church or the world. Leaving aside the occasional success stories, which are indeed significant and valuable but infrequent, most attempts to engage in critical conversation methods seem to result in superficial, uncritical, 'this is that' exegesis of the Bible which fails to achieve discernible revelation or transformation.

The Pastoral Cycle

The other dominant model on theological reflection courses is the pastoral cycle. A brief synopsis of its history within liberation theology was discussed in Chapter 1. As with the critical correlation method, a method for seeking conscientization to injustice for transformative, liberating practice (strand 3) is now frequently used for student reflective practice and the formation of Christians for ministry (strand 4). Such accessible textbooks for students that aim to teach the pastoral cycle model include Ballard and Pritchard (2006), Green (2012) and Thompson (2019).[1] I examine each of these in turn.

Ballard and Pritchard's book *Practical Theology in Action* was originally published in 1996 and the second edition came out in 2006. It begins by laying the foundations for practical theology through discussions of its status as an academic discipline and the relation of theory to practice. Ballard and Pritchard outline four 'models' for practical theology, similar to my four strands discussed in Chapter 1. They then spend the rest of their book explaining the praxis model or pastoral cycle, which they describe as offering practical theology a 'unifying methodology' (2006, p. 128). Ballard and Pritchard identify four stages of the pastoral cycle: (1) Experience – what is presently happening in a given context; (2) Exploration – the systematic analysis of the experience using research methods and insights from other disciplines; (3) Reflection – relating the analysed experience to the resources of the Christian tradition; (4) Action – what should happen now as a result of the insights gained. The book concludes with discussions on mission and spirituality, which they see as essential for the proper application and focus of the method.

Thompson's (2019) *SCM Studyguide: Theological Reflection* was originally published in 2008 and came out of Pattison, Thompson and Green's (2003) research that showed ministers' negative experiences of theological reflection. The textbook offers a range of models, methods, approaches and tools in order to provide students with 'how to' guidelines for theological reflection that are absent in Graham, Walton and Ward (2005). The pastoral cycle remains the dominant model in the textbook, reproduced in various versions. One such version is credited to Andrew Todd and has six stages: Experience, Analysis, Reflection, *Kairos* Moment, Decide, Plan. Therefore, it further expands the Reflection stage of Ballard and Pritchard's model to include a specific moment of insight or inspiration, which they refer to as *kairos*, the Greek word for the right time (as opposed to chronological time). The model also expands the Action stage into Deciding and Planning the appropriate response. Other than these additions, it is congruent with Ballard and Pritchard's approach.

The third version of the pastoral cycle frequently used by students is the pastoral spiral proposed in Green's classic text *Let's Do Theology*, originally published in 1989. Green describes how the impetus for his model came early on in his ministry when there was an 'impenetrable reluctance on the part of academic theologians to mix [theology] with ordinary Christians' (2012, p. vii). Theology was therefore seen as elitist, abstract and irrelevant. Green's intention is to enable 'ordinary' Christians to 'do theology' in a way that is contextually rooted and has the potential for context transformation. Green's four stages are synonymous with Ballard and Pritchard's: Experience, Exploring, Reflecting, Responding (see Figure 2). A minor adaptation is that the cycle does not return to Experience to complete a circle. Rather, it points to a new experience, recognizing that the reflectors do not return to where they started because of the transforming implications of the reflection. A spiral is therefore created so that the process continues through ever new experiences. Green identifies some of the possible criticisms of his model, including its focus on activity at the expense of spirituality; its reliance on group work; its rigid step-by-step process; and it not adequately privileging the Christian tradition. To each he gives a brief response in ways that clarify misunderstandings but he also defends the use of the model.

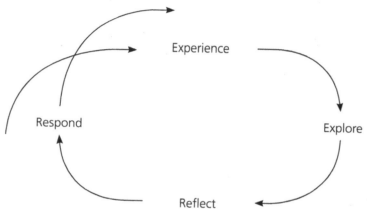

Figure 2: The Doing Theology Spiral (Green 2012, p. 42)

One of the challenges with this model is the lack of clarity about the Reflection stage of the process and exactly how to bring together the experience and Christian tradition. Ballard and Pritchard (2006) suggest a number of models for this stage, including case studies, brainstorming, workshops, stories, art or liturgy, but none of them really get at *how* the process of relating should occur. Green similarly proposes a range of creative approaches and represents this as an additional 'mini spiral' within the overall cycle so that the Reflection stage is its own cycle of Intuition, Verification and New Witness. Green refers to an 'intuitive, imaginative leap' (2012, p. 100) to describe this stage, which is comparable to Thompson's (2019) *Kairos* Moment when the gap between the experience and tradition is bridged by insight. The extent of Green's explanation of this 'leap' is to hope that the group imagination is Spirit-filled while Thompson's 'interillumination' is only vaguely related to hearing the Spirit and focuses more on ensuring open-mindedness and space. Therefore, a pneumatology that could explain this 'leap' or *kairos* moment is lacking. I return to this in Chapter 4.

In these theology-in-action methods, there is a focus on the organic nature of the reflection, in comparison with the more differentiated conversation partners of the critical correlation method. Therefore, there is a focus on the Christian tradition arising out of the exploration of the experience. There is the obvious danger here of proof-texting, as the passage or resource the reflectors assume to be most relevant to the situation is the one that emerges for discussion. All versions of the cycle would advocate for critical engagement with the emerging source, but this relies on good group facilitation, a level of theological expertise, and proficient self-reflexivity, which may not be the case. As with all models, there is the danger that students think they are using it appropriately, but it is just serving to embed their preconceived ideas.

My experience of reading student reflections using the pastoral cycle is again mixed. As with the correlation method, there are occasionally some good examples of reframed thinking, challenged assumptions and reshaped practices as students engage with the process. However, there are equally many formulaic and uninspiring examples drawing on a limited and familiar range of Christian sources doing little to challenge injustice or to reconceive praxis in ways that are creative, transformational and enduring.

Critiques of these Methods

I have highlighted above some potential issues with each method within teaching and its use by students. I recognize that a number of the above critiques may well be accounted for not by a deficit in the models as I claim but rather by the possibility of inadequate teaching, or the unfortunate restrictions of institutional higher education that I identify, such as a focus on assessing theological reflection primarily through written assignments. Ministerial practitioners who have more distance from their accredited theological education may well have much more positive perspectives on the usefulness and worth of these methods and models in their contexts and practice – and I do not wish to detract from that. I am pleased if a practitioner's experience of using these models is more positive than I have described. However, it remains the case that even if the methods have 'worked' in a given setting, in doing so they have imported particular paradigms and epistemologies, and thus there remains value in making these explicit, however 'successful' the reflections have been.

In this section, I focus on eight critiques of these two methods in order to expose their implicit theological assumptions and the implications of these. In so doing, I argue that these methods are in tension with an evangelical, charismatic theology and with an intention to educate and form Christians for Christian ministry. These critiques are in order to clear the ground to make the case for the proposed scriptural cycle model. It is worth reiterating: I am not intending to argue that these methods and related models do not make an important contribution within their particular strand of practical theology. Rather, I am seeking to make explicit the theological assumptions that inform these dominant methods in order to question the legitimacy of using these methods in forming Christians for ministry, particularly those who identify with an evangelical and charismatic spirituality. O'Neill and Shercliff review different models of theological reflection and conclude that 'design is not what is important' (2018, p. 36). However, I would strongly refute that on the basis that models are not neutral; they imply a particular understanding of the relationship between the Christian tradition and contemporary life that is fundamentally a theological claim about humanity, creation and God, and thus comes to shape how we understand and articulate the Christian faith. I highlight five areas that critical correlation and the pastoral cycle seek to privilege: experience, the present, critical incidents, other disciplines, and Enlightenment thinking; and I highlight three corresponding areas that the methods disadvantage: the Bible, Christian experience, and God's agency.

The Privileging of Experience

Many iterations of these methods explicitly prioritize experience in the theological reflection process. Browning (1996) understands experience to be temporally and logically prior to theory due to his praxis-theory-praxis dialectic and thus experience should always be the starting point for the correlation. Likewise, Graham (2013) notes that congregations are not 'blank slates' into which God's revelation comes in a pure form; therefore experience has to have primacy because it is through experience that people access the religious tradition. Other versions of these methods see the sources on an equal footing with one another and do not give priority either to experience or to the religious tradition, for example Shercliff and O'Neill (2018). However, of their four sources, which are drawn from Killen and de Beer (2002) – Tradition, Culture, Experience, Position – three relate explicitly to human experience through social structures, actions, personal convictions and feelings. Therefore, while they might claim that the Christian tradition is an equal source to experience, the conversation is weighted heavily towards human experience. As noted above, Whitehead and Whitehead's conversation model and some versions of the pastoral cycle may claim to give priority to the insights of the Christian tradition. However, when the focus of the conversation begins and ends with experience, the process has given functional priority to experience even while not intending to do so. At the end of the chapter, I discuss the implications of starting points, and in Chapter 5 I look more closely at the proper place of experience within theology. Within this critique, I simply note that the methods discussed do privilege experience, either explicitly or accidentally, and that this has theological consequences.

The prioritizing of experience is clearly seen in the frequently stated goal of theological reflection as 'human flourishing'. Cameron, Reader, Slater and Rowland (2012) make this the title of their book, while Graham (2013) identifies the goals of theological reflection as emancipation, human flourishing and liberation. Leaving aside the contested understandings of what actually constitutes 'human flourishing', I would wish strongly to argue that the well-being of humanity is not the primary goal of theology or the purpose of creation. Of course, human flourishing (whatever it may be) is desirable and important, but it should be a consequence of a rightly ordered relationship with God and not the stated goal. I do not have space in this section to argue for the appropriate goal of theological reflection – which I consider to be discerning the Holy Spirit's invitation to encounter Christ in order to participate in his ongoing ministry (see Chapters 4, 5 and 6) – my point is simply to problematize the popularly understood, and uncritically accepted, goal of theological reflection as 'human flourishing'. To further highlight why this concept might be problematic as the desired goal, it is important to recognize that any focus on human flourishing fails to acknowledge that humans do not only flourish, but also wither, perish and decay as an unavoidable part of the human condition. If theological reflection is explicitly for human flourishing, how can it take proper account of experiences of pain, suffering and death as inevitable in the life of faith?

Furthermore, Cartledge analyses the use of the term 'experience' within practical theology and observes that experience is often assumed to be universal and holistic within the discipline. He argues for two problems that this creates. First, to focus on 'experience' without defining the concept more clearly – is it cognitive, interpretative, relational, affective, passive, interactional, incidental – leads to seeing experience as a universal term such that one assumes such a thing as a 'common human experience'. Cartledge argues that this is too simplistic and therefore fails to acknowledge that all experience is 'mediated via social contexts, languages, and worldviews' (2015, p. 52) and thus even the concept of human experience is never neutral, raw or common. Second, a holistic and all-encompassing view of experience means that the category of religious experience is often not differentiated. This may be seen as an advantage within practical theology, such that all experience can be 'religious' and material for theology. However, failure to distinguish religious experience means that practical theology often overlooks people's encounters with God and fails to see them as qualitatively different and distinct for theological reflection (see Chapter 5).

Moreover, an initial focus on experience in the task of theological reflection implies that the experiential world is the world of the real. Green describes his approach beginning from experience: 'so we begin by trying to become as conscious as we possibly can of the real situation that surrounds us' (2012, p. 19). Such a concept of the experiential as the real would seem in tension with a Christian understanding of reality where 'what is really going on' is only truly comprehended from God's heavenly domain and seen only partially in the physical world through divine revelation (see Chapter 3).

The explicit or functional privileging of experience in the methods used leads to an inappropriate focus on human flourishing as the goal and purpose of theological reflection. It also unhelpfully universalizes experience in a way that ignores religious experiences and interprets the physical world as 'reality' in opposition to a theistic worldview. The methods that start from experience therefore risk placing the contemporary human at the centre of the theological task in a way that has the potential to undermine the right ordering of the Creator/creature relationship.

The Privileging of the Present

A further consequence of the prioritizing of our experience is the privileging of the present within theological reflection. Focusing on a contemporary experience as the grounds for theological reflection obscures the necessary historical and future dimension of all pastoral activity. As has been seen, the pastoral cycle and the critical correlation method are concerned to relate the present experience with the historical tradition and so are concerned, to varying degrees, to orientate our present experiences in relation to the past. As noted, this is often done in ways that privilege our (present) experience over against the insights from the experiences of our fore-mothers and forefathers in the faith. It is understandable to contemporary thinkers formed by enlightenment rationality that the 'now' of our experiences is seen to be more signifi-cant, relevant and normative than the oppressive, patriarchal insights of the past, and thus we prioritize the insights of our present experiences in our theological formulations.

However, this does not take sufficient account of the rela-tionship of the present to the future, which is fundamental to the Christian narrative. The only focus on the future within the theological reflection methods discussed comes in terms of what we will now do in the future as a result of reflecting in the present, such that future action is determined out of the privi-leged vantage point of 'now'. This is at odds with a Christian understanding of eschatology which understands the renewal of all creation and the inauguration of God's eternal kingdom as normative for present action. Anderson (2001) discusses this dynamic and argues that the Spirit comes to the Church from the promised eschatological future of God's perfect and eternal reign over creation rather than only being discerned through the traditions of the Church (see Chapter 4). A Christian eschatological vision therefore makes the prioritizing of the present experience unnecessary and illogical. The present is important and significant as the bridge between the past tradition and the future hope, but it cannot and must not be privileged over against them. The methods under discussion engage with experience in such a way as to privilege the present in a way that does not do justice to Christian eschatology.

The Privileging of 'Critical Incidents'

As discussed, Whitehead and Whitehead's model encourages the reflector to start theological reflection with a particular type of experience, often identified as a 'critical incident'. This is usually understood as a problem or crisis which provokes an emotional reaction and is seen to spark the reflection. Ward uses this focus to critique the pastoral cycle: 'this orientation toward tensions and conflict ... dislocate(s) theological reflection from the ordinary ways in which the Christian church is continually engaged in connecting theology and practice' (2017, p. 100). Therefore, the ordinary day-to-day thinking, praying and reflecting of practitioners is at best implicit and at worst invisible to the models and turns theological reflection into a programmatic response to crises. Cameron, Reader, Slater and Rowland refer to critical incidents as 'triggers' (2012, p. 16) or that which gives the reflection its energy and life. They understand this very broadly and describe how they went about identifying and establishing a trigger for the disparate people involved in their action research as a necessary instigator of the project. However, despite this broad understanding of trigger or incident, the implication is that we initiate the theological reflection process primarily by identifying a source of dissonance.

This focus on problems has two unhelpful implications. First, the selection of any incident for reflection is already an act of interpretation. To choose an event and identify it as a problem is already informed by a host of assumptions, interpretations and theological paradigms that often remain unconscious. Arguably, a 'good' theological reflection exposes these unconscious dimensions as the reflector goes through the process, but this is more reliant upon the skill of the reflector and their capacity for sustained, critical reflexivity than it is explicitly encouraged or enabled by the particular model. The methods under discussion often assume that what has most agitated us emotionally is the problem most in need of reflection in a particular context. This may be the case but is not necessarily so. While I would want to argue that emotions and intuition are indeed important sources of knowledge about the world (see Chapters 4 and 5) and necessary to holistic transformation, they are not authoritative indicators of relevance or meaning, as the focus on critical incidents assumes. Second, a focus on

critical incidents discourages reflections on 'ordinary', functional, ongoing, harmonious or familiar aspects of practice.
This moves us more into a habitus model of theological reflection (cf. Ballard and Pritchard 2006), which focuses on the
role of theological reflection in ongoing character formation.
The focus on critical incidents therefore channels students
towards identifying problems – and then presuming theological
reflection will provide 'the solution' – without necessarily challenging their interpretations that led them to identify it as a
problem, or encouraging reflection upon habitus.

This focus on problems, or 'limit situations' as Freire (2017,
p. 72) might describe them in his context, is an explicit intention of the pastoral cycle model because of its concern with
the liberation of the oppressed. Freire's praxis approach to
education seeks to make the oppressed aware of the political
and social realities that cause their oppression. He calls this
process 'conscientization', where the oppressed recognize the
oppression within their situation and then see themselves as
agents of transformation within those unjust structures. Leaving
aside for now the critique of the Marxist influences upon this
method, we can legitimately ask whether a method designed
to promote the liberation of the oppressed in acting positively
to change their oppressive situations is an appropriate pedagogical process for the educational and spiritual formation of
(predominantly) middle-class Christians for ministerial offices.
Generally, I would suggest that higher education theology
students from the Global North are not primarily in need of
encouragement to become aware of their human potential to
overcome 'limit situations', and that as recipients of higher
education they already have a well-developed assurance of
agency and control in their lives. Rather, in very generalized
terms, the students I work with have a greater need to be 'con-
scientized' about their dependency in relation to God's agency
and the oppression of others that results from their location of
privilege. I return to these themes in Chapters 3, 4 and 5.

The Privileging of Other Disciplines

We have already seen how these methods of theological reflection privilege a present experience of dissonance and how this will influence the process of interpretation. This is further emphasized by the use of other academic disciplines, which is explicitly advocated for in the two methods under discussion. In the Exploration phase of the pastoral cycle, and the Identifying a Pastoral Challenge phase of the critical correlation/conversation, both recommend drawing in insights from other disciplines to aid the interpretation of the identified situation or event. It is then a secondary stage to relate this interpreted experience to the insights of the Christian tradition. In Cameron, Bhatti, Duce, Sweeney and Watkins, it becomes apparent how this primary stage of interpretation using other disciplines is much more natural for their participants compared to the secondary stage of relating the interpretations to the Christian tradition. They observe:

> To reflect on one's own experience is, for the late modern practitioner, instinctively to reflect on one's own subjectivity, one's psychological responses to a situation. The integration of this with the language of faith is often secondary, and struggled with as a problem. (2010, p. 24)

While the insights from other disciplines are important and need a place within theological reflection (see Chapter 5), there is a danger in making it a first step in the process such that the reflector believes the experience to have been 'interpreted' before Scripture or the tradition has an opportunity to shape that interpretation.

One could argue, as Osmer (2008) does, that the secondary move to the tradition is an assertion of the normative status of the Christian faith. He identifies questions to describe each of the four stages of his theology-in-action method: (1) What is going on? (Experience); (2) Why is it going on? (Exploration); (3) What ought to be going on? (Reflection); (4) How might we respond? (Action). This suggests that the turn to the tradition gives it a privileged place by defining what ought to be. However, ordering the questions in this way prevents a theological interpretation of the 'what' and the 'why' of the experience. Theological categories such as creation, sin, redemption, judgement and forgiveness may give more illuminating insights than sociology or psychology into 'what is happening' or 'why it is happening'. The methods under discussion leave little room for theology (and more importantly, the God whom theology is about) to challenge whether the reflector is asking the right question, or whether the sociologically informed interpretation is accurate. Johns critiques Freire's focus on the social scientific analysis of situations. She suggests that 'the realm of "magic and myth" may indeed be more revelatory of the true nature of reality than human critical perception' (1998, p. 44). Social science disciplines are given a prioritized role in interpreting a situation within these models, which prevents theological insights from being able to disrupt the questions or interpretations. This makes the Experience/Exploration stage of the process seem theologically neutral, which is misleading and incorrect.

Ward (2017) further develops this critique in highlighting the Marxist influences upon the developers of the pastoral cycle. He argues that the pastoral cycle assumes that it is the participants' ignorance of the true nature of the situation that leads to their oppression, and that a greater understanding and awareness of the circumstances contributing to their oppression will result in liberating action. Therefore, as Cameron's works above showed, it is often the insights from other disciplines that are assumed to bring the desired revelation and transformation, and thus other disciplines are privileged above theological insights. Chapter 5 explores further the relationship between the Christian tradition and other disciplines.

Furthermore, theological reflection tends to privilege a rather narrow range of academic disciplines in its interpretation of experience. Insights from sociology, psychology and anthropology are usually favoured because of the focus on human action and interaction. Less often, insights from politics, economics, art, geography or history might inform an analysis, yet the use of other disciplines is nearly always limited to the humanities. This bias prevents insights from the natural sciences, for example, being brought into theological reflection. McLeish (2014) has an interesting discussion of the role of faith and wisdom in the development of the natural sciences and seeks to show a much closer integration of theology and science than popular culture often assumes. By ignoring insights about God's creation and focusing only on the social sciences, we risk further privileging our human perspective in the task of theological reflection.

The Privileging of Enlightenment Thinking

This critique builds on and is illustrated by the previous four critiques. The privileging of the present human subject, their perceived problems requiring solutions, and the insights that come through critical, reasoned study of human subjects is characteristic of Enlightenment rationality. Fowler expounds this critique, following Metz (1980), and argues that the critical correlationist practical theology method he is outlining has succumbed to Enlightenment thinking. He states: 'most fundamentally, I believe, these theologies remain trapped in a dialectic in which critical reason tries to overcome the limits of critical reasoning by the mediation of reason alone' (1985, pp. 56–7). He notes how the Enlightenment birthed the concept of the autonomous, knowing subject which relied upon the privileging of critical rationality for its legitimacy to claim truth. This led to the creation and elevation of the hermeneutical method as the grounds for both applying but also assessing the limits of subjective insight. In other words, the Enlightenment produced the concept of the 'critical thinker' as the authoritative knower, but also exposed the limits of the subjectivity of the thinker. In order to get out of this bind, rational critical methods for interpretation were developed and looked to as authoritative, without recognizing that they were created by the same rational subjectivity they were seeking to overcome. Fowler suggests that critical correlation approaches to practical theology have similarly designed a method to overcome the limits of partial knowing in an attempt to establish normative knowledge, and are thus absorbed in Enlightenment paradigms.

Hastings (2007) expands Fowler's critique of critical correlation methods to show how the praxis model has also been affected by Enlightenment epistemology. Hastings examines Chopp's (2009 [1989]) article, which critiques the critical correlationists for being too hierarchical and privileging the interpretations of middle-class congregations. Hastings argues that Chopp uses the same critical rationality in her approach by similarly privileging marginalized communities in place of middle-class congregations. Hastings notes that 'her "praxis" approach is also thoroughly normed by the modernist epistemological hesitancy to posit any "theory of divine praxis"' (2007, p. 11). In other words, Chopp is just as wedded to the authority of the interpreting subject as are the critical correlationalist models; she has simply replaced which subjects should be authoritative. Hastings goes on to show how practical theology's '(1) failure to account for divine agency; and (2) their imprisonment to an Enlightenment rationality' (2007, p. 5) has prevented it being able to engage with the concerns of the global Church. He argues for a greater emphasis on the ecumene (body of Christ) in practical theology and that this requires a shedding of the Enlightenment epistemology.

Johns (1998) similarly critiques Freire's conscientization approach to education from a Pentecostal perspective. She argues that a focus on consciousness-raising is concerned primarily with cognitive awareness of one's situation and does not give sufficient attention to affective or intuitive ways of knowing. The goal of liberationist theological reflection through the pastoral cycle is consciousness-raising through critical, situational analysis, and this creates a hierarchy of knowing that privileges rationality in line with Enlightenment thinking. Johns suggests an alternative, pentecostal pedagogical approach for Christian formation, which is examined in Chapters 4 and 6.

Furthermore, Root notes how practical theology has frequently become captive to a secular paradigm of human actuality to possibility. Root associates this with Aristotle rather than with the Enlightenment but emphasizes how practical theology has tended to assume 'the potential and potency of human action' (2014, p. 118) in its theological formulations. Practical theologians study experience because they consider that human action gives rise to actualities: that there is power, meaning and purpose in human action that can create communities, morality and knowledge about God. While perhaps deriving from Aristotle's concept of praxis, this human possibility to actuality dynamic is consistent with the Enlightenment privileging of the rational knowing and acting subject. Root argues that this understanding is contrary to the doctrine of justification, which regards humans as utterly unable to actualize their desired utopia and therefore in need of a saviour. He suggests that rather than possibility to actuality, practical theology needs to be characterized by actuality through nothingness, the *ex nihilo* of God's creative agency.

In response to this critique, some may point to the *kairos* moment of Thompson's (2019) pastoral cycle or the 'imaginative leap' of Green's (2012) pastoral spiral, which seems to leave space for the transcendence of human reason and the recognition of God's activity. I discuss the disadvantaging of God's agency as the final critique. It is sufficient to note here that even if that is what is happening implicitly in these models, it confines God's activity to the small gap to be bridged, rather than explicitly recognizing God's initiating and sustaining activity throughout the process.

The Disadvantaging of the Bible

If, as I have claimed, the dominant theological reflection methods of critical correlation and the pastoral cycle privilege present experiences of dissonance and their rational interpretation, they therefore disadvantage biblical insights, despite sometimes claiming to give them authority. This disadvantaging happens in three ways.

First, the Reflection stage of the cycle or the Christian Tradition contributor to the critical conversation are usually understood in very broad terms to encompass Scripture, doctrine, church history, liturgy, the lives of saints, and the writings of theologians, past and present. Whitehead and Whitehead (1995) rightly identify the pluriform nature of the Christian tradition. However, this diversity obscures the unique and vital role of Scripture within the life of faith. I am coming from an evangelical conviction that the Bible should be understood as the authoritative word of God's self-revelation and is unique, trustworthy and sufficient as the primary basis for our understanding of God. This is ultimately a faith conviction and cannot be fully apprehended by the Enlightenment rational epistemology discussed above. I discuss this further in Chapter 3, but it is sufficient to state here that even where this faith conviction of the authority of Scripture is not shared by other theological reflectors, the Bible has an indisputable, foundational and necessary place in Christian theology and is the primary text for the Christian tradition and through which that tradition is derived. Therefore, to have models of theological reflection that subsume Scripture within the broad category of Christian tradition and allow students to do practical theology without necessarily needing to engage with the primary text is problematic for anything claiming to be theology.

Second, even where the Reflection/Christian Tradition stage of the process is focused on the Bible, the fact that it is a secondary step dictates the direction of the conversation in a way that disadvantages the biblical narrative. Students are going to the Bible looking for answers to their own set of questions, and thus the Bible is not able to speak on its own terms. The chosen experience and its interpretation have influenced the selection of the Bible passage and are thus imposing a particular set of assumptions upon what 'the Bible says' about the issue. Given that the Bible is the living word of God via the Holy Spirit (see Chapters 3 and 4), it is of course still possible for the selected passage to challenge assumptions and problematize the accepted interpretation of the contemporary situation. However, the process continues to frame the Bible as the solution to our predefined problem without allowing (God through) Scripture to identify which actually are the relevant questions or problems for this group of reflectors to address.

Third, the theological reflection methods under discussion assume competent knowledge of the Bible and proficient interpretation skills while doing little to nurture and develop this knowledge and skill. I notice that students frequently return to the same limited canon of texts in their theological reflections – the Good Samaritan (Luke 10.25–37) and the weaker brother principle (1 Corinthians 8) are very popular 'go to' passages for a range of critical incidents. Because the models frequently ask 'what does this passage say to this incident?' or 'what ought to be happening in this situation?' there is the temptation either to short-cut the careful work of exegesis of the passage on its own terms or to turn to familiar passages where students can assume the connections. Therefore, the Bible is disadvantaged by the models that envisage a broad understanding of the Christian tradition and confine the Bible to a secondary stage. Furthermore, Cartledge conducts a survey of the use of the Bible in academic practical theology. He concludes that 'the majority of authors in academic practical theology either use Scripture in a limited manner or not at all' (2015, p. 43). The disadvantaging of the Bible is therefore not only a problem for the specific methods being discussed, but rather appears to be symptomatic of the whole discipline of practical theology.

The Disadvantaging of Christian Experience

As discussed in Chapter 1, practical theology and theological reflection is frustrating for my students, often because it seems to be giving them solutions to a problem they do not have. Theological reflection is in part a response to the fragmentary nature of theology in the academy where biblical studies and systematic theology can be taught and studied without any reference to or interest in the practices of the Church or the lives of actual Christians (strand 1). As a correlation method (strand 2), theological reflection is a response to philosophical questions about meaning and truth in the public context. As liberation (strand 3), theological reflection is concerned to provide ways for the oppressed to reflect on their situation and seek transformation. However, I argue that these concerns are not the primary ones facing Christians engaging in theological higher education for Christian/ministerial formation in the British context.

The students with whom I work are constantly engaged in theological reflection as an outworking of their relationship with Jesus, before they ever begin formal theological education. However, they seldom name their ongoing practices of faith as 'theological reflection'. Village is interested to examine how 'ordinary' Christians – 'those who have not been trained in academic biblical scholarship' (2007, p. 1) – interpret the Bible. He demonstrates that they constantly engage in the theological interpretation of their lives and actions using a variety of approaches, informed by their personality, their context and their Christian community. Therefore, when my students enter theological education, their concern is that their studies might make them more proficient in what they are already doing all the time: expecting to encounter God and grow in their knowledge and love of God so that they can discern God's ministry in the world and participate in it. The imposition of a theological reflection model can feel like a step backwards in an area where they already have proficiency.

Schon explores the differences between technical rationality and professional knowledge to understand the practical competence of practitioners. He describes reflection-in-action to characterize professional knowledge, which represents how 'our knowledge is *in* our action' (1991, p. 49). The knowledge is often unarticulated and unsystematized, but this does not mean that professional practitioners do not think about what they are doing. He highlights the phrase often used by sports professionals to describe their competence as an experience of 'finding the groove' (1991, p. 54). This 'groove' is not the meticulous application of sports theory, or a conscious decision to act based on technical knowledge; rather it is an embodied and holistic way of knowing that embraces technical knowledge but also transcends it.

Ward draws on Schon's work to critique the pastoral cycle, arguing that Schon's work implies that 'reflection is not so much a method to follow as part of the way that practitioners operate professionally' (2017, p. 101). Schon's work shows that, just like for my students, the process of reflection on action is much more integrated, nuanced and ongoing than the theological reflection models can imply. The popular models are therefore potentially disempowering for Christians who already frequently read and interpret the Bible, who hear sermons and engage in intercession for the world, who encounter God at work in their lives and somehow make sense of those experiences through reflection-in-action. It would be legitimate to ask, if reflection transcends models, why am I trying to propose a new model, which could succumb to the same criticism? In response, I would argue that the scriptural cycle is less a model to be imposed on reflectors and more a description of the type of reflection with which charismatic, evangelical Christians are already familiar and engaged. The contribution of this book is in making that method explicit as a valid and potentially preferable way of engaging with theological reflection for ministerial formation.

The Disadvantaging of God's Agency

The final critique has already been implied in the others and is the logical consequence of the privileging of present problematic experiences, other disciplines and Enlightenment epistemology. Theological reflection models have inadvertently bypassed the possibility of God's sovereign, free and supernatural 'intervention' in the life of faith.

Fowler highlights this 'lack of attention' to divine praxis as a criticism of correlation methods. He suggests that this is due to a concern to correlate the interpretation of the situation with the interpretation of the Christian tradition, which leaves 'no clear affirmation or examination of the priority and objectivity of divine initiative' (1985, p. 56). God becomes 'fossilized' in the Christian tradition and inaccessible in the situational analysis due to the methodological agnosticism of social science. Hastings (2007) puzzles as to why Fowler does not connect together his first and second criticisms, recognizing that the absence of divine agency is directly linked to an Enlightenment epistemology that does away with God in the elevation of rationality and empiricism.

Root similarly sets out to critique the lack of interest in divine agency within practical theology. He describes how practical theology has tended to focus on *phronesis* as the goal of its work. *Phronesis* is an Aristotelian concept that means practical wisdom or knowing from practice. Practical theologians therefore study experience in order to discover, formulate or test the practical wisdom evident in the Church and the lives of its members. Root shows how the goal of *phronesis* is human flourishing because it is oriented towards engaging the practical wisdom for right living. As already stated, the focus on human flourishing places humanity at the centre and thus leaves little space for divine action, initiative or agency as the transcendental reality that comes from outside of ourselves. Root is not following this line of argument in order to propose a purely metaphysical, intangible knowledge beyond and above experience. Rather, he suggests that 'experiences of transcendence, experiences of Jesus coming to us, may actually be concrete and lived ... an event of ministerial encounter' (2014, p. 30). Experiences of God's activity are real, embodied events in the Christian life – and Root has a whole chapter of examples of these divine encounters. While they might not be straightforward to interpret, models that focus on *phronesis* deny the possibility or legitimacy of examining encounters of divine agency because the focus remains on human action. It therefore becomes the practical wisdom that transforms communities rather than God's transcendent agency and activity.

As discussed, some versions of the pastoral cycle have an 'imaginative leap' or *kairos* moment to signify that a part of the reflective process transcends rational explanation. However, as noted, this confines God's agency to the gap, and does not make explicit the potential for God's activity in the identification of the experience, the selection of the relevant passage, the interpretation of the situation or the formulation of responses. The higher education context further problematizes this appeal to divine agency through its expectation of rationally comprehensible, logical and critically defensible claims, such that to write 'God told me' in an assignment would not be viewed favourably.

It is therefore possible, and perhaps even common, to carry out theological reflections without any recourse to prayer, spirituality or expectations of divine encounters. God's activity either becomes conflated with human action or indistinguishable from the wisdom of the Christian tradition. This may not be a problem for some theological reflectors who do not conceive of divine action outside of human activity or the wisdom of tradition. Again, it is a faith position to assert that there is a God who engages with creation and encounters human subjects in experiential ways that transcend rational categorization or empirical investigation. However, a theology that denies divine agency does beg the question of what it even means to say 'God' if God has no independent reality. Furthermore, it fails to account for the real encounters with God to which Christians testify. Moreover, it makes the miraculous events of the incarnation, the resurrection and Pentecost problematic to explain. This book is seeking to offer a method and model that responds to these critiques by privileging the Bible (Chapter 3), divine agency (Chapter 4), and a Christian understanding of experience as encounters with Christ (Chapter 5).

An Alternative Theological Reflection Method

So far in this chapter, I have given significant attention to the critical correlation and pastoral cycle models of theological reflection because these are the most frequently used and taught within theological education. I suggested that this is due to a combination of the simple models associated with these methods and the expectations of higher education assessment criteria. I have argued that the methods are not neutral tools, but rather they contain various theological and epistemological assumptions that are in tension with a charismatic, evangelical theology. The stating of this problem is to 'clear the ground' and create the case for the development of a new method and model that better reflects evangelical, charismatic theological convictions and is potentially better suited to the formation of Christians for participating in Christ's ministry. However, this critical engagement with two particular methods raises the question of whether other methods of theological reflection already exist that prioritize Scripture, Christian experience and divine agency. I briefly examine one such example – Killen and de Beer's (2002) *The Art of Theological Reflection* – which might seem to be analogous to my proposed method but which I argue is not. I then briefly summarize the method within which my work is situated – Canonical Narrative Theology in Graham, Walton and Ward (2005).

It could be argued that methods and models for theological reflection already exist which allow reflectors to begin from any source, and so students can use them to start from Scripture if they wish. Killen and de Beer's (2002) work is one such example. Their method is based on what they call the human 'movement to insight', which they claim is a standard human process of reflection that begins with experience and then explores the feelings associated with those experiences and seeks to illustrate those feelings with an image. Questioning the image or metaphor is what brings insight and leads to renewed actions. From this, they develop a four-stage process of theological reflection which draws on four sources: Experience, Tradition, Culture and Position.[2] Killen and de Beer envisage that the theological reflection may begin from any of the four sources and they provide a step-by-step process for beginning from each source; pages 90–5 show a model that begins with the Christian tradition and may be seen as similar to the scriptural cycle model proposed by this book. In addition, the focus on feelings, images and imagination would seem to distance the method from the critiques of captivity to Enlightenment thinking, and thus the method may resonate with the pentecostal/charismatic approach I outline in Chapter 4.

However, there are a few significant differences between my model and Killen and de Beer's method. These differences would also relate to any of the other pastoral cycle models that claim that the reflector can start from anywhere in the cycle. First, the role of divine agency within the process is unclear. There are references to the insights of the reflection coming to the participant as 'gift' (2002, p. 84), suggesting something external to the reflector. Also, there is a focus on prayer being foundational to practising what they see as a spiritual discipline, implying that they do envisage a place for divine agency in the process. However, they envisage the role of prayer not as encountering God's divine agency but rather as a means to 'nurture and support individual and corporate openness, trust, and courage' (2002, p. 78). Furthermore, they frequently describe how the relevant experience 'comes to mind' (2002, p. 69), or encourage reflectors to 'let the image lead you' (2002, p. 90). The Holy Spirit could be the implied agent behind these inspirations, but that is not explicitly stated, and thus divine agency is at best hidden in the process and at worst it is absent. Second, because the reflection can begin from any of the four sources, their methodology is different from the one I am advocating. While the reflector can start from Scripture, they can equally begin with Culture or Experience and thus risk succumbing to the critiques of privileging experience, the present, critical incidents, and other disciplines, as already discussed. Third, the Christian tradition is understood in the broadest possible terms to include 'any piece of the Christian heritage: a story of a saint, an event from church history, or a bishop's pastoral letter' (2002, p. 90), and thus it does not privilege the uniqueness of Scripture in the way I am seeking to do. Therefore, while Killen and de Beer have one version of a model that seems as if it relates to my scriptural cycle, the underlying methodologies are significantly different.

I now turn my attention to the tradition of practical theology within which my method is situated. As noted in the Introduction to this chapter, Canonical Narrative Theology is one of the seven methods of theological reflection identified in Graham, Walton and Ward (2005). It offers a different methodology from the other methods so far discussed in starting from Scripture and I situate my method within this tradition. Graham, Walton and Ward describe how for this method the story and event of Jesus is the central interpretative paradigm such that theological reflection is not about discovering new contextually appropriate truth but rather about situating the contemporary situation within the wider narrative of God's redemptive purposes. Graham, Walton and Ward trace the development of this method from St Paul's institution of the Lord's Supper – where believers are charged to re-enact the Passion of Christ as the heart of their community life – through to St Francis' Rule, Ignatian Spiritual Exercises and the Anabaptists. Barth is credited with realizing this method through his emphasis on the biblical stories of Jesus as the foundation and judge of human history. The authors show how this method has developed and been put to use through the works of Hans Frei, George Lindbeck, Stanley Hauerwas and Gerard Loughlin.

Graham, Walton and Ward (2005) conclude their discussion with an evaluation of Canonical Narrative Theology, which highlights a number of criticisms of the method. First, they question the turn towards the realistic reading of the biblical narrative, which is characteristic of modernity and, they argue, overlooks the mystical and allegorical readings of Scripture that have also been popular in different times and places. Second, they suggest that the return to a grand narrative is not possible in the radically diverse world we inhabit. Third, they challenge the often oppressive ways in which the story of Jesus is told to privilege certain groups. I consider their fundamental critique of the method to be most clearly expressed when they are assessing Barth's approach: 'Is a theology of *Krisis*, which finds grounds for hope in what lies entirely beyond human culture, really an adequate Christian response to the complex realities of the twenty-first century?' (2005, p. 96). Emphatically, I would want to say 'yes', it is the only adequate response and the very definition of 'hope', precisely in the complex realities of our time. For Root (2014), Christian theology is about possibility *ex nihilo* rather than human potential to actuality: the Creator coming from without to save a world incapable of manufacturing its own redemption. The challenge, as Graham, Walton and Ward suggest, is how to advocate for such a grand narrative without seeming to return to a pre-modern, pre-critical era and how to take proper account of when the narrative has been used to oppress and marginalize. These particular critiques are addressed in detail in Chapter 3. Here, it is sufficient to state that my method sits firmly within this tradition of 'telling God's story' but is distinctive in two ways. First, it offers a model to aid the teaching and learning of such a method, particularly for use in theological education for ministerial formation. Such a model is currently lacking in all the examples of the method they cite, and thus, students of theological reflection often struggle to know how to implement the method in their own work. Second, I draw on the work of Pentecostal/charismatic practical theologians to nuance and foreground the role of God's agency, such that Canonical Narrative Theology becomes not just about *telling* God's story but about encountering Christ and participating in the story of Christ's ongoing ministry.

The Importance of Starting Points

I have made several references in this chapter to the significance of starting points and I have stated, but not yet justified, that theological reflection starting from Scripture is the best way to prioritize the authority of the Bible, the agency of God's Holy Spirit, and a Christian understanding of experience as encounters with Christ. I have stated the need to start theological reflection from Scripture in order to have methods of theological reflection that reflect charismatic, evangelical convictions and are also, I argue, more appropriate for forming Christians for participation in Christ's ongoing ministry. However, as will be clear from the discussion so far, starting points are not straightforward.

Many practical theologians argue that starting points are important but advocate for the need to begin with experience. Browning has been particularly influential in this regard, insisting that experience must be the starting point of all theology in order to be consistent with the logic of human epistemology. Others take a more pragmatic approach to their advocacy for beginning from experience. Cameron, Reader, Slater and Rowland are critical of any model of theological reflection that wants to '"close the loop" as quickly as possible' (2012, p. 24) by bringing in the Christian tradition too early. They consider that this stifles the creativity of the reflection. Likewise, Stoddart observes that 'placing the biblical engagement after personal and social analysis frees the group to a considerable extent from the tramlines of constraining exegesis' (2014, p. 48). It is therefore often assumed within practical theology that, as quoted in Chapter 1, beginning with experience is 'the very basis of the discipline' (Ward 2017, p. 5). Likewise, to start with the Christian tradition is often considered tantamount to a one-directional applied theology (cf. Ballard and Pritchard 2006) and is consequently critiqued for not taking experience seriously. I have argued through the critiques of critical correlation and the pastoral cycle that to start with experience contains theological and epistemological convictions that disadvantage reflectors who wish to reflect from within their theological convictions of the authority of the Bible and the agency of God in the process of reflection.

For some practical theologians, starting points do not matter. Pattison (1989), Killen and de Beer (2002) and O'Neill and Shercliff (2018) propose models of theological reflection where reflectors can start from any source and they claim it does not matter for the outcome where a theological reflection begins. Such a position might resonate with Williams' observation that the theologian 'is always beginning in the middle of things' (1999, xii), and thus even the concept of starting points may be seen as a false perception. This is particularly the case when we acknowledge the interrelationship between tradition and experience. Volf (2010) argues that practices are belief-shaped in that it makes no sense to speak of Christian practices as Christian – such as hospitality, giving, praying and serving – without seeing the narrative of Christ that inspires, informs and directs the practices. These activities are only Christian because of the motivating beliefs that underlie them. Similarly, he shows how beliefs are practice-shaping; to say that 'God cares for the marginalized' is also to commit oneself to live likewise. Beliefs therefore always orientate normative action and do not, indeed cannot, live in isolation from practices. Therefore, we read Scripture from within our experiences and our experiences are informed and interpreted through the faith tradition. They can never be separated in order to start from one perspective in any pure way.

However, to acknowledge this 'beginning in the middle' through the necessary interrelationship of beliefs (tradition) and practices (experience) is not the same as admitting their equal status or interchangeability. Volf argues that because theory, tradition and beliefs are ultimately about the Creator God, it is they that ground the experiences, practices and praxis, not the other way around, stating: 'adequate beliefs about God cannot be ultimately grounded in a way of life; a way of life must be grounded in adequate beliefs about God' (2010, p. 57).

Therefore, beliefs about God, which are practice-shaped and practice-shaping, are given primacy within the interrelationship precisely because of the God to whom they relate. Volf argues that even to say 'God' is to imply our dependency on God and the fact that all life, thought, experience and knowledge begins in God's initiative to create.

Thus, while Williams is correct in that there is no such thing as a pure starting point in God that is distinct from our lived encounters with God, it is a faith assertion that recognizes God as the grounding of our lives and justifies the intention to start from God's story. Starting with Scripture is not a claim to pure, abstract knowledge that exists in isolation from our lives. As I argue in Chapter 4, following Root, theology is necessarily practical but crucially because of the initiative of God's action in ministry rather than because of the logic of human epistemology. Starting from Scripture is not a denial of our embodied reality but is the necessary movement of faith which asserts that God knows best about Godself, creation, and our own lives within that creation, and that this account of reality is most reliably revealed in Scripture. Our theological reflections go first to the Bible as our act of faith, looking for

God to tell us who God is and who we are, so that we are able to see the world rightly and to live within it faithfully. It is in Scripture where we find the language to articulate our encounters with the living God, and through Scripture we develop the ability to discern Christ's present ministry. I argue that it is this evangelical, charismatic theological worldview that is disadvantaged by the other methods of theological reflection. Furthermore, where theological reflection is used in the formation and theological education of Christians for ministry (in its widest sense), it would seem to be much more appropriate for reflectors to use methods that foreground this faith conviction of our dependency on God and that seek explicitly to nurture reflectors' ability to discern, encounter and participate in Christ's ongoing ministry – the very thing for which they are being formed and trained. The next chapter further expounds and justifies this faith conviction for theological reflection to start from Scripture.

Notes

1 Other examples would include: Swinton and Mowat (2006), Lartey (2000), and possibly Osmer (2008), whose method follows the stages of the pastoral cycle but whose model places the stages of the cycle on two-directional, intersecting axes. These approaches further nuance the pastoral cycle in their use.

2 This method has been developed more recently by O'Neill and Shercliff (2018), into a rather complicated, 16-stage model.

3

Laying the Foundations: The Bible
in Theological Reflection

Introduction

I argue in Chapter 2 that theological reflection methods have
tended to follow an Enlightenment paradigm of privileging the
witness of present 'incident' experiences, interpreted through
other academic disciplines, and thus the authoritative role of
the Bible has been disadvantaged in practical theology methods.
This book is proposing an evangelical model for theological
reflection that allows belief in the authority of Scripture to
underpin the process. This is both for the sake of reflectors
with evangelical convictions but also, I argue, a more appropriate model for use in the forming of Christians for ministry.
This is not to reject the worth of other methods that begin
from experience, for example in the context of public theology
or liberation theology, but rather to expose the implicit theological assumptions in these methods and to raise questions
of the appropriateness of their persistent usage in ministerial
formation, especially but not exclusively among charismatic
evangelicals. I argue that the prioritizing of experience, the
present critical incidents, other disciplines and enlightenment
thinking in the correlation and liberation methods consequently
disadvantages the Bible, Christian experience and God's agency
within the process of theological reflection.

   The next three chapters form the theoretical heart of the
book in this process of constructing the proposed evangelical,
charismatic method and scriptural cycle model. They provide
a theological justification for why and how the Bible, the Holy

Spirit and Christian experience should be prioritized within a charismatic, evangelical method of theological reflection for ministerial formation. This chapter attends to why and how the Bible should be prioritized, given the complexities and challenges of its composition and interpretation, and I argue for the use of narrative theology as the basis for this construction. Chapter 4 focuses on why and how the agency of God should be foregrounded, drawing on a pentecostal/charismatic theology of encountering Christ's present ministry. Chapter 5 examines the concept of Christian experience and specifies the particular ways in which it must contribute to theological reflection, through the concept of testimony.

In the conclusion of Chapter 2, I stated that the Bible is God's authoritative story for understanding who God is and who we are. It is therefore an enactment of our faith in God and our recognition of our dependence on God that we begin theological reflection with Scripture. This chapter begins with an account of what it means to say that 'the Bible is authoritative', drawing on Barth and Webster. I assess the insights of narrative theology in the works of Frei and Lindbeck to argue that the Bible is God's story of reality and I give examples of how this perspective has been variously adopted in the works of Wright, Brueggemann and Loughlin. These works illustrate the ways in which a narrative theology should particularly relate to formation for and enactment of Christian ministry. I then engage with some of the criticisms of a narrative reading of Scripture and seek to defend my position in response to them. Finally, I suggest five convictions that should inform the way we read the Bible as an authoritative, realistic narrative and that seek to respond to the criticisms raised.

The Bible as Authoritative

Before engaging in this discussion, it is helpful to clarify what I mean by 'authority of Scripture'. I am not interested here in claims about the 'infallibility' or 'inerrancy' of Scripture, or the debates surrounding those terms.[1] Following Wright, to speak of the authority of Scripture refers to 'the authority of the triune God, exercised somehow *through* Scripture' (2005, p. 17). Therefore, to speak of the authority of Scripture is often a shorthand way of affirming God's authority and priority. It requires the belief that God is uniquely revealed through the pages of Scripture, and the Bible is thus worthy of our trust, obedience and love. To believe in the authority of God exercised through Scripture means to see the Bible as normative for interpreting the Church's thinking about God and all things in relationship to God. I argued in the final section of Chapter 2 that starting points matter and that beginning our theological reflection with Scripture is the way that Christians enact and nurture their faith in God, as revealed in Jesus Christ, and affirm their ongoing dependency upon God. I must now establish on what basis the Bible is to be considered the unique self-revelation of God's authoritative word and therefore the necessary starting point for all theological inquiry.

Barth's *Church Dogmatics* has significantly contributed to an evangelical understanding of the authoritative place of Scripture in the life of faith and thus I shall briefly summarize his argument for considering the Bible to be the authoritative word of God. In response to liberal Protestantism, Barth argues that any knowledge of God is only possible because of God's own self-revelation. Jesus Christ is that perfect and pre-eminent self-revelation of God and therefore the Scriptures are to be considered authoritative in that they point to Christ and the historical events of his incarnate life. Barth describes the Word of God as a threefold form: (1) the revealed Word – Jesus; (2) the written Word – Scripture; and (3) the proclaimed Word – *kerygma*, or gospel of Jesus. These three forms of God's word are distinct but inseparable. Therefore, the Bible is not synonymous with God's self-revelation; rather, it is a witness that points to Jesus Christ and testifies to the truth of his saving death and resurrection that brought about our salvation and reconciliation. The Bible is the means by which the Church accesses God's revelation for the purpose of proclamation and is the source of all authentic recollection about God and God's activity.

Scripture's authority, therefore, lies in the one to whom it bears witness. It is because it faithfully testifies to the gospel of Jesus as preached by the Church that it 'imposes itself' upon the Church (Barth 2009a, p. 105). In one sense, this is rather circular, in that the Bible establishes its own grounds for authority. However, as Barth argues, if there were external verifications of its authenticity that we could examine and critique, we would enter into a 'self-dialogue' whereby we were the arbiters of authoritative truth. Acceptance of the authority of the Bible as authentic witness to God's self-revelation is therefore always a matter of faith. However, Barth is clear that this does not mean that it is our faith that makes the Bible authoritative; rather, it is authoritative because of God's grace-filled action of giving Godself to the human words of Scripture, which is only comprehended through faith. Barth declares that once seen through faith, the Bible proves itself to the believer to be a 'true sign' (2009b, p. 1) in testifying to the saving events of Christ and to God's sovereignty.

In the Bible, the believer encounters the biblical writers who were witnesses to the revelatory word of God, and as such the authors' written accounts 'confront us as living documents of that unique event' (2009b, p. 30). Therefore, while the witness and the revelation are distinct, the scriptural witness sets God's revelation before the reader, and in so doing God's revelation becomes for them 'an actual presence and event' (2009b, p. 7) as they encounter God through the witness of Scripture. Therefore, for Barth, the Bible is authoritative because it is the primary source of knowledge about the saving work of Christ and because it verifies itself as authoritative through its testimony in the enactment and proclamation of faith.

Scholars have consistently wrestled with how a human text may be meaningfully understood as the revealed word of God. Bacote, Miguelez and Okholm (2004) offer the analogy of the incarnation as explanation, such that the text of Scripture is both fully human and fully divine. However, Webster is apprehensive about drawing this analogy because it may threaten the uniqueness of the 'word made flesh' and also risks divinizing the Bible. The Bible is the primary and pre-eminent witness to the divine life and to the perfect relation between divinity and humanity found in Christ. Webster defines God's revelation as 'the self-presentation of the triune God, the free work of sovereign mercy in which God wills, establishes and perfects saving fellowship with himself in which humankind comes to know, love and fear him above all things' (2003, p. 13). He uses the term 'sanctification' to explain how the whole process of writing and compiling the scriptural canon was made holy by God through election and 'inspiration'. The human text of Scripture may therefore be considered as authoritative in that it is God's chosen and sanctified witness to God's gracious self-revelation. For Webster, the Scriptures are uniquely authoritative, not simply because of the content, the authors, or their function in the Church, but because of God's sovereign freedom in willing them to be God's revelation.

Clark (2003) distinguishes two types of authority that characterize an evangelical understanding of God's authority in Scripture. First, God has a moral authority exercised through Scripture, where humanity is to respect and obey God and God's commands because God is the good Creator and therefore the ultimate moral authority on matters of human behaviour. In addition, God has a veracious authority in that God is the 'expert'. In the same way a neuroscientist can be considered authoritative on matters of the brain – and we trust what she says because of her expertise – so God is the veracious authority on matters of Godself and creation. The Bible is therefore normative in this dual sense – moral and veracious – having authority to determine human action and purpose.

In summary, the Bible should be considered authoritative for Christians because it is the elected, inspired and sanctified witness to Jesus Christ as preached by the Church; because the Bible tells us it is authoritative and provides a self-witness verified through faith; and because God knows best about Godself and has willed for this text uniquely to reveal God to creation. Therefore, affirming the authority of God as revealed in Jesus Christ means giving priority to God's elected, sanctified word in Scripture as the pre-eminent witness to God and God's relationship to all things. In the next section, I argue that the way in which Scripture functions as authoritative witness in the life of the Church is as a realist, universal narrative.

The Bible as God's Story

Frei's significant volume *The Eclipse of Biblical Narrative* argues that up until the eighteenth century the Church had always read the Bible as a realistic narrative that gave an accurate account of the whole of reality, and thus was understood as authoritative and foundational for the Christian life. By 'realistic', Frei means that the narrative is history-like, where the characters and their circumstances are not 'a shadow of something else more real or more significant' (1974, p. 14). There is no meaning to be discerned or fathomed beyond the stories themselves and the focus of reading and interpretation was upon how the text shaped and defined the community reading it. Frei argues that this sense of Scripture as realistic narrative was lost during the eighteenth century when the focus became upon whether the stories were factually accurate. Exegesis became about finding the meaning behind the stories, either in author intention or in the concerns of the original hearers, such that this meaning could be detached from the stories themselves. This historical-critical approach led to the Bible no longer being read figuratively or typologically. Typological readings are where earlier stories and characters are seen as types of later ones; for example, Paul's interpretation of Adam as a type of Christ in Romans 5, Christ as the rock in the wilderness in 1 Corinthians 10, or Christ as Isaiah's suffering servant in 1 Peter 2. Historical-critical readings of the canon dismissed the legitimacy of seeing Christ in these Old Testament texts, because signalling Christ could not have been the author's intention or the understanding of the original hearers. Frei argues that the rejection of such readings eroded the unity of the scriptural narrative.

Lindbeck draws heavily on Frei in his argument that the contemporary Church must rediscover this classical, realistic narrative reading of Scripture if Christianity is in any way to recover its 'consensus-and-community-building potential' (2002, p. 202). Lindbeck argues how from the early Church to the Reformation the Scriptures were read as 'the all-embracing story of the present as well as past dealings of the Triune God with God's people and God's world' (2002, p. 207). As the early Church read the Jewish Scriptures through the interpretative framework of the life, death and resurrection of Jesus Christ, the creeds formed to articulate these new Christological and Trinitarian readings of Scripture. Church creeds and doctrines therefore provide the framework within which the Scriptures should be read and interpreted. Such an approach safeguards their unity. Lindbeck argues, along with Frei, that this break-down of reading the Bible as typological, realistic narrative prevents it from speaking to the contemporary situation on its own terms, and as such the Church comes to require expert interpreters. These interpreters come either in the form of specialized exegetes meticulously training in historical-critical methods or alternatively in the form of human scientists, translating the Bible into contemporary idioms. While Lindbeck acknowledges the benefits of both such readings – including bringing clarity about how passages should not be read or highlighting biased readings – he argues that they can never be unifying for Christian communities. This is because historical reconstructions are diverse and fluctuating, as is the present context, and Lindbeck suggests that this explains the reason for the contemporary fragmentation of theology and the Church. Lindbeck's solution to this situation is a return to these classical readings of the Bible where Scripture and tradition provide the required cultural-linguistic framework within which the Christian interprets the whole of reality. However, he argues that we should not return to anti-critical readings of Scripture. For Lindbeck, historical scholarship should inform – but not dictate – the work of interpretation.

A number of biblical scholars have developed their own articulation of a narrative reading of Scripture, and this perspective is foundational for their hermeneutics. I briefly summarize three examples of forms of narrative hermeneutics – Wright, Brueggemann and Loughlin – that have significantly informed my own approach, and particularly give examples of the ways in which a narrative reading of Scripture matters for Christian ministry. Wright critiques the post-liberal approach of Frei and Lindbeck on the basis that their history-like narrative reading becomes too separate from the facts of history. Wright takes a critical realist approach to Scripture, where the story relates to the objective world of history, even if we can only ever have partial access to that 'real' world. I therefore use the term 'realist narrative' as opposed to Frei's 'realistic' to convey both the history-like *and* history-rooted character of the story.

Despite critiquing the history-like approach, Wright makes much of the Bible as the grand story of God. Wright (1992) famously describes Scripture as a five-act play – Creation, Fall, Israel, Jesus and the Church – where the fifth act is still ongoing as we are part of the unfolding story of God's covenantal faithfulness with creation. Whether one agrees with Wright's division of the story in this particular way or not, his analogy of the Bible as a newly discovered Shakespeare play is a useful way to think about how the realist narrative of Scripture functions in the life of faith. In the analogy, the first four acts of the play are written but the final act is unfinished. The actors (Christians) must therefore complete the unfinished play (life) that has already been scripted (the Bible) and performed (salvation history) up to its final act. These actors must continue the performance of the unscripted final act by faithfully improvising the story to its known conclusion (the eschaton). As such, Christians must study the Scriptures as the primary authority for the unfolding story, just as actors would need to study the unfinished play script to determine its ongoing direction. The success of the performance is judged against its consistency with the written script, just as faithful Christian living is assessed against the witness of Scripture. Those engaging in theological education for ministerial formation need methods for theological reflection that equip and nurture reflectors deeply to inhabit and study the script of faith so as to discern the faithfulness of the ongoing performance. That is the way in which the Church discerns its participation in Christ's ongoing ministry. Christian ministers particularly must be confident to do this for themselves and to facilitate others to develop the same skills.

Brueggemann's reading of Scripture employs a comparable narrative approach and focuses on the story's role in forming and enlivening a prophetic imagination in readers. Brueggemann argues that the world as we know it is an 'imaginative construal' (1993, p. 17) and as such can be imagined differently. He sees it as the role of Christian preaching to 'fund' and 'resource' the Christian imagination in order to inspire new imaginings of ourselves, our world and our communities. The story of the Bible enables us to tell our own stories in its terms and thus imagine ourselves differently, as a created world awaiting final consummation. As the Bible is studied and preached, Brueggemann argues that it is the role of ministers 'to nurture, nourish, and evoke a consciousness and perception alternative to the consciousness and perception of the dominant culture around us' (1978, p. 13). Understanding ourselves in this biblically inspired alternative way equips us to live differently in the present and thus recognize and resist the oppressive imagined world we presently inhabit. Brueggemann advocates that this should be done not only by focusing on the larger themes of the biblical narrative but also by reading and preaching the 'little texts' that do not seem to fit comfortably within the wider narrative. Therefore, he recognizes the importance of careful study of individual texts in order to fuel the desired prophetic, world-shaping imagination.

Brueggemann's advocacy for the need to 'evoke a consciousness' is an interesting parallel to Freire's concept of *conscientização* (referred to in Chapter 1 as influencing the development of the pastoral cycle through liberation theology). Freire's concern is with how education can enable the oppressed to perceive the realities of their oppression through situational analysis and then act to bring about change. Brueggemann, on the other hand, argues for a formation that enables Christians to perceive the realities of a situation through inhabiting a scriptural worldview and then acting according to the pattern God sets. I argued in Chapter 2 that it is questionable to use Freire's approach for the education of (predominantly) globally privileged theology students. It is perhaps even more questionable to use it as the dominant method for forming Christians for Christian ministry. My renewed theological reflection method is aimed at the 'conscientization' of Christians in God's story for participation in the ongoing ministry of Christ. I am arguing that charismatic evangelicals in particular, but all students studying theology in order to participate in Christ's ministry, need methods that are oriented to the nurture of this prophetic imagination through the narrative reading of Scripture.

A third example of the relevance of narrative readings for Christian formation is Loughlin's work, *Telling God's Story*. Loughlin closely follows Frei and Lindbeck in articulating the Bible as God's unifying story, but he further develops their arguments by focusing on the 'mutually constitutive' (1996, p. 36) relationship between the Church and Scripture. Scripture makes and forms the Church as the Church lives out Scripture, and so continues God's story. Loughlin sees this happening in two ways. First, Jesus' story continues through the Church in that the Church is his body, continuing his mission and ministry in and to the world. All stories are found in the story of Christ because the end of his story in his promised return will be 'the end of all stories' (1996, p. 84). Second, the Church and Scripture are mutually constitutive because Jesus was resurrected, and therefore is alive and continuing his own story in relationship with the ongoing life of the Church. This is most clearly seen when the Church gathers to celebrate the Eucharist. In so doing, they are rehearsing the Christian story, not only through retelling and remembering but through enacting it and becoming characters and agents in the story. Furthermore, they are taking the story into themselves as they consume the elements, and thus the Church is nourished by the story to continue its performance. For Loughlin, narrative readings of the Bible are both about placing ourselves within the story and also about letting the story form and discipline us from the inside, as we take it into ourselves. Therefore, the way Christians place themselves in God's narrative is by the enacting of that story through the worshipping, witnessing life of the Church, just as the Church constitutes the telling of the story and is told by it. Christian ministry is about being the body of Christ in the world in order to participate in Christ's ongoing ministry. Christian education/formation therefore needs methods of theological reflection that are firmly and explicitly rooted in the life of the Church so as to enable this mutually constituting process.

Some may argue that this mutually constituting relationship between the Church and Scripture is justification for starting theological reflection with either the Church or the Bible. Similarly, if Christ, by the Holy Spirit, is presently ministering in the world and we can encounter that ministry, we can presumably begin our theological reflections from our experiences of Christ. I have already argued at the end of Chapter 2 that there is no such thing as a pure starting point, and that the Church and the Bible, or experience and tradition, or any other similarly expressed dichotomy, is a false one. However, starting from Scripture is the enactment of faith that affirms and trusts God and God's story as the grounding of our lives, and not the other way around. The Bible is God's elected and sanctified witness, which by God's grace provides the most solid ground from which to discern Christ's ongoing ministry in the world. Formation for Christian ministry is therefore about growing in skill, maturity and confidence to stand in the story and see the world and ourselves from its perspective.

So far in this chapter, I have argued why the Bible should be considered the authoritative and unique witness to God, God's interaction with the world, and God's story of who we are and therefore the necessary starting point for our theological reflection. This divinely elected and sanctified witness can be understood to function authoritatively in the life of faith through realist narrative readings of Scripture. This narrative reading sees the Bible as a unified story that encompasses our present and future reality as we perform our lives according to its plot lines and reimagine our world according to its patterns. As the worshipping Church, we place ourselves in its story and let the story be found in us as we participate in the ongoing telling/performance. This interpreting, proclaiming and participating in God's story and Christ's ministry as the body of Christ is what it means to be Christian. Therefore, Scripture is necessarily the starting point for all theological reflection, because it uniquely witnesses to God's world-defining story in which the Church must be found. Theological education for ministerial formation therefore requires methods of reflection that explicitly form Christians as just such interpreters, proclaimers and participants of God's story.

Difficulties with the Bible as God's Authoritative Story

There are a number of criticisms that have been made against these narrative understandings and interpretations of Scripture. I shall now turn my attention to three prominent concerns: the Bible is not a unified narrative; all grand narratives are oppressive; and the particular narrative of the Bible is oppressive. Each critique will be examined, and I present a response to each critique.

The Bible is not a Unified Narrative

Wiles (1987) finds the concept of narrative readings of the Bible problematic because much of the Bible is not in fact narrative in form. He recognizes that narrative readings of the Gospels make sense, but highlights that the wisdom literature is not narrative and therefore argues that it is stretching the concept of narrative too far to describe the whole Bible in this way. Furthermore, Wiles suggests that critical scholarship has revealed the extensive diversity present in the different books of the Bible and the extent to which each writing is the product of its particular context and culture. He therefore questions how, even if all the Bible were narrative in form, it could legitimately be considered one story. He is sceptical of how the diverse books can be considered to point to a unified, coherent 'identity description' of God. He therefore questions what the 'one story' is, given that there could be so many diverse retellings. Finally, he is critical of Lindbeck's idea that the doctrines and creeds of the Church are the interpretative rules for reading Scripture, because, Wiles argues, this prevents the insights of critical scholarship being able to challenge and change traditional interpretations, and so Scripture becomes locked in its own echo-chamber.

Tracy (1990) critiques the realistic narrative reading of Scripture of Frei and Lindbeck because it seems to mirror the concerns of their Anglo-Saxon cultural context. Thus, Tracy suggests, the realistic reading of Scripture grew out of their Western worldview and is not reflective of the fact that the global Church throughout history has read the Scriptures in a variety of non-realistic ways. Tracy highlights allegorical and mystical readings of the Bible that have emerged both pre- and post-Enlightenment and argues that a focus on realistic reading risks elevating a particular cultural hermeneutic above another. Like Wiles, Tracy also highlights the diverse retellings of the Christian story present within the Bible itself. He compares Revelation's apocalyptic story, Luke's salvation history narrative, and John's metaphysical account to argue that there was never one unified Christian story, and that pluriformity is intrinsic to the Christian faith.

In response to similar criticisms, Bauckham (2003) argues that while clearly there are parts of the Bible that are not narrative in form, the overall arc of the story, from creation to new creation, is a sufficient narrative within which the smaller, non-narrative books can be held and interpreted. He also highlights that it is a familiar device within the Bible itself to summarize and retell its own overarching story. He points to Deuteronomy 6.20–24, Joshua 24, Nehemiah 9, Psalms 78 and 105, and Acts 7 as examples of when the Bible retells its own larger story, and thus sees itself as a coherent narrative. Following Frei, Loughlin (1996) acknowledges that the Bible is clearly not a united narrative, given the diversity present in the writings, but he argues that figuration in the story is the way in which it is meaningfully held together and becomes one unified story. Figurations of earlier characters and themes in later stories located in very different cultural and historical settings enable connections to be made through the diverse writings. These figural readings, most often seen between the Old and New Testaments, where Adam, Abraham, Melchezidek, Israel, David's son and Isaiah's suffering servant (to name a few) are all interpreted by New Testament writers as prefigures of that which is fulfilled in Christ. Loughlin and Frei argue that it is this figurative reading that enables contemporary readers also to reinterpret their lives and actions within the unified story: for example, how the story of the Exodus has been frequently used by liberation theologians to tell the contemporary situation of the oppressed. Therefore, not only is the Bible unified through these figural readings, but such figural readings are what enable the Bible to transcend the boundaries of the text and have meaning for all time and situations. Furthermore, Loughlin highlights the difference between story and narrative, expressing how there can and must be numerous different narratives that retell the one story. The Gospels are therefore diverse, situated narratives that retell the one story of Jesus.

In response to the criticism about the Church's reading rules becoming an echo-chamber, insulating its claims from the critiques of those outside, Lindbeck himself acknowledges this challenge. His response is that while translations between religion and culture are necessary no one learns to speak a language only through translations. There is a point at which the speaker must speak and inhabit the language in order to be able to assess and evaluate its usage. Lindbeck argues: 'religions, like languages, can be understood only in their own terms, not by transposing them into an alien speech' (2009, p. 115). In other words, the Scripture reading rules of the Church do not prevent the possibility for new interpretations and readings to emerge; rather, this work of critique and analysis can only be done properly from the inside, in the language of the Church and not the language of a sociologist, a historian or a philosopher. Chapter 5 discusses the roles that other disciplines play in theological reflection as a resource potentially to complexify, diversify and interrogate the cultural-linguistic framework.

Grand Narratives are Oppressive

Even if there were agreement that the Bible can be read as a unified, coherent narrative, some would argue that any recourse to religious grand narratives is inappropriate within a postmodern, pluralist context. Attempts to tell the 'one story' for all other cultures and peoples was the (failed) project of modernity, which the postmodern perspective now rightly views with suspicion for its oppressive and imperialistic consequences. Elaine Graham's influential work *Transforming Practice* wrestles with how Christian communities can assert any values and norms when postmodernity has exposed all knowledge as situated and therefore, in her view, has successfully undermined the claims of the Christian metanarrative. For Graham, there can be no appeal to authority in a text or tradition when the writing and interpretation of those sources have consistently marginalized alternative voices, particularly those of women. However, rather than descend into relativism, Graham turns to Christian practices as the appropriate source of normativity for the Christian community. The values that are embedded within and emerge from liberating practices become the community's source of normative practical wisdom. These norms can only ever be seen as provisional, but are also binding on the community because of their transforming outcome. For Graham, there is no unmediated revelation or truth:

> The only vocabulary available to Christian communities in articulating their truth-claims is that of pastoral practice itself ... The faith-community acts as the guardian of *practical wisdom* by which such purposeful action gains its authenticity and credibility, and serves as the medium by which truth-claims are forged and publicly articulated. (2002, p. 203)

Graham therefore rejects the legitimacy of calling the Bible an authoritative narrative and explicitly seeks to locate Christian ethical norms in the practices of the community.

In response to such approaches, Bauckham argues that the postmodern rejection of metanarratives (itself a totalizing theory) has not actually got rid of universalizing stories but rather has enabled their replacement with the individualist narrative of consumerism that pervades our social and political context. Bauckham argues that the postmodern, relativizing perspective is powerless against this new metanarrative of globalized consumerism. Therefore, liberation is not to be found in the rejection of grand narratives; instead, 'we need a story that once again affirms universal values while resisting their co-option by the forces of domination' (2003, p. 46). Bauckham argues that the Christian story is just such a 'non-modern metanarrative'. Lindbeck sees postmodernism as a positive context for a revitalized Christian story. Bauckham and Lindbeck do not desire to return to a pre-critical era; rather, they incorporate the insights of critical scholarship into a storied, contextual understanding of the world. The focus of their narrative readings of Scripture is on Christian identity and witness rather than on superiority and domination, and thus it coheres with a postmodern perspective. Lindbeck, drawing on Thiemann, is concerned with the Bible as 'followable', and draws on the postmodern focus on whether something works in contrast to modernity's preoccupation with the empirically factual. For Lindbeck, the Bible tells a story that works, for individuals and for communities, in a way that resists the totalizing domination that made postmoderns suspicious of other metanarratives.

Furthermore, in telling the biblical narrative of God as Creator and Sustainer of the world, the Church does not seek to dominate the world, or fight with it for supremacy, attempting to subsume the plural narratives under its own. For Bonhoeffer, the Church acts as witness to and for the world through the telling of its story: 'The church of Jesus Christ is the place – that is, the space – in the world where the reign of Jesus Christ over the whole world is to be demonstrated and proclaimed' (2009, p. 63). The Church and its story exist for the world, witnessing to the fact that the world is that which is known and loved by God. Therefore, the biblical narrative to which the Church bears witness is not an oppressive grand narrative, but rather is supposed to be the service of witness, a being-for-others, that brings freedom and life.

The Bible Narrative is Oppressive

Even if there were agreement that the Bible can be seen as a unified narrative and that we still need a unifying narrative to resist the present oppressive narrative of consumerism, some would strongly argue that the Bible tells its own oppressive story. In recent decades, feminist theologians have been particularly instrumental in highlighting the Bible's patriarchal origins and norms, and I reference briefly some of those insights. There is, of course, no one feminist method of reading the Bible, but a diversity of approaches. Some feminists see the Bible and Christianity as irredeemably patriarchal and reject it altogether, as expressed by Daly: 'A patriarchal divinity or his son is exactly *not* in a position to save us from the horrors of a patriarchal world' (1973, p. 96). Trible (1984) wrestles with the various 'texts of terror' in the Bible that represent women as victims and seem to legitimate violence against them (for example, Genesis 19; Judges 11.29–40; 19; 2 Samuel 13). Trible's work seeks to remember and bear witness to the women's suffering in these stories in the hope of inspiring repentance in the face of contemporary manifestations of such atrocities. Fiorenza's feminist, critical hermeneutic recognizes the liberating and oppressive parts of Scripture and critiques both the Bible text and also the patriarchal scholarship that has interpreted the texts in an oppressive way. To do this, Fiorenza adopts a 'hermeneutics of suspicion' (1984, p. 15), which means that feminist readers must never uncritically accept the authority of the text, but rather use suspicion as a tool to expose its oppressive narrative and to retell a more liberating story. Therefore, attempts to celebrate the unifying metanarrative of Scripture as the authoritative story in which the Church discovers its identity and witness must be able to give account for the oppression and patriarchy found within its plot lines.

I do not have space here to rehearse the various responses feminists have made to this dilemma.[2] In the context of the discussion about unifying narrative, I will simply refer to Bauckham's argument, which is that the scriptural narrative subverts itself by not being an encyclopaedic explanation of the whole of reality. Within the story, there are plot lines that run counter to one another, such as Job undermining the Deuteronomic account of sin and punishment, or Ecclesiastes' ode to meaninglessness challenging the prophetic 'disobedience and judgement' accounts of events. In addition, some of the smaller Old Testament narratives testify to alternative inter-pretations of history; for example, compare Ruth with Judges; Esther with Daniel; or Jonah with Amos. This is not about establishing 'a canon within a canon', but about recognizing, as Bauckham argues, that the diversity within the biblical story enables it to resist closure. The Bible does not conclu-sively explain the enduring influence of evil, or the meaning of suffering, or the relationship between providence and human freedom. Rather, it allows Job and Deuteronomy, Esther and Acts, Ecclesiastes and Romans to sit alongside one another in a unified story, but not an exhaustive one. Likewise, from a feminist perspective, the 'texts of terror' exist alongside themes of empowerment and liberation. This does not explain why the oppressive passages exist in Scripture in the first place, but the subverting effect of the other liberating accounts means that no one group can control the story or co-opt the Bible story for oppressive ends. It is a tragedy that the Bible has been co-opted to power throughout its history. However, the Bible has also funded the impetus for resistance and reimagination. The story the Bible tells is coherent but not complete, comprehensible but not comprehensive. The Bible is therefore able, eventually and perpetually, to resist all possession and ownership of any dominant group and to embrace diverse perspectives in a non-coercive way.

Furthermore, the incompleteness of the biblical narrative is what enables readers to widen their gaze to the God to whom the story bears witness. As Stratis argues: 'The long narrative arc of the Bible ... makes sense when we attend not only to the internal logic of the story, but also, and especially, to the God whose identity gives rise to its possibility, duration, and final consummation' (2016, p. 32). Ultimately, the biblical story finds coherence as it testifies to the fact that it exists at all because of the nature of the God to whom it points. Inhabiting the grand narrative is not an end in itself but is the means by which we become aware of and, by grace, are united with the life of God that transcends the story. Therefore, the narrative is not about oppressing us by fully defining and constraining us within its worldview; rather, it witnesses to the possibility of our participation in God's triune life via the Holy Spirit (see Chapter 4). As such, the Bible is the unifying, non-modern, incomplete metanarrative that bears witness to the God who transcends the story and who is the initiator and goal of the telling.

Reading the Bible as Authoritative Narrative

Thus far in this chapter, I have argued that the Bible is the elected and sanctified witness to God's self-revelation, and the unified but not exhaustive story in which reality is to be found. The Bible is the script for our performance, mutually constitutive with the Church and funding our imaginative construction of the world in a way that can resist all other oppressive metanarratives. The Bible is therefore the authoritative and proper starting point for all theological reflection, but most especially for theological reflection that is concerned with the formation of Christians for participation in God's ongoing story. In this final section, I provide some guidance as to how reflectors should think about reading and interpreting this God-elected and sanctified, unifying, non-modern, Church-constituting, incomplete but authoritative metanarrative, particularly in light of the challenges raised. I draw on Volf to outline five 'convictions' that guide the reading of this divinely authored narrative within theological reflection.

Volf highlights 'an integrated set of convictions' (2010, p. 15) that guide his reading of Scripture. These are: (1) then and there – recognizing the historical dimension of the text and the need to study it from this perspective; (2) here and now – the Bible is a sacred text for today through which God speaks God's word and acts upon people's lives; (3) unity and diversity

– the Bible tells a unified story but includes many diverse voices that resist harmonization; (4) meaning – the Bible texts can have multiple and changing meanings, but this does not mean a 'free-for-all' as the Bible is God's self-communication, and as such readers have an obligation to discern that meaning; and (5) stance – in light of this, we read it from a position of respect and not suspicion, but do so utilizing all our critical judgement. These five convictions are consistent with the narrative reading already outlined and I shall build on them to outline my own approach to reading the Bible as authoritative narrative. These convictions are intended to be aspirational and developmental, rather than implying that any person will or can 'possess' them in their entirety.

In Humility ...

In line with Volf's conviction of 'stance', I argue that reading and interpreting God's narrative must be done with humility. As for Volf, this is not about reading meekly or submissively, but rather recognizing God's veracious authority in being 'the expert' on God's self-revelation. I read assuming I know little and wanting to know more. I also humbly assume that other readers of the Bible, throughout history and around the world, have wisdom and insight to share in guiding my interpretation. Therefore, I can, in humility, affirm Lindbeck's 'reading rules' of the creeds as the lens through which generations of the Church have encountered trustworthy meaning in the text. In humility, I recognize my small part in the larger story, standing between past and future, receiving the gospel as the Church has historically understood it and being called faithfully to pass it on to the next generation. The other, interrelated convictions ensure that this does not happen uncritically. Part of the faithfulness of transmission is expressed through rigorously testing that which is to be passed on. The central point, however, is that it is entrusted to us in order to be transmitted, not just for our own consumption. We encounter Christ through the story in order that we participate with his ministry for others.

Humility enables us to maintain a correct perspective on the small part we are privileged to play in the story, and humility consistently affirms our important but narrow field of vision. It encourages us to read prayerfully and reflexively, aware of our constant need for grace and conscious of our own prejudices and situatedness.

... as a Whole ...

The Bible should be understood as a unified narrative, and therefore it is necessary to read the story as a whole. Precisely because the story resists neat harmonization or adequate summary, the entirety of the biblical witness must be kept in view for faithful reading and interpretation. This broad vision encompasses careful study of what the texts meant to the original writers and hearers and therefore includes the hermeneutical approaches that reconstruct the *world behind the text* (for example, Historical, Form, Source and Redaction Criticisms, cf. Gooder 2008). It also requires thorough study of the *world within the text*, including Translation Theory, Rhetorical, Narrative and Structural Criticism. The requirement to read the *world in front of the text* (for example, through Reader-Response, Feminist and Postcolonial Criticisms) straddles this and the following conviction, which is to read 'with other Christians'. Tate advocates for the integration of these three worlds in the task of hermeneutics: 'meaning results from a conversation between the world of the text and the world of the reader, a conversation informed by the world of the author' (2008, p. 5). He argues that any attempt to privilege one of the worlds (author, text, reader) over the other two will result in distorted interpretation. Thus, some proficiency with the different methods of reading the Bible is necessary for faithful reading.

Such 'whole', integrated reading seems a daunting and impossible task for individual Christians or congregations. In practice, it means that we do not only read our favourite passages, but we commit to wrestle with our 'texts of terror', humbly listening to the context as well as the diverse perspectives within the text. In addition, we see it as a lifelong journey of reading, within the global and universal Church, rather than a task for one person in a two-year theology course. A commitment to lifelong study in community best enables our growing expertise and proficiency to interpret and inhabit the whole of the story.

... with Other Christians ...

The conviction to read the whole of Scripture is, of course, an impossible task for any individual reader, hence the vital conviction that faithful reading and interpretation must be done with other members of the body of Christ. Other Christians similarly need to be understood in the broadest terms so as to ensure the widest possible perspective, and so need to be conceived (1) historically – reading with theologians throughout the centuries for their insight and perspective; (2) geographically – reading with Christians around the world to ensure that the global story is inclusive; (3) academically – reading with contemporary scholars and academics to consider the latest research; and (4) sociologically – reading with Christians who are socio-economically different from ourselves in order to hear how the text is read from different social localities. The inclusion of geographical and sociological 'others' is a unique contribution which practical theology has brought to theology in recent decades. Traditionally, 'theology' has been more focused on reading with historical and academic 'others'. Likewise, a pentecostal hermeneutic that celebrates the diverse languages of Pentecost as the pattern for the Spirit's ongoing work insists on the diversity of Christian testimonies as intrinsic to faithful interpretation of God's story. Scripture tells a story that culminates in 'a great multitude that no one could count, from every nation, from all tribes and peoples and languages, standing before the throne and before the Lamb, robed in white, with palm branches in their hands' (Revelation 7.9). Therefore, for the fulfilment of this vision we must not only *read* with other Christians but also *minister* with others: ecumenical working, interdisciplinary conferences, and co-authored research projects should all be celebrated as ways to develop whole readings of the Bible with increasingly diverse others. The focus on reading with other Christians is not to say that we should never read Scripture with not-Christian others. Chapter 5 discusses the particular contribution that perspectives from other disciplines should make to complexifying, diversifying and interrogating our reading of Scripture in order to act as a resource for our theological reflections. However, following Lindbeck, God's story can only be properly understood from inside the Christian cultural-linguistic framework as it is enacted. Importantly, reading with other Christians is necessary to show us just how broad and diverse is that framework and to prevent us from perpetuating it in our own image.

... *through the Holy Spirit* ...

This conviction to read with the Church across space, time and social divide could be interpreted to mean that the Bible will have endlessly diverse interpretations. Volf speaks of the conviction of 'meaning' as understanding that the biblical text will have multiple meanings, but is clear that this does not mean that 'anything goes'. If the Bible is indeed God's story – God's elected self-communication to creation – it is incumbent upon the reader primarily to discern the meaning(s) God intended. The meaning(s) may certainly be multiple, but the reader is not at liberty to conclude any and every meaning from the text, because there is divine intent, purpose and agency in the text's construction. Volf argues:

> The reader is not called to the endeavor of the 'making of meaning' as though none were encoded in the text, but rather to the task of 'decoding meaning(s)', or, more precisely, constructing plausible accounts of the meaning encoded. (2010, p. 29)

How we 'construct plausible accounts' of God's meaning and intent is a significant question. It is my conviction that endeavouring to read the whole of God's self-revealed story, in humility, with the whole Church across time and space is part of the way that, together, the Church discerns the meaning of God's self-revelation. However, this is insufficient in and of itself. Significantly, as Anderson argues, 'the living Lord Jesus is present in the hermeneutical task of reading and interpreting Scripture' (2001, p. 77). Through God's Holy Spirit we are not left as orphans, but the Church is given, as gracious gift, the same Spirit who inspired, elected and sanctified the text to be Scripture for the Church. Therefore, we do not read alone but with the risen Jesus through the Holy Spirit and the same Holy Spirit 'serves as a common context' (Johns 1998, p. 85) between the historic writer and the contemporary reader, thus facilitating the hermeneutical process. This charismatic perspective on hermeneutics is a much neglected dimension in both biblical studies and practical theology. To return to Wright's (1992) play script analogy, not only do we have the text of Shakespeare's unfinished play, we also have been given the 'Spirit of Shakespeare' to shape and illuminate our reading and performance. How we can conceive of accessing this, and what it is that the Holy Spirit does, is the topic of the next chapter.

... for Transformation

Just as there is divine intention to communicate through the Bible, so there needs to be reader intention to receive that communication in order for a faithful reading of God's story. We do not read only for interest, or learning, or research, or even proclamation – although all these things can and should be a part of our Scripture reading. We read to hear God's word to us and encounter God's Spirit, in order to worship God and participate with God's ministry. We read to be formed and transformed, to be shaped and inspired, to train our prophetic imaginations and to enthuse our worship and witness. We read the Bible to find ourselves in its story, to learn and relearn our identity, and to live that out faithfully in the world. We read with a conviction that change is both necessary and possible – individually, communally, societally and globally. We read for encounter with God, knowing that any such encounter is always that which transforms. Our reading of Scripture should continually transform all our relating – with ourselves, with others, with creation and with God. The reader does not necessarily have to be desirous of this change in order for it to be manifested. Indeed, often we read because we do not want to change; rather we want to be confirmed in our present conviction or situation. However, a narrative reading of Scripture recognizes the dangerous and glorious reality of God's transforming power for anyone brave enough to open the pages. Even our most cherished and deeply held beliefs and practices are not safe from challenge and the invitation to change. The more we commit ourselves to reading the whole text humbly, with other Christians, and through the Holy Spirit, the more likely and frequently this transformation will occur. Through our transformed lives, we are best able to offer our worship to God and to glorify God's name. Again, this is why I argue that a theological reflection method that starts from Scripture, with the expectation of encountering God through the story and being transformed to participate with Christ's ongoing ministry, is a significantly more appropriate method for forming Christians for Christian ministry than the models presently being employed.

Summary

In this chapter, I have attempted to lay the foundations for the proposed evangelical, charismatic method by arguing for the authoritative status of Scripture in the life of faith and therefore the appropriate place to begin theological reflection for Christian formation. I articulated the Bible as God's elected, sanctified witness to the life, death and resurrection of Jesus Christ and to the history from which he arose. The Bible authenticates itself as this unique and pre-eminent witness to God's self-revelation and this is comprehended through faith. This sacred text is God's account of God's dealings with the world, from creation to new creation, and is thus a unified story of reality within which humanity finds its identity and meaning. The Bible can be understood as providing the script for the life of faith, enabling readers to improvise their performance in a way that is faithful to its plot lines. This script funds the imagination of its readers to remake the world according to its story, and in so doing constitutes the Church which is the ongoing embodiment and continuation of the story within which individuals can find their identity. This cosmic narrative, made up of diverse writings from varied social contexts, is unified by the oneness of the triune God to whom it points. It makes use of recurring figures, types and themes as later writers claim and reinterpret the unfolding story, thus enabling contemporary readers similarly to see their story prefigured in the text. It is a unified narrative which does not give a comprehensive explanation of every aspect of reality, and as such is self-subverting, resisting the totalizing impetus of modern metanarratives. This unified narrative should be read carefully and humbly, so as faithfully to recognize its authoritative status. The Bible also requires careful reading to avoid the potential pitfalls of misinterpretation, oppression and co-option to power of which the Church has been, and sadly continues to be, guilty. This faithful reading of Scripture should be done in humility, as a whole, with other Christians, through the Holy Spirit, for transformation.

If Scripture is authoritative for the Church in the ways I have argued, it must be the starting point for all theological reflection for Christian formation. Humbly, we must listen to God's account of the world before we begin to improvise our part within it or seek to reimagine our world from its vantage point. We must commit ourselves to read God's story with others so as to inform, form and transform our understanding of Christ's ministry in the contemporary world so that we can discern how we are called to participate. Obviously, in reality, life is more complex and nuanced than this. We find ourselves 'in the middle of things' and we cannot expect to achieve the aspirational 'whole reading of the Bible with all other Christians' before we can ever hope to participate in Christ's ministry. We bring all our inherited theory-laden practices and our practice-shaped beliefs with us to the text each time we read. A call to start theological reflection with Scripture is simply to recognize that, theologically, the initiative for everything begins with God. We would have no idea what 'God' meant had God not acted to reveal it to us, and we would not even exist had God not acted to create and continued to act to sustain all things. It is this initiative that determines our utter dependency on God for all thought, life and breath. To start from Scripture in theological reflection is to make explicit the faith conviction of our dependency on God's initiative. It is to acknowledge our constant need for grace as we first look to our Creator to tell us what creation is and who we are within it. Theological reflection, if it is to be theological at all, must acknowledge the contradictory theories, beliefs and practices that constitute our identity and begin by recognizing God's first move towards us through revelation and respond by finding ourselves within that story. The reading of Scripture as our first move becomes the enacting and proclaiming of our faith as we humbly acknowledge our need to have our meaning-making shaped and disciplined by God's story. By so doing, we hope to see more clearly in order to interpret and analyse our own lives and situations from its perspective.

As I have stated, the conviction that God reveals Godself through Scripture in a way that tells the story of the cosmos and our place within it such that it must be authoritative for our thinking and living is ultimately a conviction of faith. Therefore, the justification of this position argued in this chapter is unlikely to convince those who share a different faith conviction about the place and role of the Bible. My intention, even if it were possible, is not to convince those who would disagree with me about the role of the Bible, but rather to provide a basis for an evangelical approach to theological reflection. This approach takes seriously a commitment to the authority of God's revealed story, but not as a form of applied theology that disregards our experience, because our experiences are understood as sites for Christ's ongoing ministry (see Chapters 4 and 5). Furthermore, I have sought to argue that even for those who do not describe their faith as 'evangelical', an approach to theological reflection that starts from Scripture is a more appropriate method for the education of Christians as Christians than other methods that are not primarily concerned with the formation of Christians for ministry. I argue that a method that starts from Scripture foregrounds God and our encounters with God for the purpose of participating in Christ's ongoing ministry and thus better forms us as Christians – that is, those who discern, encounter and participate with Christ. Such a method better constitutes us as the Church who tell and are told by the story of Jesus because this is the method's explicit aim. So far, I have made reference to the vital role the Holy Spirit plays in the process of shaping and transforming us to inhabit God's story, and the next chapter explores this further.

Notes

1 Grenz (2004) charts the development of these different trajectories within evangelicalism.

2 A common response is the 'canon within the canon' approach. For example, Ruether (1983) focuses on the prophetic-liberation voice throughout Scripture and she considers as authoritative only those parts of the Bible that promote the full humanity of women. Walton (1993) uses a metaphor of a scriptural 'shell' that must be removed to uncover the life-giving seed that the scriptural stories contain. Alternatively, some feminists take a more evangelical approach, for example DeVries (2006), who argues for allowing Scripture to interpret itself with Christ's liberating work as the central meaning and reference point.

4

Consulting the Architect: The Holy Spirit in Theological Reflection

Introduction

So far, this book has argued that frequently used methods for theological reflection are problematic for Christians with a charismatic, evangelical theology because of the ways in which they disadvantage the authority of the Bible, the agency of the Holy Spirit, and Christian experience. I also argue that these frequently used methods, while perhaps helpful for public theology or liberation theology, are not the most appropriate ways for forming Christians as Christians – those who testify to and encounter Christ and participate in Christ's ministry. Chapter 2 examined the theological assumptions implicit in the frequently used theological reflection methods to make the case for a renewed method that foregrounds the Bible, the Holy Spirit and Christian experience. Chapter 3 argued that Christians prioritize the Bible because it is a realist, unified narrative – God's elected and sanctified witness to God and God's relationship with the world. We start our theological reflections from Scripture as the enactment of faith that recognizes that we need first to find ourselves in God's story so that we can see rightly to interpret and engage with the world around us.

However, while we start with Scripture, we do so in order to know and encounter the God to whom it bears witness. This God is a living and active God, not fossilized in the words on the page but breathing life through the words and encountering us in our contemporary lives by the Holy Spirit. The Holy

Spirit is central to articulating an understanding of Christian faith as participation in Christ's ongoing ministry. The purpose of theological reflection for Christian formation is not that we go and 'enact liberative practices' in light of our reflections, but that, necessarily, we discern the ongoing ministry of the resurrected Christ in order to bear witness to it and participate in it. Christian ministry is necessarily participation with Christ, through the Holy Spirit, and not only performing good and just actions for human flourishing. Our participation with Christ includes such actions but is not reducible to them. Theological education for formation (especially of charismatic, evangelical Christians but, I argue, for all Christian ministers) must prioritize methods that enable students to grow in this spiritual discipline of discerning encounters with Christ's present ministry in order to participate with him. This chapter draws on pentecostal/charismatic theology to articulate a pneumatology for theological reflection, which foregrounds the ministry of Christ through a focus on encounter and participation.

I am continuing the building metaphor which structures this book by referring to this chapter on pneumatology as 'Consulting the Architect'. God, as the 'architect' of creation, conceived all that is and sustains its existence, bringing creation to its promised eschatological consummation and completion. As active agent through the Holy Spirit, God guides and directs the process of Christian formation and is always Subject of theology as well as its object. I am therefore using the metaphor of God the Holy Spirit as the architect of my theological reflection methodology to further highlight God's independent, involved agency in the process of theological reflection. Clearly, one would consult an architect prior to any ground clearing (Chapter 2) or foundation laying (Chapter 3), and as such the sequencing of the metaphor has its weaknesses. However, the value of the metaphor is in making explicit the Holy Spirit as 'architect' in the process of theological reflection, and this chapter fleshes out what that means.

This chapter begins by examining the works of two influential practical theologians – Don Browning and Elaine Graham *how* – as case studies to show how they have each overlooked the role of the Holy Spirit in their practical theology. I argue that this overlooking of the Holy Spirit is symptomatic of the sub-discipline and explains the disadvantaging of divine agency within practical theology. I then articulate a pentecostal theology of encounter to explain how I understand divine agency to be apprehended within theological reflection. From this foundation, I draw on the works of four pentecostal/charismatic practical theologians – Ray Anderson, Andrew Root, Mark Cartledge and Cheryl Bridges Johns – in the construction of my own charismatic theological reflection method. This chapter argues that God is indeed an active agent in the life of faith and that God's activity can be encountered in human life. Humans access, know and encounter God's divine agency through the Holy Spirit as the mediation of God in Christ, joining human experience to God's being through our participation in Christ's ministry. Therefore, for Christians training explicitly for participation in Christ's ongoing ministry, we urgently need methods of theological reflection that are explicitly oriented towards encounter with God and participation with Christ through the Spirit.

The Holy Spirit in Practical Theology: Two Case Studies

Browning's A Fundamental Practical Theology

For Root (2014), Don Browning should be considered the big brother of practical theology because his praxis-theory-praxis methodology has been so influential upon the sub-discipline. Browning, informed by David Tracy, develops his praxis-theory-praxis approach in opposition to what he saw as the classic theory-to-practice model of theology, which for Browning was typified by Barth. Browning argues that all theology should be seen as fundamentally practical. His chief concern is how religious communities make sense to those outside and he seeks to understand how congregations engage in moral reasoning to inform their practice. Browning focuses on the practical wisdom or *phronesis* of the community to show how the claims of church communities can be seen as reasonable, and consequently as having something to offer a secular context. His concern is therefore very much in line with Tracy's correlationist method for public theology described in Chapter 1. Browning's aim is a noble one: seeking to engage with those people 'on the boundary' between faith and the world in order to evidence how religious communities are carriers of *phronesis* and therefore intelligible. This method is in contrast to Lindbeck's cultural-linguistic approach to religion, highlighted in Chapter 3 and discussed further in Chapter 5. For Lindbeck, the Christian faith can only make sense from the inside. Browning, on the other hand, contends that it is possible to gain some critical distance from our cultural-linguistic frameworks so that 'common values and rational principles can arise out of diverse traditions' (1996, p. 102) such that they can then be compared and contrasted with one another.

Browning argues that fundamental practical theology is: 'Critical reflection on the church's dialogue with Christian sources and other communities of experience and interpretation with the aim of guiding its action toward social and individual transformation' (1996, p. 36). 'Other communities of experience and interpretation' refers to the practical wisdom that emerges outside of the Church, perhaps especially in the human sciences, which are also attempts to interpret the world. The role of fundamental practical theology, for Browning, is to make explicit the assumptions and traditions that inform Christian theory-laden praxis – which is both theological and social scientific – in order to determine future transformative action. As will be seen from this description, Browning's practical theology is oriented to the world of human experience: 'church dialogue', 'Christian sources', 'other communities' and 'action', and leaves no room explicitly for the active agency of God in the formulation of theology. The correlation he envisages is between church praxis, other disciplines and religious texts. If God is conceived as an ontological reality at all in his method, it is only as that which is somehow contained within the sacred texts.

Significantly, Browning conducts three church case studies to illustrate how his praxis-theory-praxis dialectic actually works in religious communities. One of his research churches is a Pentecostal church called the Apostolic Church of God. Browning repeatedly describes how this church community see the Holy Spirit as central to their faith and theology. Browning, however, deliberately eschews their enlivening belief in divine agency to focus only on the phenomenological accounts of their practices and to assess the consequences. He is trying to demonstrate how Christian practices give rise to questions that lead the church community to 'a fresh confrontation with the normative texts' (1996, p. 49). However, he clearly illustrates that this is not primarily what the Pentecostal church think that they are doing. They are not simply dialoguing with a normative text but engaging directly with the God who speaks through the text and through their religious experiences. Browning gives examples of how his participants frequently refer to God telling them to do something, but his method leaves no space to engage with this central aspect of their theological understanding. Instead, Browning tries to show that they are in fact engaged in hermeneutical conversations between their practices and the religious texts and attempts to represent their theory-laden practices as reasonable in the language of psychology and anthropology. He states that the Apostolic Church of God 'can never communicate what it has to offer to the secular world on strictly confessional grounds' (1996, p. 249), and as such this drives his methodological agnosticism.

This eschewing of divine agency for the sake of demonstrating the comprehensibility of the church's practices would seem to be disingenuous to the religious community he is studying. The practices of the Apostolic Church of God community only make sense to the practitioners because they are done in response to God's self-revelation in Scripture verified through their experiences of the Holy Spirit in their contemporary lives. Browning's method therefore is informed by his biases, which he freely acknowledges:

No church I have ever belonged to spoke much about the Holy Spirit ... In my communities of faith, even those of my youth, God is discussed indirectly. Only rarely are God and Jesus spoken of directly and intimately as matters of first hand religious experience. (1996, p. 65)

Therefore, he rules out the confessional paradigm of his participants not only because of his aim to present them as reasonable to those outside the church, but also, arguably, because of his own lack of experience of their encounters with God. It is not clear whether Browning considers experiential encounters with God to be impossible – despite the frequent attestations of his case studies to their experiences of divine initiative – or whether he deliberately ignores the idea. Either way, he chooses to see 'God' contained within the religious texts so as to appeal to those who would not take a confessional stance. While this may be a noble aim for apologetics, it is puzzling that a correlation method that explicitly 'brackets off' confessional concerns has come to influence methods of theological reflection used for the formation of Christian ministers.

Root's critique of Browning's methodology states that 'Browning has little conception (and where there is little, there is disdain) for conceiving of a qualitative distinction between time and eternity' (2014, p. 57). In other words, there is, for Root, an ontological distinction between Creator and creature which Browning's approach does not acknowledge and for which he certainly does not take account. Talk about God as an ontological reality is either forbidden in Browning's method or it is contained within discussions of the religious texts. Root notes that Browning critiques Barth for being too theoretical in his theological method, but in doing so Browning fails to see that Barth starts not with abstract theory but rather with divine action in revelation. Therefore, for Root, Barth's approach can be seen as a practice-theory-practice approach, it just begins with divine practice rather than human practice. I return to Root's argument later in the chapter. For now, it is sufficient to note that Browning's practical theology method explicitly overlooks the active agency of God. His intention is to communicate with those outside the Church to show how the Church can be understood as meaningful and reasonable, by correlating their *phronesis* with other forms of practical wisdom. It is therefore surprising that Browning's method has come to inform the way in which the Church internally reflects on its praxis and seeks to form its members for ministry.

Graham's Transforming Practice

Elaine Graham has been similarly influential upon the development of practical theology method, particularly for feminist practical theologians. Graham further develops Browning's method through focusing on the gendered nature of all human practice and experience. Graham contends that it is no longer possible for theology to build on a consensus of normative values in society due to the deconstructive insights of postmodernity and pluralism. The Church can no longer take for granted the authority of traditional Christian sources and norms because they are gendered in their construction and therefore patriarchal and oppressive. For Graham, the Church needs new ways of developing truth claims that can have meaning for a postmodern world without descending into relativism. For Graham, any claim to normativity must be built upon practical wisdom emerging in communities of transforming practice.

Graham follows Browning in apprehending the 'value-directed nature of Christian pastoral practice' (2002, p. 96) and agrees with his goal to unite pastoral practice to the life of the Church in a way that is mutually critical, public and pluralistic. However, Graham sees Browning's method as too wedded to notions of rationality because of his focus on practical moral reasoning. For Graham, Browning does not take into account embodied, symbolic or affective types of Christian activity. His exclusive focus on rationality causes a continued dualism in Browning's thinking, according to Graham, between theory and praxis such that Browning understands theory to be insights that can be extracted from their narrative and cultural contexts. Therefore, Graham wishes to broaden the pastoral theology approach of Browning to focus on the variety of Christian practices (beyond moral reasoning) and the practical wisdom that emerges from diverse (gendered) practices. Graham sees no separation between theory and practice: all is *phronesis* – wisdom embedded in embodied practice. This extends to any human engagement with God such that 'any Divine, ultimate and transcendent dimension to human experience will only be authentically and reliably apprehended in the midst of human practice' (2002, p. 10). In other words, human practice is always culturally and linguistically bound so that there can be no objective or absolute truth or insight that comes from beyond human practice or bypasses our human contingency. Christian pastoral practice must therefore be the only grounds for any normative truth-claims for a faith community.

Graham follows Pierre Bourdieu to argue for the centrality of practice. Sociology has long debated the interaction between structure and agency in terms of their influence on human life. 'Structures' are the external factors that determine human life, such as institutions, political and economic systems, and religious traditions. 'Agency' describes the internal factors that determine how people choose to live their lives within the societal structures. Following Bourdieu, Graham argues that practices are the things people actually do between structure and agency and therefore should be the focus of study. For example, structure may dictate a gendered division of labour in society while a woman's agency may assert her desire to work outside the home. For Graham, the only thing that can be studied is the practices by which people negotiate these competing expectations, such as the practices of domestic arrangements, childcare choices and parental leave within the given context. A focus on practices can encompass both the community's shared memory of the wisdom of the past and also its contemporary reinterpretations in the present. Therefore, a focus on practices 'transcends the polarization between structure and agency' (2002, p. 103) and is necessarily where the norms for living are generated, replicated and negotiated.

This is similarly the case in religious contexts where pastoral practices mediate tradition and beliefs and are therefore foundational to theological understanding. This means that practices are necessarily generative of theology, not merely the application of external theory.

For Graham, the norms of a Christian community are generated and contained within the practices of that community. They are therefore contingent and situated, but also authoritative and binding. Graham is dismissive of narrative approaches to theology (see Chapter 3), because while they acknowledge the situated dynamic of human knowledge, she argues, they assume the Christian story to be ahistorical and absolute. A narrative approach to theology 'refuses to regard the ultimate claims of faith as contingent upon human authorship' (2002, p. 138). There can be no appeal to that which is outside of human practice. The Holy Spirit is not mentioned by Graham, but where the divine is referenced it is contained entirely within human practices, such that 'Divine grace comes as the words and meanings expressed are heard and then enacted by the whole people into something more than surface experience' (2002, p. 182). It is therefore not clear whether for Graham there is any ontological reality to 'Divine grace' outside of human interactivity. In concluding, she states: 'If such a Divine and transcendent dimension is available to human apprehension, it will only be realized in the practical and concrete arena of purposeful action' (2002, p. 207). Thus, for Graham, it makes sense to study human pastoral practice in order to be able to make any theological claims about the transcendent.

Browning and Graham, in their different ways and for slightly different reasons, do not give space for the initiative and agency of God outside of human practice and the writings of the tradition. They either 'bracket off' discussion of the Holy Spirit in order to dialogue with those outside of a framework of faith; or ignore the Holy Spirit altogether. Each asserts that any engagement with the divine can only be accessed through concrete human action and therefore make human action the primary starting point for their theological projects. These approaches have significantly informed the sub-discipline of practical theology which focuses on carrying out research into human practices, usually through social science methods, in order to generate theological insights. This approach is essential if God can only be apprehended through human religious practices. In response to this, I argue that, while we cannot (ordinarily) transcend our embodied experience (cf. Paul's description of his encounter with Christ in 2 Corinthians 12.2–3) to know God outside of human actions, God can be encountered as a present, active agent in the world and as something ontologically distinct from ourselves. I argue later that according to Anderson this is not a metaphysical claim but rather is centred on the reality of the resurrected Christ. It is the Holy Spirit who mediates God in Christ to us and enables us to apprehend and encounter God through the risen Christ's practice of ministry. Therefore, the focus of practical theology should be upon human practices only because they are locations for an encounter with the person and work of the risen Christ through the Holy Spirit. To argue this, I must first expound what I mean by 'encounter', drawing on a pentecostal epistemology.

A Pentecostal Theology of 'Encounter'

So far in this book, I have argued that the Christian life (and theological reflection as far as it seeks to form Christians within and for that Christian life) is about encountering Christ, through the Spirit, in order to participate in Christ's ministry. In this section, I clarify a theological basis for 'encounter' from a pentecostal perspective, in order to argue that God, through the Holy Spirit, can be known or (as I prefer) 'encountered' as active agent in our human lives and that this should therefore be the focus for our theological reflection.

Warrington describes 'encounter' as the primary theological category which characterizes Pentecostalism. He understands 'encounter' to be 'the central Pentecostal expectation of a radical experience of the Spirit' (2008, p. 20), where the believer experiences God as 'acting upon' them from outside of themselves. It refers to an experiential knowledge of God that is necessarily emotional, affective and transforming. This does not need to eschew the intellectual, rational and cognitive dimensions of knowledge (even if Pentecostalism may sometimes be accused of doing this), but importantly, a pentecostal spirituality resists elevating these latter ways of knowing above the former, which was a product of the Enlightenment period. Warrington points to Acts 19.2, when Paul asks the Ephesians whether they received the Holy Spirit, to illustrate the pentecostal expectation that encounter with the Holy Spirit is recognizable, tangible and evidential in some way beyond intellectual understanding. Theologically, upon confessing faith in Jesus, the Ephesian disciples may be said to 'have' the Holy Spirit, but their lack of tangible, experiential evidence to this effect means that after their baptism Paul lays hands on the Ephesian disciples so that they may encounter the Holy Spirit: in this case, through tongues-speaking and prophesying (Acts 19.6).

Warrington does not clearly define what constitutes an encounter with the Holy Spirit, but he provides numerous illustrations through his systematic discussion of a pentecostal perspective on central Christian doctrines. So, he argues that for pentecostals salvation is experienced – it is felt as well as understood – through feelings of peace, joy, assurance and hope. The Holy Spirit empowers believers for mission, evidenced by inspiration, encouragement and confidence to proclaim. The Spirit unites the community of believers by bringing a sense of love, joy and comfort. The Spirit convicts people of their sins, and brings transformation and guidance. For pentecostals, the fruits of the Spirit (Galatians 5.22) and the gifts of the Spirit (Romans 12.6–8; Ephesians 4.11; 1 Corinthians 12.8–10, 28–29) are ways in which the expected encounter with Christ is evidenced within the life of the believer and through the Church. In each case, the Holy Spirit is conceived as an external agent, acting upon the believer in a way that is known to them through the experience.

Tomlin emphasizes the importance of experience within all Christian epistemology, which affirms knowledge of God as a gift of faith. Tomlin argues that reason cannot lead a person to a certainty of faith; only the Spirit can do that by engaging the heart. Therefore, 'the life into which the Spirit brings us is intended to be *experienced*' (2011, p. 64, emphasis original). We need to feel a sense of guilt in order to repent, as well as know ourselves rationally to be sinners; we must feel a sense of gratitude in order to praise, as well as cognitively to understand God as provider; we require the feeling of love in order to worship, as well as logically to deduce God as the object of worship. The Holy Spirit may be seen as the agent initiating these emotions and thus mediating an encounter with God. Of course, these feelings are not expected to be ever and always present in the believer, nor are they seen as the only grounds for faith, but there is an assumed felt dimension to the Christian life that is not only characteristic of pentecostal spirituality.

Smith argues how and why pentecostals focus particularly on experiential encounters with God by expounding a pentecostal epistemology. He examines pentecostal spirituality to make explicit the worldview that informs them. Smith identifies five key aspects of this pentecostal worldview: (1) 'radical openness to God' – an expectancy that something will happen, often something new; (2) an '"enchanted" theology of creation and culture' – that the Spirit enthuses the whole of life, as also do other 'spirits'; (3) a 'non-dualistic affirmation of embodiment and materiality' – through the focus on bodily healing; (4) an 'affective, narrative epistemology' – the importance of feeling and story; and (5) an 'eschatological orientation to mission and justice' – a strong sense of the end times that informs 'this worldly' engagement (2010, p. 12). From this, Smith argues that pentecostals have an implicit, holistic anthropology, where humans are body *and* spirit, thinking *and* feeling beings. Their focus on experience assumes that humans '*feel* our way around the world more than we *think* about it, *before* we think about it' (2010, p. 72, emphasis original), and pentecostal spiritual practices tap into that affective foundation to human life. Felt encounters with God are therefore fundamental ways in which pentecostals know, embody and live out their faith. Of course, at its worst, a focus on felt encounter may be dismissed as experientialism and emotionalism; however, for Smith, pente-costals are not 'anti*rational*, but antirational*ist*' (2010, p. 53). In other words, their focus on experience is not a rejection of cognition but rather a rejection of the elevation of intellectual knowledge at the expense of the holistic ways in which humans know. Humans are not just 'thinking heads' but embodied, affective creatures, and these dimensions of our humanity must find expression within an account of Christian faith.

The foregrounding of encounter with Christ in my method does not negate the need for rational, critical, logical engage-ment, but it sees this as only one way in which humans interact with the world and with God. Christian theological reflection is fundamentally *to discern and testify to the Holy Spirit's initiation and mediation of contemporary encounters with Christ for our participation in Christ's ongoing ministry in the world.* Such a definition requires a pentecostal epistemology and spirituality that highlights affective and embodied know-ledge of God alongside cognitive ways of knowing. This approach to theological reflection sees God the Holy Spirit as active agent in our knowing. God through the Holy Spirit is the one who encounters us in the space and time of our lives as that which is outside and beyond ourselves. It is through being encountered in this felt, embodied way that God is known to us as 'other'. The practical theologies of Browning and Graham do not allow for the exploration of these events within their methods, nor do they acknowledge their possibility. Again, I argue, it is surprising that methods that ignore encounters with Christ are used to train Christians for the work of participating in Christ's ministry. In the remainder of this chapter, I examine four works that construct a practical theology method from within this pentecostal/charismatic epistemology of encounter with Christ, and that form the basis of my method.

Pentecostal/Charismatic Practical Theology

Anderson's The Shape of Practical Theology

Anderson writes *The Shape of Practical Theology* in a context that is sceptical and dismissive of practical theology in favour of the objective truths of the Bible and systematic theology. In this context, Anderson argues that praxis is at the heart of all theology, not, like Browning, on the basis of the way humans think but on the basis of God's interactions with creation. For Anderson, theology is practical because it is concerned with God's ministry to the world: past, present and future. God is at work in the world and in the lives of people, bringing revelation and reconciliation, and it is this activity of God that precedes all theological formulations and all church praxis. Therefore, all theology is grounded in praxis, but this is not a pragmatic turn to the authority of experience or a rejection of theological theory. Anderson identifies the key issue in this debate as the relationship between theory and practice, and explores the history of how these terms have developed and influenced theology, often with the prioritization of theory over praxis. Anderson argues for their interactive relationship such that theory is always praxis-based, and praxis is always theory-laden. As such, he affirms Browning's fundamental practical theology outlined at the beginning of this chapter and sees Browning's method as appropriately articulating the mutually dependent theory-praxis relationship. However, Anderson seeks to adapt Browning's approach because he considers it to lack a 'Christological concentration at the core and a trinitarian theology at the foundation' (2001, p. 29). I briefly explore what Anderson means by these critiques and modifications of Browning's method.

Browning distinguishes between the 'inner core' of practical theology – by which he means the concrete experience that raises the questions of 'what then shall we do?' and 'how then shall we live?' This 'inner core' exists within an 'outer envelope', which in Browning's case is the Christian story, community and doctrines within which the pastoral concern has been raised. The Church must work out the inner core problem in the context of the 'outer envelope' of the Christian faith. Anderson argues that the inner core of 'experience' should be replaced by a concept called Christopraxis, which refers to the contemporary ministry of Jesus Christ. In any experience, the risen and ascended Christ is already present and at work and is therefore a present reality in any situation. Browning's model locates Christology in the 'outer envelope', whereas Anderson makes it central to the whole task of interpretation. Anderson prefers the term Christopraxis to Christology because the focus is on Christ's active ministry in the present rather than simply on ideas about Christ's life and work. For Anderson, in seeking to answer the questions 'what shall we do?' and 'how shall we live?' the primary task is to discern the present activity of Christ and to join in with his ministry. The present-day working of the resurrected Jesus is the key hermeneutical principle for all theology – and why theology is fundamentally practical. Theological reflection therefore must seek to interpret how the present works of Christ align with the words of Christ in Scripture in order to answer the questions of faithful living. Anderson agrees with Browning and Graham that God cannot be apprehended outside of human practice; however, he shifts the discussion from metaphysical concerns to the objective reality of the resurrected person of Jesus who is actively at work in revelation and reconciliation and presents himself to us by the Holy Spirit as a reality to be encountered.

Anderson stresses the trinitarian nature of all practical theology to further ground Browning's method in a theological framework. For Anderson, Christ's praxis of ministry is fundamentally to serve God the Father on behalf of the world. Therefore, Christopraxis is not driven by human need but by God's mission to the world. Furthermore, Christ is empowered by the Holy Spirit to carry out this ministry, and the Church is also joined by the same Spirit to participate with the ongoing ministry of Christ. It is the Holy Spirit who binds the past ministry of Christ as recorded in Scripture with the present activity of Christ in the world, and with the eschatological fulfilment of that ministry at Christ's return, thus ensuring the consistency and unity of Christ's ministerial praxis. The Holy Spirit also unites the Church's ongoing ministry with Christ's praxis so that the Church participates with God. This is made possible because it is God the Holy Spirit who gifts the knowledge of God to creatures (revelation) and also enables the creatures' appropriate response (reconciliation). Practical theology is therefore necessarily a pentecostal theology in that it is about discerning the work of Christ's ministry in the world through the Holy Spirit and participating in that ministry by the empowering of the same Spirit.

An obvious question in response to this method is how to discern which human activities are to be considered Christ's praxis of ministry and which are not. The history of horrendous abuse and evil perpetrated by the Church makes clear that not all Church praxis can be considered Christopraxis. Similarly, many non-ecclesial activities can bring healing and can minister to people in need and thus may be considered to align with the work of Christ. Anderson's response is that Christopraxis is only that which reveals Jesus Christ, and which brings reconciliation through joining persons to the body of Christ, his Church. Christ's praxis is inseparable from the purpose of the action, so the praxis of preaching is only 'preaching' when one encounters its goal of revelation of Christ and reconciliation with him. Likewise, the practice of caring is only Christopraxis when its purpose and outcome is linked to Christ's revelation and reconciliation. Therefore, Christ's praxis is inseparable from the purpose of revealing Christ to the world and reconciling people to God in Christ.

Anderson acknowledges that in making the contemporary work of Christ normative for Christian living, this does not in any way detract from the authoritative place of Scripture in the life of faith. Scripture is the normative deposit of apostolic truth which helps the Church to interpret and identify Christ's present praxis. Anderson argues that just as Jesus perfectly fulfilled the requirements of the Old Testament covenant while doing something new, so the Holy Spirit unites Christ's ongoing work with the earthly life of Jesus of Nazareth, ensuring perfect congruence in new contexts. Anderson regularly refers to the story of Peter and Cornelius in Acts 10 as a significant example of the ministry of the risen Jesus being the primary criterion for faithful Christian living. It is the contemporary work of the Holy Spirit coming upon the Gentile Cornelius that causes Peter to reinterpret his Old Testament understanding of God's promises being only for the Jews. Anderson argues that this new eschatological reality is not a doing away with the commands of Scripture purely on the basis of new human experience. Rather, Anderson shows how Paul seeks to defend the inclusion of the Gentiles on the basis of the biblical account of Abraham chosen and called before he was circumcised. For Paul, if Abraham's faith was credited to him as righteousness prior to his circumcision, Abraham is thus 'the ancestor of all who believe without being circumcised' (Romans 4.11). Abraham is the biblical antecedent which verifies the outpouring of the Holy Spirit on the Gentiles as a work of Christ. Thus, Anderson seeks to retain a primary focus on the Church's praxis along with the authoritative role of Scripture through a theology of the work of the Holy Spirit. For Anderson, God the Father in Christ through the Holy Spirit is active agent in the life of faith and in the Church, revealing Godself and reconciling the world to its Creator. Furthermore, this active God is accessible to our human experience because of the objective reality of the risen and ascended human Christ, who is ever present to us via the Holy Spirit. In this way, encountering Christ's present ministry in order to participate with Christ must be the purpose, motivation and goal of any theological reflection that claims to be Christian.

Root's Christopraxis: A Practical Theology of the Cross

Root draws heavily on Anderson to formulate his *Christopraxis: A Practical Theology of the Cross*. Root is arguing against practical theologians such as Browning and Miller-McLemore on the one hand to assert that God's agency exists outside of human action, and is also seeking to argue against Barthian practical theologians such as Purves (2004) on the other hand who seem to leave little space for human action within the defence of divine agency. Root argues that all theology is practical because all human knowledge of God arises from the events of human encounter with God's self-revelation. A focus on the practical is, therefore, not in order to distil practical wisdom but rather to attend to our participation in the very being of God, and Root uses 'ministry' as the central category.

Root understands the risen Jesus to be constantly mediating God's ministry to the world, and this ministry is something we encounter, and participate in, during the ordinary course of our lives. Christ's praxis of ministry is therefore inseparable from our experience of it, but Christ's praxis is also not contained by our experience of it. Root carries out qualitative research data into people's testimonies of encountering God and observes that each description of encountering God is in the context of ministry: either as the person engages in ministry to others (caring, listening, helping); or as they experience God ministering to them (comfort, peace, healing). For Root, ministry is so central because:

> *Ministry as the act of God is the event of God's being* coming to humanity; this being is always becoming because this being is always moving and active. It is, then, the *event* of God's moving that makes ministry an ontological encounter of the divine with the human; it is the infusing of time with eternity, the making of the event in history the place of the transcendent God's becoming. *God's being as becoming is God's very ministry, God's giving Godself to humanity so humanity might be with God* ... God does stuff in Christopraxis; however, it is not really stuff (functions) but rather the unveiling of God's self (becoming) – it is the event of ontological encounter. (2014, p. 94, italics original)

In other words, in practical theology we attend to human action not for some vague theological insights but rather to encounter the living, active God as revealed through Christ's ministry to us. Significantly for Root, this attending to human action is not primarily scientific (in the form of social science methods) or doctrinal (in the form of systematic theology) but rather ministerial. The experience of God's becoming in the encounter of Christ's ministry precedes theology. For Root, as for Anderson, theology is necessarily and always practical, but crucially not because of human ways of being but because of God's being as becoming in ministry. The focus of practical theology is therefore not empirical research of human action – although, as Root argues, this will be part of the task as it recognizes 'living human documents as locales of ministry' (2014, p. 100). Rather, the focus is upon describing God's becoming in the lives of communities encountering God's ministry. These experiential encounters with God, and the descriptions of them, are not for their own sake but rather to lead us into the praxis of ministry so that we might participate in the divine life.

As for Anderson, it is through the Holy Spirit that persons are able to participate in God's being as becoming in ministry. It is the Spirit who reveals the ministry of Christ and invites people to participate, uniting them to God through the action of ministry. The union with God in Christ through the Spirit is therefore not a mystical or abstract concept but concrete, lived and experiential – encouraging a friend, caring for children, feeding the hungry, participating in a march for justice, writing to an MP, sharing assets with others. Each act of ministry is a possibility to encounter the event of God's becoming. Crucially, the possibility of encounter with Christ is not based upon human potential to actualize the transcendent through their practices, as for Graham. For Root and Anderson, it is rather the actuality of Christ's past, present and future ministry to God through the Spirit that enables the possibility for human action to be the occasion for divine encounter and revelation.

Anderson and Root are fully committed to the need for theology to be practical, and to foreground praxis as the necessary context for all knowledge of God. They do so, however, not by making human action central, but by making Christ's praxis the foundation of theology and its primary hermeneutic. God as encountered in Christ is therefore the active agent at the heart of all theology, and our theological reflection methods must reflect this. However, despite their extensive work in articulating a method for pentecostal/charismatic practical theology, neither work offers a model that could be easily taught and used by theological educators and students. I turn my attention now to two works of pentecostal practical theology that do propose such a model for theological reflection.

Cartledge's Mediation of the Spirit

Where Anderson and Root focus on the ministry of Christ, Cartledge's pentecostal practical theology attends more to the Spirit's role in the joining of us to Christ's ministry. He also goes further in proposing a model for theological reflection that implements his pentecostal method. In *Mediation of the Spirit*, Cartledge argues that pentecostal/charismatic scholarship focuses upon the authoritative place of Scripture, the significance of religious experience, and the role of the Holy Spirit in the life of faith. Crucially, for Cartledge, pentecostal/charismatic theology has a particular view of how these three focuses relate to one another. He reviews academic writings in practical theology and observes that the three themes (Scripture, religious experience and the Holy Spirit) do not receive much attention within practical theology and argues that a charismatic/pentecostal approach might help to address this. Cartledge notes that Anderson is one of the few exceptions within practical theology of a scholar incorporating a pentecostal perspective into his understanding of practical theology. Cartledge follows Anderson's approach but wants to explore further *how* the Holy Spirit operates. He uses the concept of the mediation of the Spirit from within pentecostal studies to formulate his argument.

In any relational exchange, there is a communicator, a recipient and a message being communicated. The communicator and the recipient are distinct realities (especially in the case of God and humanity) and so the communication needs to be mediated from one to the other. Cartledge argues that from a trinitarian perspective Christ is the mediator of God, perfectly revealing God to the world, being both the communicator and the message. The Holy Spirit is that which mediates Christ to the world, uniting the communicator with the recipient. The Holy Spirit *is* the mediation of Christ, but there is also 'a set of intermediary material, processes, events, or moments, what we may call the creaturely and created means' (2015, p. 65). In other words, the mediation of the Spirit is always received through the creaturely 'intermediary material' of thoughts, emotions, language, bodies, practices and social relationships. For Cartledge, God chooses to work through these frameworks while not being bound by them.

Cartledge draws heavily on Acts 2 as the foundational text for a charismatic/pentecostal theology to further explore the nature of the Spirit's mediation. He argues from Acts 2 that the mediation is both internal and external. It is internal to people in being affective and cognitive. It engages the emotions and transforms worldviews, enabling people to understand the world and their lives differently – 'when they heard this, they were cut to the heart and said to Peter and the other apostles, "Brothers, what should we do?"' (Acts 2.37). It is also external in that it necessarily incorporates human ritual practices, such as praising God's deeds of power (Acts 2.11), speaking in other languages (2.4) and preaching (2.14ff). The mediation of the Spirit is therefore mental, emotional, embodied and relational as it is enacted in the community of faith to which the Spirit comes.

For Cartledge, a pneumatological practical theology must emphatically say 'yes' both to God sustaining both sides of the mediation in the divine/human encounter and also to the importance of our human situatedness. A pneumatological practical theology embraces the concept of Christ the mediator of God to us *and* the Holy Spirit as the mediation, and it therefore foregrounds both God's divine agency and our experiences. It takes with utter seriousness our created and contextual life, because it has already been taken up into Christ through the Spirit. When we encounter the mediation of the Spirit in a variety of (familiar and unexpected) ways through our emotions, thoughts, bodies and social relationships, we are enabled to do so because the Spirit unites us with Christ, who perfectly reconciles God to God's creation.

Cartledge proposes a diagrammatic model for his charismatic practical theology in his earlier work *Practical Theology: Charismatic and Empirical Perspectives*. He describes the model as focused on the dialectic of encounter between Creator and creature, and oriented towards personal transformation for the purpose of faithful participation in the *missio Dei*. His method comprises a three-stage process of search, encounter, transformation, which Cartledge argues is reflective of the process of a charismatic spirituality. Along with the process, a diagrammatic model maps the relationship between the different parts of the theological reflection. The model has two intersecting axes: a horizontal axis representing a dialectic between the researcher and a charismatic spirituality, and a vertical axis showing a dialectic between the lifeworld (lived reality) and the system (theological and social science theory). He describes how the researcher engages in both of these dialectics in the process of theological reflection. The reflection begins with a question for exploration, which may arise from either end of the vertical axis, and this constitutes the initial 'search' phase of the process. However, Cartledge explicitly gives priority to the 'system', because the whole process is oriented to Christian theology.

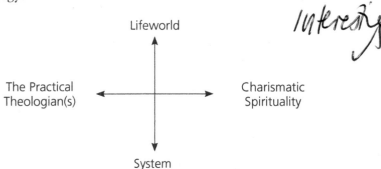

Figure 3: Cartledge's Dialectic Model of Practical Theology (2003, p. 28)

The dialectic then moves along the vertical axis, as many times as necessary, generating insights. This constitutes the 'encounter' phase of the process, where 'the beliefs and practices found in the lifeworld are made to encounter the beliefs and practices of the metanarrative' (2003, p. 29). This 'encounter' may allow the experience to bring insights to the system, while the system also informs and changes the praxis of faith. This encounter therefore leads to 'transformation', which is the final phase of the process. A transformation may happen at either end of the vertical axis and is always acknowledged as the work of the Holy Spirit.

I have been influenced by Cartledge's model in the development of my method, drawing on the back and forth dialectic process and the acknowledgement of the role of the Holy Spirit. However, I consider that his model has three problems for use in the formation of Christians for ministry. First, a model of a dialectic between distinct poles of the lifeworld and the system seems to reinforce the theory/practice divide which his own later pneumatology of mediation rejects. Second, the book is not very accessible for undergraduate students in that Cartledge's descriptions of the process assume that the reflector is engaged in higher-level academic research, with references to literature reviews, the analysis of data and formulating hypotheses. Third, despite acknowledging the priority of Scripture in the task of theological construction, the model conflates theological and social science theory under the description of 'system', which does not sufficiently theorize the relationship between God's story and the insights from other disciplines (see Chapter 5). Therefore, in Chapter 6, I propose a new model of theological reflection for formation which avoids these criticisms, but is built on the same pentecostal/charismatic theological convictions. The final text I examine in this chapter offers a simple, formation-focused and pedagogic model for a pentecostal approach to theological reflection rooted in Bible study, and it has been significant for the formulation of the scriptural cycle.

Johns' Pentecostal Formation

Johns seeks a method for Christian catechesis and formation that is consistent with a pentecostal theology. She engages with Freire's *Pedagogy of the Oppressed* (see Chapters 1 and 2) in order to critique his understanding of his concept of conscientization from a pentecostal perspective. Johns argues that the Latin American communities where Freire focused his educational reforms are also the very communities that have been significantly influenced by pentecostal Christianity. Johns argues that a pedagogical approach that does not adhere to a pentecostal worldview will be less successful among these communities. She critiques Freire for being too focused upon cognitive knowledge and not paying enough attention to the affective, oral and communal dynamics of pentecostal epistemology. Johns considers these to be central aspects of a pentecostal theology, and therefore argues that a pentecostal approach to conscientization is necessary to nuance Freire's method.

Johns argues that Freire's focus on theory/praxis is too dualistic because it relies predominantly on one's cognitive awareness and analysis and is therefore not the holistic understanding of knowledge offered by a biblical worldview. Johns examines the biblical concept of *yada*, which she argues is a holistic means of knowing, such that knowledge of God is relational, affective and connected to the human will. *Yada* knowledge of God is not only information about God, but necessarily a relationship of love and obedience that is evidenced in the way a person lives their life. There is no knowledge of God without this loving, obedient living. She argues that any understanding of praxis needs to be incorporated into a biblical epistemology informed by *yada*. Furthermore, Johns argues that a cognitive conscientization focused on theory/praxis is too human-centric and she identifies the need for a transcendent transforming reality. For pentecostals, it is God who transforms, and there needs to be space for God's active agency within a pedagogy for transformation. However, Johns acknowledges that pentecostals sometimes focus too much upon God's transforming agency and can forget their responsibility to participate with

God by being Holy Spirit-empowered agents of transformation in God's world. Hence, there is a need to integrate a focus on praxis into a pentecostal worldview.

Johns understands a pentecostal theology to be conducive to Freire's conscientization process because of pentecostals' focus on conversion, personal transformation and the ongoing sanctification of self and society. As in Freire's pedagogy, which assumes the equality of all people, pentecostals do not just logically deduce this equality of humanity but experience it as a lived reality through their every-member approach to worship and mission, and through Holy Spirit baptism. Pentecostals have a vision for transformation that is spiritual, social, global and cosmic. Johns highlights the dialectic pentecostals inhabit between Scripture and their experiences as evidence of the ongoing 'consciousness raising process' that is intrinsic to pentecostal spirituality and maintained by the Holy Spirit. Pentecostals therefore are not passive fatalists or self-actualizing agents of change, but rather active participants with God in the transformation of the world through the Holy Spirit who is the agent of 'conscientization'. Johns argues that 'the conscientization process among Pentecostals ... must be a conscientization of the Spirit, unveiling God's will for the world' (1998, p. 107). Therefore, conscientization is not focused upon becoming more aware of oppression only through situational analysis and a human vision for justice and equality; rather, pentecostal conscientization is about the Holy Spirit revealing God's will for creation through Scripture and bringing God's kingdom, which establishes the desired justice, equality and peace. It is a conscientization to God's will – inhabiting God's story and learning our place within it – which references back to the narrative theology discussed in Chapter 3.

In Johns' final chapter, she notes the differences between Freire's pedagogical approach (and its use in Christian education through the works of Groome 1980 and Schipani 1984) and a pentecostal paradigm. For Freire, the goal of education is fulfilling a vocation to full humanity, whereas for pentecostals, the goals are knowing and worshipping God, seeing God's kingdom come, and recognizing that 'full humanization is a redemptive process which is given to people as a gift of grace' (1998, p. 122). For Freire, the content of education is not predetermined, but relates to the historical realities of the lives of the oppressed, whereas for pentecostals, the content for education is both the authoritative story of God in Scripture and also the testimonies of people's lived encounters with God. For Freire, the student is to be understood as a subject of history, whereas for pentecostals, humans are both subjects of history but also objects of God's active working through history. For Johns, the pentecostal community is the primary agent of conscientization, and this happens most explicitly through corporate worship, as participants are educated and formed as disciples through pentecostal liturgical practices.

In light of these differences, Johns proposes a 'pentecostal paradigm for catechesis', which is a model of Bible study for enabling the Holy Spirit-empowered and directed process of conscientization. It is a four-movement process beginning with Sharing our Testimony, followed by Searching the Scriptures, Yielding to the Spirit and finally Responding to the Call. This process is analysed in more detail in Chapter 6 when I discuss my scriptural cycle model. For the purposes of this chapter, it is sufficient to note that Johns proposes a method of theological reflection that is distinct from Freire's liberationist pastoral cycle approach in being specific to a pentecostal theology while also being oriented towards the authoritative narrative of Scripture. Johns' four movements recognize the dialectic of Scripture and experience maintained by the Holy Spirit; the importance of testimony; the active agency of the Holy Spirit; and the authority of Scripture. Johns' pentecostal formation through Bible study brings us back to Chapter 3 and illustrates the necessarily interrelated dynamism between Scripture and pneumatology envisaged in my evangelical, charismatic method. I adapt Johns' model slightly in my scriptural cycle, in light of her own arguments, and I return to this in Chapter 6. What Johns shows is that a distinctly pentecostal methodology for theological reflection for Christian formation is necessary because non-charismatic approaches fail to account for the agency of Christ, through the Holy Spirit, in the life of faith.

Summary

This chapter began by examining the work of two influential practical theologians as case studies to show how and why the Holy Spirit has been overlooked in much practical theology. For Browning and Graham, God cannot be accessed outside of human practices and experiences and this leads them variously to conclude that human practices should be the central feature and starting point for the formulation of theology. The examination of a pentecostal epistemology of encounter showed how pentecostals consider that they encounter God's active agency through the Holy Spirit, and I explored four pentecostal approaches to practical theology that focus on this understanding of encounter as central to their method. These practical theologians agree that God cannot be accessed outside of our embodied human experience, but significantly, they resist making human experience the authoritative focus of their practical theology by turning instead to the person of Christ, who is encountered within those experiences through the Holy Spirit. This pentecostal perspective avoids the separation of, on the one hand, an experiential theology focused on contingent human praxis and, on the other hand, an applied theology focused only on timeless Scripture/doctrine. I have sought to argue that a focus on the risen Christ through the Holy Spirit allows for a third way between these dichotomous approaches – a way that focuses on word and Spirit through encounter.

The Holy Spirit is the mediation of Christ, mediating God to us in the particularities of our human lives and uniting us to God's work of ministry in Christ, as revealed through Scripture and continuing into the present. Experiential knowledge of God is both divinely given and humanly apprehended and it is the Holy Spirit who joins and unites this process, without collapsing the human into the divine or vice versa. Therefore, within theology, there is both continuity with human experience and disruption as God's Holy Spirit comes from outside creation to be encountered in specific, contextual human lives. Practical theology focuses on human experience because this is where God – the living, active and ontologically 'other' – is encountered as an agent within human life. We study human experience to know and encounter the being of God's becoming in Christ through the Spirit and to be joined to the very life of God through participating in God's ministry. Through the Holy Spirit, our stories become testimonies of encounter with this living God and sources of theological reflection. Through the same Holy Spirit, binding the risen Christ with Jesus of Nazareth in the Bible, Scripture is enlivened as the authoritative witness to and interpreter of Christ's present ministry, which is normative for Christian living. Scripture is therefore vital for understanding and interpreting the ongoing ministry of Christ as the Holy Spirit unites the readers of the text with the divine author *and* empowers them to participate in its ongoing story. The Spirit enables us to apprehend and experience God's agency in our lives and also does not eclipse our human reception of and participation in that revelation. Significantly, the encounter of and participation in Christ's praxis of ministry through the Holy Spirit is both personal and corporate – individually experienced and communally manifested through corporate worship, testimony, mission and ministry. It is also past, present and future, as the Spirit unites the work of God in the past with our present experience and with the promised eschatological future of God's eternal reign in Christ. A pentecostal/charismatic approach to practical theology is concerned with transformation and conscientization for justice, equality and human flourishing, but these are understood as the outcomes of Christ's praxis and not as the goals in and of themselves. The vision is a renewal of the entire cosmos and the right ordering of creation under the righteous and eternal reign of God in Christ. It is concerned with the removal of oppression but also with the forgiveness of sins and the reconciliation of all things to their Creator.

This pneumatological epistemology requires a specific method of theological reflection for formation that makes explicit the mediation of the Spirit in the encounter and participation in Christ's ministry. Anderson and Root have argued that new methods need to be developed that facilitate this pentecostal approach to practical theology, and Cartledge and Johns have offered such models for pentecostal theological reflection. Their approaches have significantly informed the development of my scriptural cycle model, which is presented in Chapter 6 and builds upon the themes of 'encounter' and 'participation in Christ's ministry' discussed in this chapter. However, before turning to the proposed model, the next chapter attends to the ways in which frequently used methods of theological reflection disadvantage Christian experience. I argue that experience, as testimonies of encounter with Christ, should be foregrounded in the task of theological reflection for ministerial formation.

5

Selecting the Materials: Experience in Theological Reflection

Introduction

In constructing a new method of theological reflection particularly for the formation of Christians for Christian ministry, so far in this book I have: *cleared the ground* by critiquing frequently used models of theological reflection to show that they are informed by concerns that make them less suited to the formation of Christians for ministry; *laid the foundations* by outlining an understanding of the Bible as authoritative story interpreting our lives and therefore the proper starting point for any reflection considered theological; and *consulted the architect* in focusing on the active, ongoing agency of the Holy Spirit, mediating Christ's ministry to us so that we might participate in it, which is the primary justification for any theology considered practical. In this chapter, I *select the materials* for theological reflection, in addition to Scripture, by examining the role that experience plays.

In Chapter 4, I drew on the Christopraxis practical theology of Anderson and Root to justify the need to pay attention to contemporary human lives because they are the sites of encounter with the risen Christ's ministry, through the mediation of the Holy Spirit. Reflection on human experience is therefore essential for our knowledge of God, when experience takes the form of testimonies of encounters with Christ. This chapter begins with expounding a pentecostal/charismatic approach to testimony, building on the previous chapter, to clarify why religious experiences are especially important for theological reflection. I then explore how the interrelationship between testimony and Scripture must be conceived as asymmetrical, such that Scripture is seen as the consistent and trustworthy authoritative witness to God's self-revelation. Following this, I briefly examine the methods needed to access testimonies as sources of theology. This leads into a discussion about the role of human experiences as reflected upon in other academic disciplines. I argue that other academic disciplines, which are frequently employed in practical theology, are to be seen as resources for theological reflection in three specific ways: complexity, diversity and interrogation. I make a few brief observations about how tradition and reason, as additional materials for theological reflection, are implicitly understood within my method. Finally, I examine the story of the road to Emmaus as an illustrative case study for the proposed inter-relationship between experience and theology.

Experience as Testimony

Chapter 2 argued that correlation and liberation approaches to practical theology prioritize experience in their methods and advocate that experience is the foundational source of theological enquiry and therefore the appropriate place to begin theological reflection. However, it is often not clear what 'experience' means within practical theology, or which experiences count as sources of theological enquiry; or how the different concepts of experience relate to one another; or why the identified experience can tell us anything about God. Cartledge (2015) surveys different understandings and interpretations of the concept of experience within practical theology and laments that they are often not sufficiently theorized. He observes:

> Experience has been used in a general sense of referring to the whole of life or as providing an incident or crisis upon which to reflect theologically. However, very often the theological narratives of those having religious experience are given only cursory attention, if any at all. (2015, pp. 52–3)

repentance
heart warming
dependence

It is somewhat ironic that the sub-discipline of practical theology that focuses on experience fails to attend to, arguably, the only experiences of truly theological significance – those religious experiences of encounter with God. This lack of attention given to religious experience is surprising also given how experience has been understood historically within theology. In the seventeenth century a movement arose within Lutheranism called pietism, which proclaimed the need for faith to be living and lived out. It focused on a crisis experience of repentance and salvation which motivated the Christian to live a pious life. In the eighteenth century John Wesley, influenced by pietism, led a revival that focused on one's inner feeling of faith, after his famous 'heart strangely warmed' experience. Wesley identified four sources of theology – Scripture, Tradition, Reason and Experience – which later came to be known as the Wesleyan Quadrilateral. For Wesley, Experience refers specifically to the personal experience of the assurance of salvation. Therefore, it was particularly a religious experience of inner encounter with God's truth that Wesley saw as a source of theology. Schleiermacher, also influenced by pietism, did much to develop the concept of religious experience. For Schleiermacher, faith emerges from the human feeling of absolute dependence, and religion is the outward expression of that inner feeling. Therefore, the experience that was foundational to Schleiermacher's theology was a *religious* experience. Contemporary practical theology seems to have lost this earlier focus on religious experience as a source of theology and instead understands experience much more broadly, so that any and all human experiences become a legitimate source of theological knowledge.

As argued in Chapter 4, a pentecostal/charismatic practical theology is essentially concerned with our religious experiences of encounters with Christ's present ministry. It is Christ's activity in our lives that justifies the need to conceive of theology as fundamentally practical, and to see our experiences of Christ's ministry as sources of theological enquiry. Theological reflection on religious experience therefore becomes about interpreting 'the "where" of Jesus Christ in our experiences of the now' (Root 2014, p. 99). Arguably, this is especially necessary when theological reflection is for the training, formation and practice of Christian ministry by Christians. We must attend to our lived experiences in theology primarily because that is where we encounter God and are united with Christ by the Holy Spirit as we participate in Christ's ongoing ministry as his body, the Church. This is what Christian ministry is and what theological education needs to form Christians to discern. Theological reflection for formation therefore must attend specifically to experience as testimonies of encounters with Christ.

A testimony is telling one's story of encountering God and God's ministry in Christ. In his discussion of pentecostal spirituality, Cox quotes an unnamed pentecostal scholar who observes that pentecostals understand their faith as 'a narrative theology whose central expression is the testimony' (1995, p. 71). Therefore, the concept of testimony unites a narrative reading of Scripture with pneumatology and practical theology. As discussed in Chapter 4, Smith argues that narrative is central to a pentecostal epistemology and identity, such that the story of a divine encounter is not simply conveying an abstractable principle but the 'narrative *is* the knowledge' (2010, p. 64, italics original). Pentecostals tell God's overarching story and narrate their place within that story through their testimonies of encounter, and this is how they 'know' their faith and the God to whom their faith is oriented. Therefore, the Christian faith is not only the logical deduction of and assent to systematic propositions; rather, Christian faith and theology is oriented around the encounter and participation with God's own life and the witnessing to that through the telling of one's story. Faith is therefore performative, embodied and affective, as well as being cognitive and rationalized. Smith demonstrates how this pentecostal epistemology is consistent with a postmodern philosophy and also with recent developments in Pauline studies which see Paul's thought as primarily narratively structured.

Land identifies three experiences that form the basis of pentecostal testimonies: (1) justification – testimonies of 'forgiveness, new birth, regeneration, adoption, and being in a new world'

(2010, p. 75); (2) sanctification – testimonies of daily growing in holiness, love, joyfulness and thanksgiving; and (3) Holy Spirit baptism – testimonies of the equipping and empowering of the Holy Spirit for mission and ministry. These testimonies, Land argues, bring uniformity to pentecostal believers and make their faith relevant and living. Land notes that pentecostal testimonies are oriented towards their apocalyptic fulfilment. Therefore, the pentecostal practice of testimony-sharing is not only about creating a history and a present identity but doing so in light of a known destiny and destination. Testimonies are understood and told through the lens of God's eschatological perspective. Thus, the focus on the 'now' of our encounters is not a prioritizing of the present as for correlation and liberation methods (see Chapter 2); rather it is the practice of interpreting 'now' through God's story, revealed in the past, and orientating ourselves towards the apocalyptic future fulfilment of God's glorious reign.

Testimonies are personal stories of encountering God, and through those encounters locating oneself as participant in God's story. However, they are also necessarily social and 'a means of social knowledge construction' (Cartledge 2017, p. 17). It is as Christians hear the testimonies of others (both contemporary and historic) that they come to know and interpret their own encounters with God. Cartledge draws on Audi's five sources of knowledge – sense perception, memory, consciousness, reason and testimony – to show that 'the individual aspects of knowing are integrated socially by the notion of testimony' (2003, p. 53). In other words, we need to hear what other people know in order to make sense of what we know from our own embodied perspective. For Johns, testimony-sharing is therefore much more than simply reporting a 'critical incident' or telling a story. It is recognizing our personal encounters with Christ and bringing them to a group for critical engagement and mutual encouragement. Testimony-sharing is 'a confessional movement of self-denial in which the members of the group acknowledge (implicitly or explicitly) the incompleteness of their existence and therefore their need for ongoing transformation' (1998, p. 132).

For Anderson, the Christopraxis shape of these testimonies is vital. For Christian practical theology, the testimonies cannot be vaguely religious encounters with some otherwise unknown transcendental or numinous 'force'. Rather, in order to be sources for Christian theology, testimonies must be stories of encounters with Jesus Christ. Anderson argues that 'there are forms of ministry that appear to be comforting and even reconciling, but if they do not reveal Christ, these ministries are not of God' (2001, p. 54). Such experiences, however enriching, therefore cannot be sources for *theological* reflection. A Christopraxis approach to religious experience focuses the concept of experience on its Christ-proclaiming goal and content: if the experience reveals the risen Christ, then it may be considered as a source for theological enquiry. This is because God continues to make Christ known to us through our encounters with his present ministry and we testify to those encounters so that others might hear the Holy Spirit's invitation also to encounter the risen and present Christ. Crucially, any and every experience may become an occasion to encounter Christ's ministry. As soon as we say, 'I discern Christ is at work here', our experience has become a testimony. However, we cannot assume that an experience can be a source of theological insight if it does not also witness in some way to an encounter with Christ.

Finally, it is vital that we are exposed to diverse testimonies in our theological reflection. Yong (2017) articulates a particular pentecostal hermeneutic for interpreting Scripture that sees the events of Pentecost as the lens through which all Scripture is read, exemplified through Peter's use of Joel in his Acts 2 sermon. Such a hermeneutic draws particularly on the Pentecost imperative for the gospel to be preached in many tongues and God's promise that the Spirit will be poured out on all flesh. For Yong, the diversity of languages at Pentecost witnesses to the inevitable contextuality of all theology. Theology is never separated or separable from our testimonies of encountering the Holy Spirit within our particular cultural-linguistic locations. However, this does not mean that theology-through-testimony cannot transcend the local – Yong argues that over time there will emerge trans-cultural, systematic theologies, precisely because of the work of the one Spirit in the diverse contexts. Diversity is therefore essential to his theological method, and to his understanding of the Church and the work of the Holy Spirit. This is why the Bible must be read with others, through time and space, to prevent the diverse tongues of the Spirit being universalized and homogenized.

Yong envisages the diverse speaking of the Spirit throughout the global Church, but also anticipates discerning the Holy Spirit through other religions and academic disciplines. While I affirm his commitment to diversity in reading the Bible and interpreting the work of the Spirit, I disagree with the way that Yong's reading of Acts 2 leads him to assume a parity of the Holy Spirit's speaking through other academic disciplines and religions. In Acts 2, the apostles spoke in diverse languages, but they did not speak about diverse topics. Those present heard a shared testimony of the work of the Holy Spirit articulated in diverse languages (Acts 2.11 – 'in our own languages we hear them speaking about God's deeds of power'). Joel's promise of the Spirit poured out on all flesh is that they might prophesy, dream and see visions. The outpouring is for the purpose of relational knowledge of God, not any and every type of knowledge about the world. The diverse speech is initiated by the Spirit and testifies to the present work of God through the Spirit. It is therefore diverse testimonies of Christ that can be considered a necessary source of theology, and not just diverse perspectives or insights about the world. Yong acknowledges the need for discernment in identifying the speaking of the Spirit, and he is clear that this discernment requires a Christological, Trinitarian and therefore canonical framework. We read Scripture through the Spirit, and we discern the Spirit through Scripture. A pentecostal approach to theological reflection is therefore, necessarily and permanently, word and Spirit, Scripture and testimony, belief and encounter.

Testimony and Scripture

This interrelationship between our testifying to God's story and
God's story telling us may be interpreted to imply an equality
between these ways of knowing God which could be used to
legitimate a 'beginning from testimony' method. For example,
Johns pentecostal method of catechesis begins with testimony
and moves to reading Scripture. Scripture itself may be seen as
a written collection of historical testimonies by God's people
of their encounters with God, and thus understood as of the
same kind as the testimonies of our contemporary experiences
which I am describing. However, as argued in Chapter 3, I
consider the Bible to be unique in always witnessing to God's
self-revelation, whereas our testimonies of encounter with the
Holy Spirit are not always, reliably and consistently, God's self-
revelation to us. I refer to Lindbeck, Anderson and Hunsinger
to show that testimony and Scripture are interrelated in an
asymmetrically ordered way, such that Scripture remains the
authoritative witness to God interpreting our testimonies.

For Lindbeck, religion is not a product of experience; rather
he sees religions as 'producers of experience' (2009, p. 16). In
accordance with the narrative theology of Chapter 3, Lindbeck
argues that God's story is what gives form and shape to our
experiences, not the other way around. He argues against, on
the one hand, a traditional, propositional view of religion that
sees religion as objectively true and cognitively apprehended
and, on the other hand, what he calls an experiential-expressive
view of religion that bases religion upon experience. Lindbeck
instead proposes a cultural-linguistic understanding of religion
where religion is like a language or a culture that is internal-
ized and which gives meaning to everything else. On this view,
there are no religious experiences that can be independent of
the language and concepts used to interpret and understand
them. Even to name something as an 'encounter with Christ'
requires a narrative of 'Christ' with which to relate it. Religious experiences are secondary to the texts, doctrines and
liturgies of religion that give shape to the experiences. Therefore, Scripture and the Bible-reading Church give the necessary

story and language of Christ in order for an experience to be discerned and articulated as an encounter with Jesus Christ of Nazareth. However, this is not a one-way process, as the religious experiences necessarily verify, interpret and perhaps challenge the inherited understandings of the texts, doctrines and practices.

Anderson helpfully describes this fluid but asymmetrical interrelationship of testimony and Scripture as 'eschatological preference' and 'biblical antecedent' (2001, p. 109). He argues that whenever the Holy Spirit seems to lead the New Testament Church into something new (eschatological preference), there is always a mandate in Scripture (biblical antecedent) to justify the practice. For example, Paul argues for the inclusion of Gentiles not just on the basis of his experience of Gentile faith but through Abraham, who was called and declared righteous prior to circumcision (Romans 4). Likewise, Peter justifies the Spirit's working at Pentecost as the fulfilment of Joel 2 (Acts 2). The Spirit's empowering of women for ministry can be seen as having biblical antecedents in Deborah (Judges 4.4–5), Miriam (Exodus 15.20) and Huldah (2 Kings 22.14–20). Furthermore, God's declaration to Peter that the foods in his vision are clean (Acts 10.15) may look to Genesis 9.3 as an antecedent to this declaration. In this way, Anderson argues, the 'new' things of the Holy Spirit which we may encounter and to which we testify must always be tested and verified against the witness of Scripture. Of course, the Holy Spirit may, and often does, initiate an encounter with Christ that prompts our theological reflection (which in this case would mean examining Scripture for help to interpret the encounter). However, starting theological reflection from Scripture is the enactment of faith and the process of Christian formation which affirms that we need to be immersed in the scriptural story in order to recognize where Christ, through the Holy Spirit, is at work. We root ourselves in the Bible and from there we learn to read the world and our experiences within the world, so that we can discern Christ's present ministry in our lives. Scripture is the unique and authoritative witness to God and God's dealings with the world against which our testimonies must be compared;

hence the interrelationship between Scripture and testimony is asymmetrical in favour of Scripture.

I have borrowed the term 'asymmetrical' from Hunsinger (1995) to describe the relationship of testimony to Scripture. Hunsinger seeks to understand how her Barthian theology should relate to her training in psychology and her practice as a pastoral counsellor. She draws on the Chalcedonian formulation which describes the relationship between Christ's divine and human natures as a pattern of 'indissoluble differentiation', 'inseparable unity' and 'indestructible order'. She sees in this pattern – differentiation, unity and order – categories for helpfully articulating the relationship of theology to psychology, where the two disciplines remain distinct but united in an ordered way. For Hunsinger, theology has the logical priority over psychology in a comparable way to the logical priority of Christ's divine nature over his human nature. She describes this relationship as asymmetrical. Similarly, Scripture has logical priority over our present testimonies because the Bible is God's elected, inspired, sanctified and trustworthy witness to Jesus Christ, and the Bible (read and proclaimed by the Church) gives the cultural-linguistic framework for our testimonies, not the other way around. Therefore, testimony and Scripture are differentiated and united in an asymmetrical way: Scripture provides the interpretative framework for our testimonies, our testimonies inform our reading and interpretation of Scripture.

This asymmetrical interrelationship may be best illustrated with a few brief examples. A practical theologian may carry out interviews with 80 lay women in Uganda to hear their testimonies of encountering Christ through Holy Communion. The data of their testimonies is evidently not an equivalent or symmetrical contribution to a sacramental theology as are Jesus' words of institution as recorded in Scripture. Therefore, even if they were found to be inconsistent with Scripture, the women's testimonies could not and should not convince the Church to reject Jesus' words of institution. However, this is not the same as saying that their testimonies are irrelevant to a sacramental theology. Because of the mediation of the Holy Spirit in the church community, the Ugandan women can encounter the same person of Christ who spoke the original words of institution recorded in Scripture, and thus the two perspectives are inseparably united. Therefore, the women's encounters with Christ's present ministry in the Eucharist (discerned through Scripture) can be a source for theological understanding and knowledge. Their encounters with Christ may initiate in their church a renewed appreciation of Jesus' words of institution; or a transformation of the ways in which the Eucharist is practised, or a new interpretation of the interaction between the celebration of the Eucharist and the practice of hospitality. This process may be understood as 'revelatory' in that Christ continues to reveal himself to his Church, by the Holy Spirit, and to bring knowledge and understanding of God which guides them into truth. This revelatory experience of God through the encounter, which is initiated by Christ through the Holy Spirit, may be 'new' knowledge of God to the people involved while also being already revealed by God in Scripture.

Similarly, encounters with Christ's ministry through the leadership of women might be the catalyst for a congregation to reinterpret Paul's prohibitions on women in 1 Corinthians 14 through drawing on the example of women deacons and apostles in Paul's letters; or an encounter with Christ through the suffering of the oppressed might inspire a rereading of humanity's role in creation care, and initiate engagement with social activism; or a testimony of Christ's ministry of forgiveness might bring new life to reading Jesus' parables of the kingdom and inspire new practices of generosity. In the introduction to *Advancing Practical Theology*, Stoddart (2014) recalls his own 'conversion' to the importance of practical theology by recalling a story of how a particular South African congregation wrestled with apartheid: 'the theological bulwark defending Apartheid was crumbling under the pressure of people's experience of one another ... The *practice* of interracial communion was, in this particular congregation, challenging the prevailing theological paradigm' (2014, p. 9, emphasis original). It was a congregation's encounter with Christ through one another, worshipping as a multi-racial congregation, that caused them to reimagine the theological traditions of apartheid that they had inherited. They substantiated this revision through drawing on Scriptures that speak of unity and equality. Thus, their testimonies were an essential and necessary source for the reconstruction of their theology.

These examples illustrate that we start theological reflection from Scripture as the faith assertion of our dependence on God and God's story, but we expect our testimonies of encounters with Christ, through the Holy Spirit, to generate theological insight; to form and test our theological paradigms; and to transform our reading, understanding and living in ways that more faithfully cohere with God's story. Thus, it is as testimony of encounter with the risen Christ that our contemporary human experiences should be considered a source of theology, in an asymmetrical way when compared with the uniquely authoritative source of Scripture.

Methods of Accessing Testimonies

This focus on testimonies raises the question of how one can be considered to experience an encounter with Christ through the Holy Spirit in order to theologically reflect upon it. Traditionally within practical theology, methods from the social sciences have come to dominate as the appropriate way to access and study human experience as theological source. Osmer describes how 'empirical research is a disciplined way of attending to others in their particularity' (2008, p. 39). Osmer sees this 'attending to others' as necessary to answer the questions, 'what is happening?' and 'why is it happening?' before drawing on the Christian tradition to inform 'what should be happening?' Within practical theology, social science methods are generally accepted to be the most rigorous way of 'attending to others' to study human experience as a source of theological reflection. These methods generally include, but are not limited to, interviews, participant observation, case studies, ethnography, questionnaires, action research, documentary analysis and journalling. They are informed particularly by the academic disciplines of sociology, anthropology and psychology. A number of helpful textbooks are available describing these different methods and how to use them (Cameron, Richter, Davies and Ward 2005; Swinton and Mowat 2006; Moschella 2008; Osmer 2008; Cameron and Duce 2013), and I will not rehearse their contributions here.

However, despite this prevalence of social science methods in practical theology, there are clearly significant challenges in their use within theology, and especially in theological reflection focused on testimonies. This is because Christian theology advocates a theistic worldview where faith, belief and spirituality are essential categories, whereas the social science methods frequently employed within practical theology deliberately adopt a methodological agnosticism where questions of faith and spirituality are bracketed off as unverifiable for the researcher. Social science primarily employs a social constructivist view of its field of study, where there is no objective reality beyond the negotiated interactions of social agents. A theological perspective affirms that there is a God who is independent from these social interactions, and therefore is a reality outside of our socially constructed world. These different methodological assumptions are equivalent to different languages and are not easily reconciled. Therefore, it would seem especially problematic to use these agnostic/atheistic methods to access and study testimonies of encounters with Christ as a source of theological reflection.

Rather, it is my conviction that theological reflection for the formation of Christians for ministry must shift its focus from social scientific methods of research in order to attend to Christian 'methods', if they are to access Christian testimonies as sources of theology. Such methods include traditional Christian spiritual disciplines, for example Bible reading, prayer, intercession, Eucharist, preaching, thanksgiving, *lectio divina*, confession, service, worship, fasting, giving, mission, community, meditation, silence, solitude and obedience. It is these 'methods' that theological reflection for formation must prioritize and nurture, if reflectors are to encounter Christ and participate in his ministry. These traditional spiritual disciplines are the methods given to the Church as gracious gift for its constitution and nurture as the body of Christ. This is because it is God in Christ through the Holy Spirit who encounters us in our humanity – rather than we who find God in our experiences. Our methods therefore must prioritize and nurture the ways in which all theology is dependent upon God's grace. This is not to say that the spiritual disciplines become methods to initiate encounters; rather, they provide the most trustworthy conditions through which to receive and recognize an encounter with Christ's ministry. The next chapter discusses some ways in which these Christian 'methods' or disciplines are to be employed within the scriptural cycle model for theological reflection. I now address what role other academic disciplines play in theological reflection, given that I have significantly questioned the use of their methods.

Experience as Other Disciplines

I now outline the ways in which experience, as reflected upon and conceptualized in other academic disciplines, contributes to theology. As discussed in Chapters 1 and 2, correlation methods of theological reflection have been particularly concerned to correlate theology with insights from other disciplines, and liberation methods have used other disciplines as part of the conscientization process of social analysis. Therefore, other disciplines – particularly the social sciences – have come to have a central role in practical theology, and in some ways their usage has come to define the sub-discipline. My method of theological reflection for formation acknowledges the importance of other disciplines by seeing them as *tools for* rather than *sources of* theology.

This concept of other disciplines as tools for theology is similar to what Osmer describes as the transformational model of interdisciplinary working. He describes this transformational model as an *ad hoc* use approach to other disciplines: 'where literary and hermeneutical theories are helpful to theology, they are used; where they are not, they are discarded'

(2008, p. 170). There is no systematic programme for how theology relates to the insights of other disciplines because there can be no systematic translation of one 'language' into the other. Rather, insights about experience, accessed through the scholarship of other disciplines, are 'reappropriated' (Loder 1999, p. 366) or 'converted' (Swinton and Mowat 2006, p. 92) in the service of theology. Using Lindbeck's cultural-linguistic metaphor, a language may appropriate or convert words from other languages to express something that cannot be communicated as clearly in the native tongue, for example in English the use of *déjà vu*, *Zeitgeist* and *siesta*. This process of appropriation transforms both the original meaning of the word and the host language, in an asymmetrical, *ad hoc* way. In this model, unlike for correlation models of interdisciplinary working, theology is the primary discourse and other disciplines serve the task of theology. This is because God's story revealed in Scripture, and our encounters with Christ's ministry, tell us who and what we are. Our partial estimates of who we think we might be, generated using methodologically agnostic paradigms in a world marred and broken by sin, is a significantly less reliable perspective than God's elected, sanctified witness contextualized through God's initiative to encounter us in Christ's present ministry.

However, as discussed in Chapter 3, various scholars have critiqued Lindbeck's cultural-linguistic framework model because Christianity could be seen as an echo-chamber, where Scripture and testimony perpetuate a particular (white, male) cultural or social reading of God's story which excludes other minority perspectives. I consider that careful attention to diverse cultural testimonies of encounters with Christ and reading the Bible with globally and culturally diverse Christians are already significant ways that the Church can avoid narrow, exclusivist retellings of the story by one dominant cultural expression of Christianity. However, it is the case that the Church too is marred by sin, and even given God's trustworthy revelation in Scripture and the Holy Spirit's mediation of Christ to us, we do not always read, see, know or live aright, even when we do it with diverse others. Furthermore, the patriarchal contexts in which the Bible arose further problematizes for many its status as Scripture. Given, then, the challenges of the sin of the Church and the patriarchy of the text's history, I consider that other disciplines can serve theology by potentially providing accountability, humility and reflexivity to prevent the Church telling its story in a way that makes one cultural expression normative. Other disciplines can help us to examine our reading of Scripture and our discernment of Christ-encounters in order that our participation in Christ's ministry might be genuinely to and for the world.

In this section, I clarify three specific ways in which other disciplines may act as a resource in the service of theology: complexity, diversity and interrogation. These ways are not intended to be exhaustive, nor are they understood as categorically distinct from one another. Rather, the articulation is to give clarity and purpose to the use of other disciplines in theology. I analyse each in term, illustrating their contributions to theology with examples from other practical theologians.

Complexity

One of the main ways in which other disciplines serve theology is by bringing an awareness of complexity to our understanding of testimonies. Essentially, other disciplines enable theologians to recognize that life and faith are more complex than we may often be tempted to present. Swinton and Mowat describe complexifying situations to be one of the purposes of practical theology, and they define this as 'to take that which at first glance appears normal and uncomplicated and through a process of critical reflection at various levels, reveal that it is in fact complex and polyvalent' (2006, p. 13). They argue that the questions often asked in academic theology are very different from those being asked by people of faith in local churches. For them, the process of complexifying is a significant way in which the range of possible questions can be opened up to ensure that academic theology is engaging with the life of the Church in the world.

Feminist scholarship has made significant contributions to theology through complexifying the human condition. What had previously been thought to be true of all people has been shown by feminists to be gendered, and by postcolonial scholarship to be racial also. For example, Gilligan's (1982) significantly influential work into psychological development shows how mature moral decision-making had previously been thought to be characterized by separation from others. Gilligan uses psychology to show that this model is not consistent with women's processes of attachment and relating, and thus mature female moral reasoning does not conform to the previously accepted male models of human maturity. Such an awareness of the gendered nature of moral reasoning may be drawn on, for example, to nuance a person's testimony of encounter with Christ which emphasized their individual calling at the expense of community vocation. The insights of other disciplines enable us to say to such a testimony-giver: 'Are you aware that your interpretation of your encounter with Christ could be informed by a male bias?'

In another example, Miller-McLemore's (1994) work on motherhood draws on sociological analysis and psychological and feminist theory to complexify understandings of motherhood. This is in order to question traditional theological categories of work and care to challenge gendered divisions of labour according to these categories. Her work shows that the concept of 'mother' is complex and polyvalent and thus she critiques simplistic notions of, for example, seeing one's mothering as a site for encountering God's motherly care. Such insights enable us to ask ourselves: 'Is my testimony of encountering God in my mothering informed by a particular social construct of "mother"?'

In a further example, Swinton's 2012 work *Dementia* draws on psychology to show how the experience of dementia complexifies traditional theological understandings of humans as individual, cognitive persons. Seeing persons in these terms leads to viewing dementia sufferers as non-persons. Swinton argues that instead, our theological understanding of persons should reside in the human as contingent, embodied creature in relation to a Creator God. Thus, the experience of dementia, articulated by other disciplines, may be drawn on to bring complexity to how we perceive persons as the site of Christ's present ministry. For example, we may ask our church: 'are we expecting people to articulate a particular cognitive assent to Christian doctrine during this evangelistic event?'

These examples are cited to illustrate the ways in which practical theologians already draw on human experience accessed through other disciplines to complexify understandings of God and the ways in which God encounters people. Seeing the insights of other disciplines as resources or tools means that they are utilized in an *ad hoc*, transformational way to inform our reflexive discernment of our participations in Christ's ongoing ministry. The insights, in and of themselves, do not necessitate a reinterpretation of our understanding of encounter with Christ or the Scriptures, because it is God's story revealed in Scripture and through the Holy Spirit's mediation that is given primacy as a source for theology and which narrates us, rather than the other way around. However, the process of complexifying through the insights of other disciplines is necessary to prevent naive, simplistic perspectives influencing our theological reflections and to enable us to be more careful, humble, reflexive and inclusive readers and tellers of God's story to and for the world.

Diversity

Another way in which other disciplines serve theology is by bringing diverse perspectives to our reading and interpretation of the Bible. When done well, the process of complexifying our testimonies, and their wider contexts, helps voices that were previously hidden to be noticed and heard, and this is particularly necessary for diversifying the ways we read Scripture. Cameron, Reader, Slater and Rowland argue that 'it is a key task of practical theology to identify the unheard voices and missing conversations in the life of the Church and make them audible' (2012, p. xi). For so long theology has been written by men who have been at the centres of power and establishment in the institutional churches. This historic lack of diversity has excluded and marginalized people and their perspectives from the theological task and thus not allowed them to find themselves in God's story. When the insights of other disciplines complexify and diversify, for example, concepts of sin, forgiveness or the atonement, we are able to hear different perspectives and ways of reading Scripture and understanding doctrines, and this exposes the partiality of our own perspectives.

For example, Jagessar and Burns (2014) show how, from the perspective of those who have been colonized, 'kingdom of God' language communicates superiority, privilege, domination and violence – and this is how Christian language has often been used by colonizing nations. Jagessar and Burns also examine other prominent Christian metaphors used in worship, such as 'light', 'blind' and 'body of Christ', to argue for how the language of Christian worship can be experienced by people of colour and disabled people as perpetuating their stereotyping and oppression. Thus, these diverse perspectives enable us to read and tell God's revealed story in more inclusive ways. Another example of the importance of other disciplines for diversifying theological perspectives is the work of Lewis (2007), who privileges the stories of deaf people to construct a deaf liberation theology. She uses sociological models of disability to critique theological constructions of sin, sickness, healing, salvation, the image of God and suffering, which have often been based on a medical understanding of deafness. These perspectives highlight ways in which deaf people have been subjected to oppression, and Lewis focuses particularly upon ways that liturgical practices must be transformed to overcome this injustice. In a third example, Jones (2019) draws on trauma studies to show how trauma influences the ways victims encounter and remember the Christian story of Christ's crucifixion. She examines how experiences of trauma challenge theologies of grace and suggests ways in which the tradition might be reconceived through these perspectives.

As for the previous theme of complexifying, a situation of injustice or exclusion is not necessarily a source of knowledge about God. Just because someone experiences marginalization, that is not justification, in and of itself, to make the theological changes they identify as necessary towards their understanding of a just inclusion. So, for example, Daly (1973) draws on feminist theory to critique the misogyny at the heart of the Christian faith and uses this as grounds for rejecting God as Father and the entire patriarchal religion. Feminist critiques of Christian Scripture and tradition are necessary to complexify and diversify the Christian story, to expose the androcentricity of traditional tellings of that story, and to make the Church reflexive about its own located tellings. However, such critiques also themselves need to be transformed in light of God's story and God's Christocentric account of liberation, justice and inclusion. Therefore, insights of other disciplines are tools that can aid the process of discerning Christ's contemporary ministry through Scripture and testimony by enabling our reflexivity and accountability, which can make the case for theological reimaginings.

Interrogation

The third way in which other disciplines contribute to the task of theological reflection is through the interrogation of church practices. In his contribution to *Perspectives on Ecclesiology and Ethnography*, Webster (2012) argues that phenomenological accounts of the Church, grounded in experience, cannot be a foundational source for theology. This is because the doctrine of the Trinity tells us about the Church, not the Church telling us about the Trinity. Brittain, however, responds to Webster's argument, claiming that this view of the Church as grounded in God leads to an overemphasis on the eschatological perfection of the Church. This results in an inadequate treatment of the Church's present sinfulness, where any failures or struggles of the contemporary Church are dismissed as not the true Church. Brittain argues that this causes the Church either to deny its present sinfulness or to acknowledge its sin as a universal condition, therefore overlooking the need for specific actions to rectify particular sins. He argues that 'ethnography is potentially one way that the church can attend carefully to the blessings and failings that it is presently experiencing corporately' (2014, p. 29), and thus help to address the issues of sin and injustice which the study of experience has exposed. In other words, the study of practices and beliefs within the contemporary Church is necessary to interrogate church practice and expose where the Church is failing to live out its gospel hope.

This theme is linked to Freire's concept of 'conscientization to injustice' as discussed by Johns (see Chapter 4). Johns argues that a pentecostal pedagogy needs to incorporate Freire's understanding of praxis because pentecostals 'often neglect to acknowledge that via [God's] transformation humans become partners with God in the redemptive process. They have failed to respond appropriately in obedience as historical subjects' (1998, p. 39). In other words, pentecostals have often got caught up in rejoicing in God's transforming agency, such that they have forgotten to join in with that transforming process as worldly agents of change themselves. Using other academic disciplines to complexify and diversify our interpretations of our testimonies and the Scriptures may lead to an increased conscientization to situations of injustice that require a response.

Scharen's *Public Worship and Public Work* is an example of studying congregational life as a way to interrogate theological teaching on the role of worship. Scharen examines character ethics advocated by Hauerwas and others and questions whether Christian worship does indeed form Christian people who engage in public work. Scharen suggests that such a view is too linear, simplistic and idealistic in how it sees both worship and formation, and he attempts to nuance and complexify this picture through case studies. He argues that a congregation's communal identity is a significant factor in forming their public engagement and that the Church/world dichotomy proposed by Hauerwas does not do justice to the ways in which the congregation's engagement with the world informs the telling of its story. Scharen finds that 'worship is less formation as con-formation, a reinforcement and reminder of what is important in life as they envision it in that place' (2004, p. 221).

Another example is Fulkerson's (2007) *Places of Redemption.* She uses postmodern place theory and ethnography to study the practices of an interracial, diverse church. She examines how the practices of the church are much more significant than their beliefs for constructing an inclusive place where all may be seen. Her interrogation of practices of welcome reveals that a church may express its belief in hospitality and the importance of inclusion, but the place of welcome is constituted through the interaction of affective, visceral, embodied beings – the way our bodies and emotions react to other bodies shapes and communicates welcome far more than beliefs. Clark describes this interrogating function of practical theology as a necessary 'feedback loop' (2003, p. 190) that prevents a linear application of Scripture/doctrine to the church's life by highlighting where and why there might be dissonance between practice-shaping beliefs and belief-shaped practices. Other disciplines are therefore a necessary resource in this process of highlighting such dissonance.

This articulation of three contributions of other disciplines to theology – complexity, diversity and interrogation – is not intended to be exhaustive. However, the identified contributions give specific shape and content to vague statements of 'the importance of experience to theology' or 'the necessity of insights from other disciplines' which dominate within practical theology. Discerning experience as Christ-encounters is necessary for theological reflection that enables us to read the Bible in light of Christ's present ministry, and Christ's present ministry in light of Scripture. This is so that we can discern the 'here and now' activity of Christ through the Holy Spirit in order to participate. However, due to our own sinfulness and locatedness, this reading and discerning may require insights from the empirical study of human experience and resources of other disciplines to complexify, diversify and interrogate our theology and practice so that we do not see the world or God according to the narrow perspective of our particular location. The other disciplines help us to be reflexive and accountable in our reflections so that our participation in Christ's ministry is genuinely to and for the whole world. However, they too may need to be transformed in light of God's story.

The Role of Tradition and Reason

This chapter has focused particularly on the relationship of Scripture and experience as sources of theology. This is due to the particular need to justify how and why I have given precedence to Scripture in a method purporting to be practical theology. However, consequently, the roles of reason and tradition within theology seem to have been ignored in the articulation of my method. I do not have the space to examine fully these concepts, but rather I shall state significant ways in which they have been implicit throughout. This is so that readers can recognize that, although not explicitly named, tradition and reason are necessary to the practice of the scriptural cycle theological reflection model.

I understand 'tradition' to refer to 'a living and active process of passing on the Christian faith, rather than as a static source of revelation, independent of Scripture' (McGrath 2000, p. 220). The relevance of this passing on of the faith, from one generation of the Church to the next, is particularly evident within my method in four main ways. First, in Chapter 3, I discussed the importance of reading the Bible with other Christians and listed these 'others' as historical, geographical, academic and sociological. How previous generations of Christians have read and interpreted the Scriptures is vital for informing our contemporary reading. These historical 'others' and their writings are necessary for our theological interpretations because their theology and practice shaped the faith that we have received. Second, through church history, we hear the testimonies of how our ancestors in the faith encountered Christ's ministry in their own time and context. Christ was active by the Holy Spirit in every generation of the Church, and each generation's articulation and interpretation of their testimonies, and their consequent participation in Christ's ministry, is vital to help inform our own interpretations of Christ's present ministry. Third, Lindbeck's cultural-linguistic understanding of faith highlights the doctrines and creeds through which Scripture is interpreted by the community of faith. Study of these doctrines and creeds, and the history of their development, is necessary for a Christian reading of Scripture. Fourth, I highlighted in this chapter the importance of Christian spiritual disciplines as the trustworthy ways in which we may facilitate an encounter with Christ's ministry. These methods draw attention to the importance of traditions of liturgy and worship for theological reflection. Therefore, within the scriptural cycle model, there is clear evidence for the importance of these four interrelated aspects of Christian tradition – historical scriptural exegesis, church history, doctrines and creeds, and liturgy/worship. Tradition does not have its own stage or step in the cycle model precisely because it may be incorporated into any of the five stages of the model (see Chapter 6). Tradition, therefore, has an integral role in helping reflectors to discern an encounter with Christ through Scripture and testimony in order to participate in that ministry.

I understand 'reason' to refer to humanity's capacity for rational reflection upon God's self-revelation through word and Spirit. Again, this has been implicit throughout the preceding chapters in three main ways. First, reading the Bible in humility, as a whole, with other Christians, requires tools of enquiry, critical engagement, attending to different evidence, comparing interpretations and making judgements, all of which are associated with and dependent upon rational thought. Essentially, the practice of 'reading the Bible with others' undermines any view of a universal rationalism, as Christians from different locations and situations bring their different rationalities to the task of interpretation. Reason is employed in the engagement with these different perspectives, without elevating it or universalizing it. Second, pentecostal/charismatic epistemology necessitates an interaction between reason and testimony. Testimonies are not just an emotional, embodied, intuited experience, they require reasoned analysis of an event to produce a narrative that is a coherent, interpretative and ordered testimony. Reason is an essential component in translating a felt experience into a narrative testimony. Third, the necessity of reason is evident in the use of other disciplines and informs the complexifying, diversifying and interrogation that other disciplines bring. Within the scriptural cycle, these interrelated aspects of reason – interpreting Scripture, interpreting testimony and interpreting experience through other disciplines – are again incorporated into all five stages of the model to be outlined in the next chapter. The focus on discernment in the third stage of the process may particularly relate to the exercise of reason, when reason is understood as in partnership with the Holy Spirit, seeking after God's revealed wisdom. Essentially, the scriptural cycle envisages this discernment as a practice of communion – with other Christians and with the Holy Spirit. So it is the exercise of corporate reason/discernment, through the Holy Spirit, within worship, that is necessary for theological reflection.

The Road to Emmaus: A Case Study

To conclude this chapter, I examine the story of the road to Emmaus in Luke 24 to illustrate the proposed asymmetrical interrelationship between Scripture and experience in theological reflection. O'Neill and Shercliff refer to the story of the road to Emmaus as 'a parable of theological reflection' (2018, p. 142) and Cameron, Reader, Slater and Rowland state that 'the process of theological reflection can be illustrated with reference to the description of the walk to Emmaus in Luke's Gospel' (2012, p. 9). The road to Emmaus story therefore seems like an appropriate place to test out my description of theological reflection.

For both Cameron, Reader, Slater and Rowland and O'Neill and Shercliff, the road to Emmaus story is a helpful illustration of a pastoral cycle-type theological reflection because it begins with the disciples reflecting together and conversing about the strange events they have just experienced. O'Neill and Shercliff ask: 'Isn't this what we do, in our groups, in our reading? A theological reflection is often a discussion that comes out of a tension, or something that doesn't make sense. Something is not quite right, something has disappointed us' (2018, p. 143).

Into this 'Experience' (the first stage of the pastoral cycle), Jesus comes alongside the disciples and asks them what they are talking about, inviting them into further reflection on the situation (the second, Exploration stage of the pastoral cycle). In response to their analysis of the situation, Cameron, Reader, Slater and Rowland note that 'Jesus draws into the conversation the resources of the faith tradition' (2012, p. 10), and so they engage in the third, Reflection stage of the pastoral cycle. This leads to a moment of transformation as Jesus breaks the bread and they recognize him as the risen Lord. This transformation precipitates their Action (the fourth and final stage of the pastoral cycle), as they run back to Jerusalem to tell the others what they have seen. There is much in this reading of the story that may be helpful for understanding theological reflection. However, I consider that the story powerfully illustrates the asymmetry between experience and Scripture in five important ways, calling into question the appropriateness of theological reflection starting from experience for those 'doing' theology for ministry. (av q)

First, it is God's activity in Christ on the cross that precipitates the disciples' experience of theological reflection. God's initiative precedes their questions such that our experiences, and our reasoned reflections upon them, are always a response to God's first move. Starting our theological reflection from Scripture is the act of faith that testifies to this truth that as Christians our lives are understood as responses to God's creating, sustaining and redeeming work. We start our reflecting by making space for God to have the first word, to initiate an encounter and to invite us to participate in Christ's ministry.

Second, the disciples were 'talking with each other about all these things that had happened' (Luke 24.14), but this process of reflection and analysis is unfruitful. They could have walked on that road for ever, talking and trying to reason, analyse and understand what happened, and still they would not have arrived at the mysterious truth. This is analogous to using other disciplines in the process of theological reflection.

woo'. diss'.

For example, the disciples could have interviewed everyone present at the crucifixion, examined medical models of death, conducted a sociological analysis of the institutional powers of the day; and applied psychological theories of trauma to interpret the witness testimonies, and still they would not have arrived at the theological interpretation that Jesus gives. Jesus even rebukes them, following their explanation of the situation: 'Oh, how foolish you are' (Luke 24.25). It is only the encounter with Christ, interpreting the Scriptures for them, that gives them the necessary framework to understand their own experiences. The narrative comes from outside of themselves, in the form of Christ and the words of Scripture, and without that they remain unenlightened. This is not to say that their attempts at 'situational analysis' are pointless. What their 'talking together' seems to bring to the situation is confusion and sadness (Luke 24.17) and thus their attempts at interpretation become 'resources' of despair, which ultimately enable them in their desperation to enter into the encounter with Christ which he initiates.

Third, it is through the Scriptures that Jesus tells them the story of the Messiah and connects their experiences with that wider story – 'Then beginning with Moses and all the prophets, he interpreted to them the things about himself in all the scriptures' (Luke 24.27). Jesus uses Scripture to narrate their story so that their testimony is located in that grand narrative. The Bible tells them what they have witnessed because they cannot understand it for themselves. Furthermore, it is the encounter with Jesus that helps them to interpret the Scriptures and only through the encounter can they hear the story anew, in light of Christ's present ministry. The pattern of Jesus interpreting the Scriptures to them shows the necessary interrelationship between Scripture and testimonies of encounter with Christ. The asymmetry of the relationship between Scripture and testimony that I have argued for in this chapter is less apparent in this passage precisely because the risen Jesus is physically walking alongside them and talking with them, and thus is the authoritative interpreter of the story that witnesses to himself. However, the story itself anticipates Jesus' departure and the sending of the Holy Spirit upon the disciples (Luke 24.49). Therefore, in the absence of Jesus' physical, embodied presence in the contemporary Church, Scripture remains the primary source, with the Holy Spirit empowering the Church's witness to the story.

Fourth, as Cameron, Reader, Slater and Rowland and O'Neill and Shercliff acknowledge, even after this Bible study, the disciples still require a moment of recognition and transformation. The discussions with Jesus on the road may have brought understanding of the events, but something further is needed for them to connect their newfound knowledge about the Messiah with this person in front of them. This testifies to the initiative and active agency of the Holy Spirit within the process of reflection and understanding. We are told at the beginning of the story that the disciples' 'eyes were kept from recognizing him' (Luke 24.16) and then that 'their eyes were opened' (Luke 24.31) after he broke the bread. The Holy Spirit is the implied agent of these concealing and revealing events and this testifies to the unseen but essential work of the Holy Spirit which initiates and guides the whole process of theological reflection. It is God the Holy Spirit who enables the disciples to encounter Jesus as the Christ of whom they have learnt, within the context of worship – 'he took bread, blessed and broke it' (Luke 24.30). Likewise, it is necessarily the Holy Spirit who invites us in our ordinary lives into an encounter with Christ's ministry and this experience becomes a source of our theological reflection – 'Were not our hearts burning within us while he was talking to us on the road, while he was opening the scriptures to us?' (Luke 24.32). The enlightening encounter with Christ, initiated by the Spirit within worship, is what turns their cognitive understanding into living knowledge of God in Christ, and thus is an essential source of their theological interpretation.

Fifth, the outcome – 'That same hour they got up and returned to Jerusalem' (Luke 24.33) – is not just 'action', nor is it simply a response to what they have experienced. Rather, having encountered Christ in Scripture and through the Holy Spirit, the disciples are compelled to return to Jerusalem in order to participate in Christ's ministry of proclamation to the other disciples. It is as they participate in Christ's ministry, by sharing their testimony of encounter, that Jesus initiates another encounter – 'While they were talking about this, Jesus himself stood among them' (Luke 24.36) – and ministers his peace to them. Thus, participating in Christ's ministry by sharing with others our testimonies of encounter with Christ initiates further opportunities for encounter. Furthermore, the subsequent encounter is also necessarily rooted in reading Scripture – 'Then he opened their minds to understand the Scriptures' (Luke 24.45).

The story of the road to Emmaus is less an illustration of the pastoral cycle in action and more a radical affirmation of the Holy Spirit initiating encounters with Christ through the Scriptures, and inviting humans to participate in the ongoing story of Christ's ministry. In this story, we see Jesus forming his disciples for participating in his ministry of proclamation and reconciliation. He does it through facilitating their theological reflections rooted in Scripture, encounter, testimony, participation and worship, not the equivalent sociological, anthropological and psychological wisdoms of their day. One could argue that their theological reflections 'begin' with testimony (Luke 24.17, 36) and move through encounter to Scripture, as Jesus comes alongside them, encountering them where they are by first asking them to tell him what has been happening. However, I have already noted the tension between Jesus as physically present compared with Jesus mediated by the Holy Spirit, which accounts for this difference. Moreover, Jesus beginning where they are would seem to be the result of Jesus' graciousness, which is necessitated by their foolishness, rather than a model for us to emulate, as suggested by Jesus' rebuke. Jesus began where they were because they did not know any better. Revelation only came to them when he brought them to where he was through expounding the Scriptures and breaking the bread. Thus, we start our theological reflections through reading Scripture in the power of the Holy Spirit, recognizing the necessity of our testimonies as sources of theology in an asymmetrical way, and we seek to be open to the possibility of insights from other disciplines being potential tools in that process.

Summary

In this chapter, I have stated that experience has been understood too broadly within practical theology and that this is not reflective of the role that experience has traditionally played in theology, which is as religious experience as a source of theology. I have argued that only testimony can be considered a source of theological reflection because of the work of the Holy Spirit mediating Christ's present ministry through the Church. Thus, human experience as encounters with the risen Christ is revelatory of God in Christ and therefore necessary for our theology. Our testimonies of Christ's present ministry are related to Scripture in an asymmetrical way, which gives logical priority to Scripture as God's elected and sanctified witness to Christ in the absence of Christ's physical, embodied presence with us. The Bible has priority as the cultural-linguistic framework that gives the necessary worldview and language to identify our testimonies as encounters with Christ. We see how this works through the New Testament pattern of interpreting testimonies of the Holy Spirit's work through biblical antecedents. Scripture therefore reveals to us Christ's present ministry in our lives and our testimonies of this ministry help us to read Scripture anew. Both are necessary sources of theological reflection, in an asymmetrical way. We start from Scripture as the move of faith that recognizes the Bible as prioritized witness to God and God's relationship to creation. The present ministry of the risen Christ may, and indeed will, cause us to read Scripture in new ways as the Holy Spirit leads the Church into all truth. Theological reflection focused on encounter with Christ through Scripture and testimony requires particularly Christian methods, and the spiritual disciplines are the ways in which the Church has traditionally encountered Christ; thus they should be foundational for our practice of theological reflection for formation. Of course, the initiative remains with God through the Holy Spirit to invite us into an encounter with Christ, so the spiritual disciplines do not initiate testimonies. Rather, they provide the most reliable and trustworthy conditions through which to experience Christ's ministry.

I have argued that experience accessed and interpreted through other academic disciplines is a potential resource for theological reflection in three particular ways: to complexify our testimonies and their wider contexts; to diversify our reading of Scripture; and to interrogate our church practices for consistency with beliefs and/or as carriers of belief. These contributions may nuance, problematize or inform our discernment of the ways in which we encounter Christ through Scripture and our testimonies in order to discern how we might participate in Christ's ministry. This process of complexifying, diversifying and interrogating our discernment of Christ's present ministry is important for an authentic and global theology and is part of the way we read the Bible with others to ensure the faithfulness of our own reading of Scripture. The relationship between theology and other disciplines is necessarily *ad hoc* and transformational, where insights from other disciplines are appropriated by theology and converted in its service. This process has the potential to transform both theology and the other discipline, but not equally or necessarily so. God's authoritative story, interpreted through our testimonies, may need to be told in light of our complexifying, diversifying and interrogating, but only where that telling coheres with our encounters with Christ's ministry, illuminated through Scripture. The Bible will likely need to retell our testimony and the other disciplines in light of its story.

I concluded the chapter by exploring the story of the road to Emmaus to illustrate the necessary relationship between encounter and Scripture within the narrative. I examined the role of the Holy Spirit as agent in the process and showed how our attempts to interpret our situations using 'worldly wisdom' cannot be sources of theological insight but may be tools that God can use in the process. The next chapter draws these insights together to propose the scriptural cycle model for theological reflection, which encapsulates the methodological convictions so far discussed.

6

Building the Structure: A Model for Theological Reflection for Formation

Introduction

Having done the necessary preparatory work, this chapter finally 'gets to the point' to outline the proposed 'scriptural cycle' model for theological reflection. The model is intended as one way for theological reflectors to implement the theological convictions advocated: the prioritizing of Scripture as God's self-revelation (Chapter 3); an understanding of the Holy Spirit as active agent in the process of theological reflection mediating Christ, so we can encounter his present ministry in order to participate with him (Chapter 4); and testimonies of encounter as sources of theological reflection with other disciplines as resources (Chapter 5). The foregrounding of the Bible, the Holy Spirit and testimonies gives a method for theological reflection particularly suited to the theological convictions of evangelical charismatics, but also, I consider that it is better suited than the other methods for forming Christians for Christian ministry. The chosen name for the model – the scriptural cycle – highlights the prioritizing of Scripture within the process and obviously relates it to the pastoral cycle in order to encourage comparison and provoke methodological discussions. The danger of the name is that it potentially perpetuates a dichotomy between 'pastoral' and 'biblical' such that one is understood to be in opposition to the other. It is my conviction that the scriptural cycle model inspires greater pastoral practice than the other models because it begins by orientating people towards God and seeks to discern an encounter with Christ in a way that enables our participation in God's pastoral ministry. While it is my intention that the scriptural cycle should act as a critical friend to the pastoral cycle to expose the methodological assumptions implicit within it, it would be a disappointment if this positioning led to a stereotyping of the scriptural cycle as 'not pastoral'.

Any model may be critiqued for being too formulaic and superficial when it is used without reference to the wider methodological intentions. As stated in Chapter 1, I am proposing a step-by-step, diagrammatic model for the enactment of my theological reflection method because diagrams tend to be easier to teach students, particularly when students are new to the discipline. Pictorial models are also more readily remembered and implemented, and I think a reason for the popularity of the pastoral cycle among students is the simplicity and memorability of the diagram. The scriptural cycle is intended only as a starting point for learning a way of thinking and being that hopefully becomes a habitual spiritual discipline rather than a process to be always slavishly followed. I hope that any accusations of superficiality made against the model's use are at least minimized in the scriptural cycle because its primary aim is to give space for the living God to speak through word and Spirit as a first move. Thus, it foregrounds God's grace to inspire depth and authenticity of engagement throughout the process.

This chapter begins with an articulation of four characteristics for theological reflection drawn from the discussions of the previous three chapters. I then return to Johns' pentecostal paradigm for catechesis discussed in Chapter 4 to show how I have built on and adapted her method in the formulation of the scriptural cycle model. Following this, I outline the five stages of my theological reflection model: Scripture, Testimony, Discernment, Encounter, Participation. The chapter concludes with possible critiques that might be made of the model and my responses to those critiques.

Four Characteristics of the Method

My charismatic, evangelical approach to theological reflection advocates for the authority of Scripture in an asymmetrical interrelationship with testimonies of Christ-encounters as the necessary sources of theological knowledge. Other disciplines are used as resources in *ad hoc* ways, especially as they contribute to complexifying our testimonies, diversifying our reading of Scripture and interrogating our church practices for their faithfulness. On the basis of this, we are in a position to articulate four characteristics for theological reflection which govern the method:

1 Theological reflection starts from Scripture as God's authoritative story.
While in some senses starting points are arbitrary, the appropriate beginning for anything claiming to be theology is that God knows best about Godself and that the Bible is God's gracious self-revelation. This choice to start with Scripture is a hermeneutic of faith, where reading Scripture teaches us the necessary cultural-linguistic framework which enables us faithfully to discern which experiences are testimonies of Christ's present ministry. It also enables, as a first step, the transformation of who we think we are in light of God's story, subjecting our own interpretations of our experiences to God's revealed truth. When we see ourselves as God sees us, we are then best able to interpret the world around us. Scripture funds our prophetic imagination and immerses us in the script in which our lives are performed so that we can encounter its author through the story. Thus, by encountering God through God's revealed world, we are formed and transformed to perceive and encounter Christ's present ministry in our lives.

2 Theological reflection seeks to testify to the agency of the Holy Spirit mediating Christ's ministry.
Christ is not only revealed through the words of Scripture; the Holy Spirit mediates Christ's ongoing ministry in, to and for the world such that we can expect to encounter that minis-

try in our ordinary lives as something distinct from ourselves. The Christian life is about being a disciple of Jesus and we learn about Jesus both through the revelation of Scripture and through our encounters with his present ministry. Our encounters, mediated by the Spirit, are sources of theology in enabling us to read anew the faith tradition in ways that are consistent with the story's narrative. We seek to recognize and testify to where Christ is at work in our lives in order that we might participate by God's gracious invitation. It is the asymmetrical relationship between Scripture and testimony – Scripture interpreting our testimonies and our testimonies informing our reading of Scripture – that enable us to discern Christ's present ministry in order to participate. Theological reflection is therefore an act of worship where our prayerful reading of Scripture prompts our recognition of Christ in our lives such that we can give testimony to his present ministry. The Holy Spirit is initiator, guide and active agent for the whole process of theological reflection.

3 Theological reflection is a spiritual discipline of discernment in community.

Understanding the relationship between our Holy Spirit-mediated testimonies and our Holy Spirit-inspired reading of Scripture is a process of discernment where the Holy Spirit continues to be Subject of the reflection, guiding us into truth. The Holy Spirit joins Christ in the word with Christ in the world and joins us with that ongoing work. Therefore, theological reflection is mostly about listening to the Holy Spirit as the active agent of God's mediation. This is why the appropriate methods for theological reflection for formation are Christian spiritual disciplines – prayer, worship, Eucharist, Bible reading, meditation, service – because these are the ways the Church has always sought to know and encounter God. These spiritual disciplines all aid our listening to the Holy Spirit, which is best done in community so that together, as the body of Christ, we may discern God's guidance into truth. Bonhoeffer's *Life Together* is a practical portrait of the character of a Christian community living together, and his approach has informed my commitment to discernment in community as essential for faithfully hearing and interpreting the word of God. For Bonhoeffer, Christian community is a grace of God which is gifted to each person differently; it is not something that is chosen or some ideal to be realized, but is an essential part of being in Jesus Christ.

> God has willed that we should seek and find God's living Word in the testimony of other Christians, in the mouths of human beings. Therefore, Christians need other Christians who speak God's Word to them ... They need other Christians as bearers and proclaimers of the divine word of salvation. They need them solely for the sake of Jesus Christ. (2015, p. 6)

While theological reflection for the formation of Christians for ministry is necessarily rooted in the Church as the body of Christ, it is seeking to participate in Christ's ministry to the world, and to testify to the story in which all are included. Therefore, our corporate discernment of the ways in which the Holy Spirit is uniting Christ witnessed to in Scripture and Christ testified to in our encounters needs to draw on other disciplines so as not to be narrowly focused on a particular location. Other disciplines are valuable resources to aid our theological reflections in that they bring accountability, humility and reflexivity, potentially enabling us to see how our testimonies are shaped by privilege and exclusion and facilitating a retelling that is more inclusive.

4 Theological reflection discerns our encounters with Christ in order to worship Christ through our participation with his ministry.

Unlike other theological reflection models where the stated goal is transformative action, the focus here on encounter with Christ and upon God's initiative through the Holy Spirit means that the aim and purpose of theological reflection is to participate with Christ's ministry for the glory of God. We discern Christ-encounters in order to be united with his present ministry, in order that Christ's kingdom may extend, and in order that God might be worshipped and glorified in the whole of creation. This should always be the purpose and goal of our theological (and indeed all our) activity. Therefore, the primary criteria for 'success' in theological reflection should not be the actions and activities that result, important as they may be, but rather the extent to which love and worship of God has been extended in creation through our participation with Christ. By God's grace, what results from our participation is transformed individuals and communities, as the Holy Spirit forms God's people more into the likeness of Christ. The transformation of our theology or the transformation of our practices may be an outcome, but these are always the overflow of our worship through participation rather than ends in themselves.

These four characteristics of an evangelical, charismatic method for theological reflection relate to the five stages of my theological reflection model. Before describing these five stages, I return to Cheryl Bridges Johns' work to examine how my five characteristics relate to her four-stage process.

Johns' Pentecostal Paradigm for Catechesis

As discussed in Chapter 4, Johns has already proposed a pentecostal approach to theological reflection for formation, which integrates Freire's liberation pedagogy with a pentecostal theology and spirituality. She grounds her pentecostal epistemology in the biblical concept of *yada*, which is a relational, affective way of knowing God and inhabiting that knowledge as a way of life. Her method is the closest thing I have found to my own work and my model is a development of her proposed four-stage process. Johns acknowledges that:

> [Pentecostals] have, however, failed to integrate adequately the epistemological features which are found in communal worship with Bible study. In many ways, this failure reflects

a false dichotomy which is found among most Christians between content and process ... Methods are considered value-free tools which do not affect the truths they mediate and, therefore, may be borrowed from any number of sources, the social sciences being currently favoured. Consequently, Pentecostals have failed to consider the implications of their dynamic belief system for issues of epistemology and pedagogy. Often methods utilized in teaching by Pentecostals militate against the experiential and relational dimensions of their faith. (1998, p. 130)

In other words, *how* Christians do their reflection is as significant as *what* they reflect upon, and charismatic Christians need methods that are authentic to their theological and spiritual convictions. Johns' solution to this is to propose a pentecostal approach to Bible study with four stages: (1) Sharing our Testimony, (2) Searching the Scriptures, (3) Yielding to the Spirit, and (4) Responding to the Call. I have largely kept these categories in my model, along with her particular interpretation of them. The major change is my reversal of Johns' stages 1 and 2. This is for three reasons. First, to retain the explicit evangelical focus on Scripture as the primary place of encountering God and hearing God's word to us, I have chosen to put it first. The engagement with Scripture then prompts testimonies or situations for further reflection and thus allows God's Holy Spirit to bring to mind those testimonies that are most relevant for reflection. Second, even though Johns' understanding of 'testimony' is very different from the pastoral cycle understanding of 'experience', retaining Johns' original order of beginning with testimony could lazily be interpreted as a beginning with experience in a way that undermines the arguments I have been advocating so far in this book. Third, Johns herself argues that pentecostal worship should inform the pedagogic processes, but it is not clear how pentecostal worship is a part of her proposed model. By making worshipful engagement with Scripture the start of the process, I hope to retain explicitly a focus on worship as the beginning of the theological reflection process as well as the end.

Furthermore, as will be seen in my model, I have added a stage between Johns' stages 2 and 3 which I have called Discernment. Johns argues that Freire's liberation theology must contribute to a pentecostal worldview 'an awareness that the community does not exist in isolation from society and that it has the role of critiquing the dominant order' (1998, p. 128), yet it is not clear how this happens in her four-stage process. The addition of a stage in the process which focuses on discernment and includes insights from other disciplines as a resource potentially enables this 'critique of the dominant order' in the Church and the world. I use Johns' understanding of each of her stages to construct my own model.

The Scriptural Cycle Model

Scripture

As has been discussed throughout this book, the model starts from Scripture as God's authoritative story. The diagram I am constructing is a cycle, but with intersecting axes in the centre to illustrate what Johns describes: 'the four movements are best understood as interdependent organic functions of a dynamic system' (1998, p. 131). In other words, there is a chronological flow to the five stages, but they are necessarily interrelated, and the central axes makes this explicit.

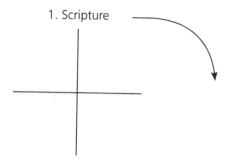

Figure 4: The Scriptural Cycle, Stage 1: Scripture

The model begins, then, with reading the Bible. Returning to the principles of reading the Bible discussed at the end of Chapter 3, my model starts by reading Scripture in humility. Reading in humility means acknowledging our dependence on God's word of life and our need to be found within God's story. Johns claims that 'a Pentecostal approach is to bring life to the text so that the word of God might interpret us' (1998, p. 133). This is a recognition that we always come to the Bible with our pre-understandings, but that pentecostal/charismatics subject these pre-understandings to the words of Scripture so that their lives are interpreted in its language. In humility, we know our need for God to retell God's own story in us and through us each time we read. The text must speak for itself on its own terms and we do not presume in advance to know what that might be. Approaching the text in humility is therefore about coming with an attitude of worship and prayer. The process might begin with an act of worship, or reading the Bible in a prayerful, meditative way such as *lectio divina*.

Second, we read the text of Scripture as a whole. Clearly, this does not mean reading the whole Bible at every theological reflection. However, it does mean forming habits that enable an engagement with the whole of Scripture, not just the bits we like the best or with which we happen to be most familiar. A lectionary is very useful for this, with set readings for each day, and this is often a good way to begin with choosing which passage to read. This process is intended to be part of an ongoing spirituality in community, rather than only used *ad hoc* when situations arise (although it can also be used in this way – see Chapter 7). Therefore, a process for engaging with different parts of the Bible as part of a rhythm of discipleship is most effective. For example, a ministry team or home group might meet each week to read the set passage for the day/week prayerfully, and then follow this model together as part of their spiritual rhythm. Reading Scripture as a whole may also mean referring during the theological reflection to other passages which relate to the particular passage being discussed.

Third, Scripture is read with other Christians. This means principally three things, the first being reading with others in a group. For Johns, the process of Bible study should be both personal and corporate in that the readers' individual lives are found in the words of Scripture, but their interpretations of those words are subjected to corporate discernment as part of a group of readers. This corporate discernment necessarily extends to include, second, the use of insights from biblical scholarship. These scholarly 'others' bring a necessary perspective to the interpretation of the text which grounds the passage in church history and tradition and not just within a reader-response paradigm. In addition, some theological training is strongly advised for anyone wishing to engage more frequently in this process to build up competency and confidence in biblical interpretation. This part of the process is essential for enabling the passage to speak on its own terms. The third group of 'others' is other Christians globally and socio-economically, to whom we might not have easy access. This is where the complexifying and diversifying through other disciplines can contribute to the process and relates to the third stage of the model (hence the interconnecting axes at the centre of the cycle).

Fourth, we read Scripture through the Holy Spirit. Relying only on the tools of scholarship is not sufficient. For Johns, 'this process of interpretation when illumined by the Holy Spirit puts us in touch with the source realities of the Scripture so that we know ourselves to be addressed by the author himself' (1998, p. 134). Therefore, within the context of a worshipful engagement with the text, this means reading both with scholarly, rational lenses and with intuition, emotion and discernment, trusting the work of the Holy Spirit through the group to guide the group into insight and truth. This might involve having times of prayerful silence for people to listen to the prompting of the Holy Spirit to raise questions or highlight particular themes within the text or the discussion. Both personal and corporate discernment must be brought to bear on this task, as we see particularly in the subsequent stages.

Fifth, Scripture is read for transformation. There is an expectancy inherent in the process which is brought by the pentecostal epistemology that the living God is present by the Holy Spirit's mediation. The expected transformation may be personal in terms of changed understanding, awareness or feeling. It may be corporate in terms of changed relationships, actions or praxis. It may also be social in terms of the need for changed structures or policies. Whichever way, an expectancy of transformation rests upon the theological conviction that the Holy Spirit of God is the agent of change, at work in all of life to establish God's just and gracious reign over creation. Reading the Bible prayerfully and expectantly with others helps to establish God's reign first in our own hearts so that all theological reflection might flow from this place of transformation. An expectancy for transformation is therefore also a willingness to be transformed, personally and corporately. Allowing God's story to tell our lives will transform who we think we are and what we think we know, and reflectors need to be willing, in humility, to lay down any behaviours, attitudes, convictions or interpretations if they are found to be at odds with what the group discern the Holy Spirit to be saying. This is therefore a vulnerable process but ultimately a deeply formative one, grounded in the faith conviction of God's goodness, graciousness, kindness and mercy as well as God's holiness, righteousness and judgement.

The question that initiates and guides this stage of the process is: *What does this passage of Scripture reveal to us about God/God's interaction with the world/God's story of who we are?* Or, put more simply: *What does the passage tell us about God and ourselves?*

Testimony

The agency of the Holy Spirit continues into this next stage of Testimony. As the passage has been prayerfully read and discussed on its own terms, the Holy Spirit is at work in the hearts and minds of the participants: stirring thoughts, making connections, highlighting situations, triggering memories. Our brains naturally make connections in this way, responding to stimuli and sparking new avenues of thought. The obvious question is: 'Why does this thinking process need to be spiritu-

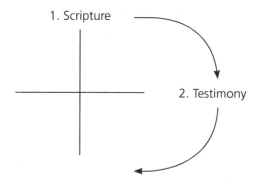

1. Scripture

2. Testimony

Figure 5: The Scriptural Cycle, Stage 2: Testimony

alized to be the work of the Holy Spirit rather than just the way our brains work?' Of course, not every random thought is of the Holy Spirit, hence the need for ongoing, corporate discernment. However, a pentecostal/charismatic epistemology acknowledges the work of the Holy Spirit in those intuitive connections in a way that is entirely consistent with the road to Emmaus story: 'Were not our hearts burning within us while he was talking to us on the road, while he was opening the scriptures to us?' (Luke 24.32). It is this 'heart burning' that this second stage of the process tries to highlight.

Following on from Chapter 4, testimony is the story of our encounters with Christ, illuminated by the text. This does not mean (necessarily) a jubilant account of what God has done, which it can often mean in pentecostal/charismatic settings. It is about telling a story of ourselves as actors in God's ongoing narrative of creation and redemption. It may be a story of praise, thanksgiving or 'success'. It may also be a story of pain, confusion or struggle. Testimony is the way in which we bear witness to the ongoing realities of our day-to-day relationship with Christ. The testimony might not be entirely known or worked out; the seeming absence of Christ's present ministry or a confusion about what Christ is doing might be the testimony. The group is trying to discern Christ's present ministry in their lives, which the Holy Spirit is illuminating through the reading of the biblical text.

This stage of the process is about discerning which life situation the Scripture passage has stirred or prompted in each reader. It is about articulating things such as 'this situation has just come to mind ...' or 'this has made me think of the time when ...' or 'I wonder how this connects with this present problem ...' and following those stirrings as potential 'inner burnings' of the Spirit. The connections might seem very obvious – such as a passage about conflict bringing to mind a situation of conflict. In these scenarios, the group need to be careful in stage 3 to explore the tensions between the passage and the testimony as well as the areas of resonance, to avoid simply applying the Bible in a naive way. The insights of other disciplines that come into stage 3 can be particularly helpful for this. The passage and the shared testimony might appear at first to be tangentially connected or even unrelated. It may not be obvious to the testimony-sharer how Christ is ministering in the situation, and it might just be an intuitive stirring that says, 'I think something might be going on here ...'. The third stage of Discernment is working out how and why the testimony might inform the Scripture passage and how the passage illuminates Christ's ministry within the testimony. Asking the testimony-sharer to speak about why or how they think the passage might resonate with the testimony can be a helpful way to lead into this discernment stage.

The question that initiates and guides this stage of the process is: *What particular life situation is the Holy Spirit bringing to our attention through the passage within which we might give testimony to Christ's present ministry?* Or, put more simply: *Which part of our lives does the Holy Spirit bring to mind to share as testimony?*

Discernment

This third stage could variously be called 'analysis', 'reflection' or 'exploration'. However, I have chosen to use the language of Discernment to relate it more explicitly to the traditional spiritual disciplines that underpin theological reflection for

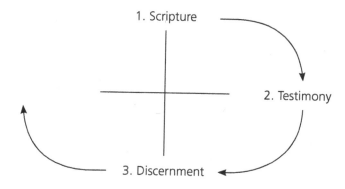

Figure 6: The Scriptural Cycle, Stage 3: Discernment

formation and also to foreground the role of the Holy Spirit. Johns criticizes other Bible study methods for domesticating the Spirit to a 'mild-mannered coach' rather than the authoritative agent of God's transforming power. Many theological reflection methods talk about discernment, but their lack of pneumatology reduces the concept to something like common sense. Kim examines global perspectives on the Holy Spirit and notes the diversity of perspectives on how the Spirit works and where the Spirit comes from – is the Spirit from above or below, within or outside us, in the Church or also in the world, a presence or an event? Also, who decides the criteria for discerning the Holy Spirit, given the diversity of theologies? Kim emphasizes the importance of ecumenical community, specificity and provisionality in discerning the Spirit and gives four biblical criteria for Christian discernment: (1) ecclesial – that which points to Jesus Christ; (2) ethical – seen in the fruits of the Spirit; (3) charismatic – evidenced through the gifts of the Spirit; and (4) liberational – give preference to the poor. However, Kim argues that discernment can never be the result of common sense of the application of criteria; rather, it is wisdom that comes from God and is relational, more encountered than rationalized. Therefore, common sense, rationality and scholarship have their place, but necessarily alongside intuition, emotion, wisdom and testimony. Kim refers to the process of discernment in the road to Emmaus story, arguing that 'in the last analysis, this is a story of revelation ... the fact that "discernment of spirits" (1 Cor 12.10) is listed as a gift of the Holy Spirit shows that the Spirit is needed to discern the spirits' (2008, p. 169). The central theological point is that it is the Holy Spirit who is the agent who activates the various sources and resources in any given context to unite the group to Jesus Christ who is the truth, and this is what is meant by discernment.

There are three interconnected 'movements' or discernments that this stage seeks to address, represented by the central intersecting axes. First, there is discerning how Christ, by the Holy Spirit, as encountered through the passage of Scripture illuminates the identified testimony. This stage then returns to examining the Scripture passage, from the perspective of the testimony, to continue to discern what God is saying to the group through the Bible passage. Second, there is discerning how Christ, by the Holy Spirit, as encountered in the testimony informs the reading of the passage. The discussion of the biblical passage helps the group to discern where Christ's present ministry might be evident within the testimony and how an awareness of what Christ is doing now informs and shapes the interpretation of the encounter with Christ through the passage. Third, there is discerning whether and how this interrelated interpretation of testimony and Scripture might need to be complexified or diversified, or whether our church practices need to be interrogated. This stage particularly seeks to discern where the encounter with Christ's present ministry interacts with the world beyond the Church and draws on other disciplines as resources to aid this process, particularly in terms of our own reflexivity. This is to ensure that the mutual engagement of the testimony and our reading of Scripture is not simply reinforcing our power, or our sense of our own rightness, or our positions of privilege at the expense of others. We therefore draw on other disciplines as a resource to ensure our reflections are reflexive and accountable to the diversity of the world, for whose sake we bear witness to Christ's ministry. At the same time, we discern how the other disciplines might need to be critiqued and transformed in line with God's story.

As in Chapter 4, the Holy Spirit is active agent and Subject, initiating and guiding this process of corporate discernment.

There are various ways in which this third movement of discernment through other disciplines might happen. For example, to complexify the situation of the testimony, particular tools from psychology might inform the analysis; or to diversify the reading of Scripture and bring in hidden voices, the group might draw on gender or postcolonial hermeneutics; or the group might need to interrogate its church practice through empirical methods to test the ways in which the church thinks it is participating with Christ's ministry discerned in the testimony through the passage. It is difficult to be too prescriptive about this stage because its particular focus will depend upon the chosen passage, the identified testimony and the guidance of the Holy Spirit in that particular context.

These three interrelated movements of discernment potentially make this stage seem overly complicated, but I have resisted using yet another metaphor/diagram to illustrate this interrelationship. The intersecting axes in the centre of the model are intended to illustrate the interrelationships I am trying to describe, between Christ as encountered in the Scripture passage; an encounter with Christ's present ministry in the form of a testimony; and the complexifying, diversifying and interrogating of our discernment through other disciplines for our reflexivity – which themselves may need to be transformed and interrogated. This process is for the purpose of discerning the one crucified, risen and ascended Christ whose united ministry is revealed by Scripture, encountered in our lives through the Spirit, and is for the sake of participating in Christ's ministry to the world. The examples in the next chapter illustrate how this might work in practice.

The question that initiates and guides this stage of the process is: *Where do we discern the Holy Spirit inviting us into an encounter with Christ's ministry through the passage and the identified testimony, and how might this need to be complexified, diversified or interrogated? Or, put more simply: How do we reflexively discern an encounter with Christ through the passage and in our lives?*

Encounter

This fourth stage is not really a separate stage, as it expresses what is central to the whole theological reflection process: discerning how we encounter Christ through Scripture and in our testimonies, hence why it sits in the middle of the model. However, there is a particular focus on articulating the encounter with Christ's present ministry at this point in the process as the group try to clarify the discussion for the sake of faithful, transformative participation. Anderson describes discernment as 'the recognition of the congruence between the Christ of Scripture and the Christ in ministry' (2001, p. 56), and so this stage focuses on discerning the ways in which the Holy Spirit unites the witness of the Scripture passage with Christ's present ministry in the context of the shared testimony. This uniting work of the Spirit enables the group to determine the particular way in which they encounter the manifestation of Christ's ministry in the particular context. As discussed in Chapter 4, an encounter with Christ through the Holy Spirit is not for its own sake so that we feel all 'warm and fuzzy'. Rather, the encounter is the invitation to participate in the ongoing ministry of God for God's glory. As Root describes it: 'practical theology may be (and even is) ethical, political, liberative, and even doctrinal, but *only* as an outgrowth of being first and

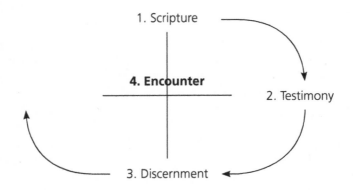

Figure 7: The Scriptural Cycle, Stage 4: Encounter

foremost *ministerial*, of participating in the praxis of Jesus in and through human experiences of encounter' (2014, p. 93).

The focus on encountering Christ's ministry is about trying to articulate specifically what Christ is doing in and through the particular situation of the testimony, illuminated through the Scripture passage. Examples of Christ's ministry may include reconciling, encouraging, comforting, healing, sanctifying, empowering, transforming, enlightening, convicting, forgiving, redeeming, blessing, restoring, strengthening, providing, removing obstacles, opening doors, judging sin and injustice, and growing the fruits of the Spirit. The discernment of stage 3 is now articulated in a particular way to name how we encounter Christ's ministry, informed by the Bible passage and the wider context of the testimony, for the sake of determining our participation in that ministry.

Again, there are no formulas that can be prescribed for how this works in any given setting. Of course, different personalities, group power dynamics, and even what people ate for breakfast, can potentially all influence a group's sense of their encounter with Christ, through the Holy Spirit, and the group may get it wrong. However, it is hoped that the principles guiding this model – humble expectancy, attentive reading of Scripture, prayerful listening to the Spirit, group discernment, spiritual disciplines, reflexivity through other disciplines, space for diversity and complexity – aim to create the best possible conditions for people to discern the guidance of God's Spirit.

The question that initiates and guides this stage of the process is: *How is Christ ministering in and through the Holy Spirit's invitation to encounter through Scripture and testimony?* Or, put more simply: *How are we encountering Christ's ministry?*

Participation

Once the group have discerned where the Holy Spirit is inviting them to encounter Christ and the nature of Christ's ministry in that encounter, they are able to discern the ways in which the Spirit invites them to participate in that ministry. Unlike other

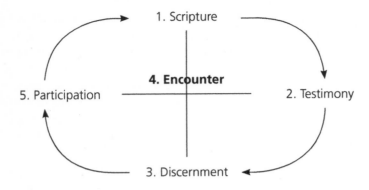

Figure 8: The Scriptural Cycle, Stage 5: Participation

theological reflection methods which aim for the enactment of transformative action as their stated goal, Participation understands that action to be a response to God's initiative in ministry. 'Action' focuses on what we the reflectors will do rather than seeing all our activity as a response to God's gracious invitation for us to join in with God's ongoing ministry to the world. Thus, participation ensures that the focus remains upon the activity of God. Furthermore, it is not just about 'doing stuff'. For Ward, theological reflection is itself participation in the divine life. Through theological reflection we engage in a reasoned, cultural practice that is, at the same time, indwelt by God, and so the process of reflection mediates the divine life. Theology that is faith seeking understanding is 'simultaneously then a personal sanctification and glorification and a participation in the mission of God' (2008, p. 104). Therefore, our participation begins in our reflection and necessarily involves prayer and worship, perhaps praising and giving thanks to God for the ways in which the group have discerned and encountered Christ. It will also likely involve intercession for God's ongoing ministry in Christ within the particular testimony. The actions then flow out of this primary participation with God as we seek ways in which God invites us to be the answers to our own prayers.

For Johns, pentecostal pedagogy is not a form of applying theological truths worked out elsewhere. Rather,

As God's word becomes known, the individual and the group are known and named for who they are ... But God is also critiquing the world ... The Spirit contextualizes the Scriptures, working within the believer to interpret the world. As God's word becomes known, the world is also known and named for what it is. To yield to the Spirit is to join oneself to the presence and mission of Christ in the world. (1998, p. 136)

For Johns, the primary aim of this sort of reflection on Scripture is to know and encounter God; thus it is about recognizing God's goodness, love and glory, and living in a way that witnesses to this recognition of who God is. She highlights how responding to God's invitation to participate in Christ's ministry through the reflection needs to be both individual and corporate. Again, the initiative remains with God to guide and determine any invitation to participation, rather than the group presuming to know how to act. This is why the process cycles back to the first stage of Scripture, so that any activities of participation may be submitted back to the guidance of God through God's word. This in turn informs the ongoing reading of God's story.

The question that initiates and guides this stage of the process is: *In light of where we discern an encounter with Christ's ministry, how does the Holy Spirit invite us to participate?* Or, put more simply: *How is God inviting us to participate?*

Discerning our encounters with Christ through Scripture and our testimonies, in order to participate with Christ's present ministry for the sake of the world and the glory of God, is exactly what theological education for ministerial formation is designed to do, or at least it should be. The Church is called to form and train Christians to testify to Christ in a way that coheres with God's story revealed in Scripture, and to participate with Christ in ministering reconciliation, forgiveness, peace and hope to a broken world. This is what it means to be a Christian, and theological education for the formation of Christians for ministry requires methods and models that explicitly nurture them to interpret the Bible in order to testify to Christ, discern encounters with Christ, and participate with Christ. The five stages of the scriptural cycle provide just such a model for Christian formation for ministry which, it is hoped, can be taught and implemented in an accessible way.

Potential Criticisms of the Model

In the next chapter, I describe four case study examples to show how the model can work in practice. However, before moving on to that, I address here some of the questions and concerns that the scriptural cycle model might raise. In doing this, I am aware that criticisms will likely be made from a variety of perspectives. Practical theologians advocating for theological reflection beginning from experience will have different criticisms from theologians committed to a more doctrinal approach. Therefore, I have tried to anticipate criticisms that might be made from both these perspectives, while responding to them in ways that show that the model cannot be drawn into this dichotomous way of thinking.

It is just another form of applied theology.

Starting with Scripture may be seen by some as a method of applying to the particular situation truths that have been worked out elsewhere. I have already critiqued this interpretation through the discussions of 'encounter' and 'testimony' in previous chapters. The Bible is not seen as truth detached from the life of faith, but rather as God's self-revealed story that is always encountered and interpreted by people in the midst of their lives. There is a differentiated, asymmetrical unity between testimony and Scripture such that testimony can be a source for theology and takes extremely seriously lived experience as the location of encounters with Christ's present ministry. Therefore, a process of interrelated interpretation is very much embedded in the model through the Discernment stage. I have been explicit that this relationship is asymmetrical with priority of interpretation given to Scripture. An acknowledgement of asymmetry is not the same as a devaluing of experience or a form of applied theology, it is simply appropriately recognizing the contingency of our experiences in relation to God's eternal reality as revealed through Scripture by the Holy Spirit. The Bible story is therefore not *applied*, but rather, guided by the Spirit, it is dynamically encountered in the midst of a particular life situation in order to discern and participate in Christ's present ministry.

It is just Bible study.

While I have presented this as a new theological reflection model, I am keenly aware that there is nothing new under the sun, and much of what I have outlined is comparable to other methods of studying the Bible. As I have shown, I am particularly indebted to Johns' work and she calls her method 'a Pentecostal approach to group Bible study'. The scriptural cycle is therefore intentionally very much in line with the way that ordinary Christians, particularly those schooled in an evangelical, charismatic tradition, go about the daily task of theologically reflecting on their lives, unlike other methods (see Chapter 2). I see this resonance with ordinary ways of being Christians in the world as a particular strength of the model. The particular 'new' contribution of this book is to bring this method into the sub-discipline of practical theology and claim it as a legitimate model for theological reflection in a context where it has become taken for granted that practical theology can only be so named if it is that which begins with experience. While the model is therefore very similar to what many Christians are already doing in their rhythms of spirituality and Bible reading, it provides a structure that can facilitate greater rigour, discernment, self-examination, accountability, corporate engagement and critical thinking.

It focuses too much on the agency of the Holy Spirit and risks making reflectors mere passive recipients.

First, I would want to respond by questioning whether there is such a thing as focusing 'too much' on God, especially for those engaging with theological education for formation for Christian ministry. Second, I would advocate strongly that reflectors on this model are very far from being passive. The model is not about simply asking God what God wants us to do and then doing it – which would not be possible in any 'pure' form even if it were the stated intention of the model. Prayerful, attentive, analytical reading of Scripture and careful, critical listening to testimonies to discern where we might participate with God is very hard work indeed when done with the necessary self-examination and rigour. It requires a significant amount of active energy, commitment and skill. The process is essentially about seeking to encounter God afresh by recognizing where we already perceive encounters with Christ in our lives and through God's word. A focus on 'encounter' stresses the relationality of the process, which is always bi-directional and never passive. Again, there is an asymmetry to that relationship, with God taking the initiative in encountering us, but this does not make humans into passive recipients. Furthermore, an assumption of God's initiative does not mean that God simply tells people what to do. The Holy Spirit's guiding is an invitation to participation, not a command. Essentially, the model is about humbly approaching God and recognizing, in the first instance, God's authority as Creator, Redeemer and Sustainer to orientate our lives for our own good and for God's glory. This is not the same as God the puppet-master dictating every eventuality, but it is about recognizing the asymmetry between Creator and creature as the starting point for the encounter. The theological reflection may, and often does, result in the Spirit giving agency to the participants to use their God-given reason, talents and wisdom to determine their own activities. Crucially, the model recognizes human agency as a gracious gift rather than as an inalienable right. It is ever open to the possibility that God may act in a situation in ways that are at odds with our choices and common sense.

It is too focused on the Bible and on religious experiences to be useful in a public/secular forum.
The Bible is about the whole of reality, from the creation of the universe to the end of time, as per the grand narrative argu-

ment in Chapter 3. Therefore, I argue that nothing is outside of its remit or beyond its scope. The whole of life is told by Scripture and so its story is relevant to all of public/secular life, even if it is not always easy to interpret. The Church witnesses to this story for the sake of the world, and this is the Church's primary vocation, rather than judging itself in terms of what secular forums might consider useful. Furthermore, I have stated that this model is particularly for the formation of Christians for participation in Christ's ongoing ministry to the world; thus it is not primarily interested in being useful in a secular context beyond enabling Christians to discern what their participation with Christ might look like in that context. A method of Christ-encounters through Scripture and testimony means that the scope of the theological reflection is focused but not narrow. Any experience can become an occasion for an encounter with Christ's ministry and therefore all of life can potentially be examined within the model. Crucially, we do not assume the relevance of any particular experience at the outset, but rather we allow the Holy Spirit to prompt the particular testimony that the Spirit determines is relevant for further discernment on this particular occasion. There are, of course, many valuable approaches to situational analysis which promote reflective practice and are useful in secular contexts. The correlation method is designed to do just this work. This book does not reject these, but it questions the wisdom of using these as primary methods for forming Christians for Christian ministry. By naming our reflections *theological*, this means that we want to be able to say something about God. I have argued that the prayerful reading of Scripture and the discernment of Holy Spirit-mediated Christ-encounters is the only way to trust that the process does indeed reveal God to us and thus form Christians for ministry.

Christians being formed for Christian ministry need to develop greater awareness of the insights of other disciplines than this model allows, in order to minister to the world.
In response, I would say that Christians do not minister to the world, Christ does, and we are invited by God's grace to

participate in that through the Holy Spirit. This is our distinctive vocation. Therefore, discerning Christ's ministry primarily needs Christian 'methods' and Christians who are sufficiently formed in God's story to know what Christ's ministry looks like in the world, rather than perpetuating therapeutic 'ministries' from other contexts. This is not to devalue the contributions of, for example, counselling, feminist theory, postmodernism, ethnography, transference, Myers-Briggs, and all manner of other theories, methods and tools for helping people make sense of their lives. Each of these may be a resource for theological reflection in bringing greater complexity, diversity and reflexivity to our process of discernment. However, the formation of Christians for participation in Christ's ministry needs to be distinctively Christian and theological. We may discern that someone is encountering Christ's ministry of healing through counselling, but we come to that discernment through the gateway of Scripture and testimony. The world is well equipped with doctors, psychologists, sociologists, historians, political theorists, leadership gurus, economists and activists seeking to 'minister' to the world, and often with great success. However, Christians, whatever their profession, are called primarily to follow and witness to Christ and participate in Christ's ministry for the sake of the world, and they desperately need methods of training that best form them for this purpose.

It may be useful for ongoing group reflection, but it is not so useful for exploring particular pastoral issues.
This is a common assumption made by students who have been using the scriptural cycle, and it may be that it is less obviously applicable for resolving a particular issue. As discussed, there are many other reflection models and methods for problem-solving, and my model is not intended simply to replace all of those. It is simply questioning the wisdom of forming Christians to begin always with problems/pastoral issues, looking to the Bible for solutions and then acting to solve the problem as we have diagnosed it. Whatever our personal circumstances, the scriptural cycle begins in faith by letting God 'speak' first. A group may have gathered together

in the midst of a devastating pastoral crisis, and another theological reflection method would advocate starting from that place of crisis. However, while the group might consider the particular pastoral crisis to be the thing most in need of their immediate attention, a process of stopping and humbly going to God's word as a first move allows the agency of the Holy Spirit to highlight a different testimony which may be more important for the group to attend to than the so-called pastoral crisis. It may be that the Holy Spirit makes strong connections between the chosen passage and the pastoral crisis such that the crisis forms the substance of people's testimonies. However, crucially, within the scriptural cycle the group approach the crisis from the perspective of God's wider story as the first move, rather than simply examining it from their own point of view. In Osmer's (2008) practical theology model, reflectors begin in asking 'what is happening?' and 'why is it happening?' A group using the scriptural cycle is allowing God's narrative to frame answers to those questions before we presume to answer them from our own perspectives. Thus, it can be used in relation to particular pastoral issues, but only by first humbly laying down that which we think is a problem, allowing the Holy Spirit, through Scripture and testimony, to illuminate what Christ is already doing in our lives in order that we might participate with him.

There is a significant danger that the scriptural cycle can be used manipulatively with claims of 'God says ...'
This is, of course, always a risk when we entertain the idea of God's active agency in human lives. Some Christians may find it more comfortable to deny the possibility of God's agency or to dismiss our human capacity ever to discern it, even if it were a reality. As we are painfully aware, the Christian tradition has been used in horrific ways to oppress and exclude people throughout its history, and tragically this continues in different ways within the contemporary Church. However, the scriptural cycle model is not seeking to apply a static tradition in a particular way but rather to facilitate an encounter with the person of Jesus Christ, who is presently active in our con-

temporary world through the Holy Spirit. 'God says ...' is not about producing truths that can be owned and used by one group over another, but about groups of Christians coming together, prayerfully and humbly, to discern what God's Spirit might be saying to them in their context. The very existence of the model resists oppressive application of God's word by one group over against another because the recipient group can engage in their own scriptural cycle reflection to discern if what is presented to them as God's word is in fact what the Spirit is revealing. By engaging in their own scriptural cycle reflection, they can critique the presented 'word' as not what they discern God in Christ to be doing. The model itself seeks to minimize its oppressive use by encouraging the reading of the Bible with diverse others and through the inclusion of complexifying and diversifying perspectives. Likewise, the focus on transformative participation means that from the outset there must be a willingness on the part of the reflectors for themselves and their views/behaviours to be changed by the reflection process, before any change can be advocated to others. Furthermore, it is not as if pastoral cycle/critical correlation models are exempt from claims of manipulation and abuse. Choices made in the process of reflection using any model may be made in ways that seek to influence a particular outcome. Invariably, any model may be misused, but models therefore cannot be judged by the worst examples of their use.

We cannot know what God might be saying or doing in any particular context.
Those who would wish to reject or question a pentecostal epistemology might struggle with this method. Chapter 4 gives a pentecostal/charismatic pneumatology which articulates the confessional claim that the Spirit can and does mediate to us the active agency of God in Christ's present ministry in a way that we can expect to encounter. It is clear that we cannot know in a positivist, empirically verifiable way how Christ is ministering in any particular context. However, as Johns argues, *knowing* God is not just rational and cognitive knowledge but affective and obedient knowing in relationship. The scriptural cycle

seeks this knowledge, which is embodied, holistic, relational knowing, grounded in rigorous scholarship of God's revealed word and discerned with and through the body of Christ, the Church. It is by the grace of God, through the Holy Spirit, that we are able to have this relational knowing of God's being and life as a gift of faith and to participate in God's ministry through the Church. Therefore, while we can never be certain about what the Spirit is saying or how Christ is ministering, the only 'means' the Church has ever had for discerning the will of God have been: discerning in the community of the Church united by the sacraments; prayerfully and expectantly reading God's revealed word; carefully watching for where Christ is at work in our lives; and trusting the guidance of the Holy Spirit to unite these perspectives. It is these traditional disciplines of Christian faith which the scriptural cycle seeks to prioritize within the context of theological reflection.

The leap from Scripture to testimony is a form of eisegesis.
This criticism may come from two perspectives. First, scholars committed to a historical-critical or literary reading of Scripture may question the legitimacy of appearing to read the biblical texts for what they are saying to us. However, as discussed in Chapter 3, I follow Tate in seeing the need to integrate historical readings with literary and reader-response perspectives for understanding the Bible as Scripture with relevance for us today. The scriptural cycle advocates for the inclusion of historical-critical and literary readings of the Bible, but also seeks to incorporate reader-response hermeneutics due to the work of the Holy Spirit in prompting testimonies from our contemporary lives. Second, practical theologians may criticize the method for starting from Scripture in a way that does not allow readers to acknowledge their own preconceptions and pre-understandings of the text before reading, and so a criticism may be that readers discover what they wish or expect to find. Again, it is hoped that the principles of reading Scripture with others in humility and expectant of transformation will enable the necessary reflexivity within the act of reading. Also, engaging the scriptural interpretations with particular

testimonies is a process of exposing those preconceptions to critical analysis and being open to their revision. Moreover, the commitment to read with the Holy Spirit as Subject of the interpretation process creates space for the Spirit to unfold the passage in ways that are not bound by reader preconceptions. Finally, the inclusion of other disciplines as resources for complexifying, diversifying and interrogating our discernments also militates against finding what we want to find. A pentecostal epistemology is not about submitting our thinking to any particular hermeneutical tool or reflexive technique as if they are neutral and 'foolproof', but rather about the expectation of encountering the person of Christ who shapes our thinking and interpretations through relationship. Thus, while we might come to the text looking to 'read in' our own experiences, we trust the work of the Holy Spirit through the Bible and the testimonies of others, along with the transformed insights from other disciplines, to disrupt our preconceptions as we engage with the process.

This chapter has outlined the proposed scriptural cycle model for starting theological reflection from Scripture within a pentecostal/charismatic epistemology and spirituality. I stated four characteristics which inform the particular method proposed and draw on the discussions in the earlier chapters. Johns' pentecostal approach to Bible study was highlighted as a framework for my model and I described how I have adapted her approach. I then outlined the five stages of the process – Scripture, Testimony, Discernment, Encounter, Participation – each of which has an associated question. Finally, I anticipated some possible critiques of the model and formulated responses. The next chapter gives case study examples of how the model could be used in different contexts for further illustration.

7

Moving In: Examples of the Scriptural Cycle in Use

Introduction

The previous chapter described the scriptural cycle as a model for theological reflection based upon the theological convictions argued throughout this book. This chapter provides some case studies to illustrate how the model might be used in practice. They are not intended as ideals to be emulated; rather, in drawing on life-like examples, the aim is to give a sense of the benefits and complexities of the scriptural cycle when used in practice. I have chosen not to conclude each case study with an analysis of the process and outcomes, in order that readers might develop their own critical engagement. This then informs how readers might facilitate such a process in their own contexts. The chapter concludes with a brief, step-by-step guide for facilitators, which lays out the suggested questions for each stage of the process for those wishing to lead others in using the scriptural cycle.

As has been argued in the previous chapter, the scriptural cycle assumes a community of Christians reading the Bible together as Scripture in a way that is open to the agency of the Holy Spirit in the unfolding discussion. It focuses on the Holy Spirit illuminating personal testimonies of encounter with Christ with the intention of uniting the reflectors with Christ to participate in his ongoing ministry. It has been specifically designed for theological education or ministry settings where Christians are wanting to be formed and grown in their habits of discerning and participating with Christ. In the first case study, I begin by focusing on how the model might work in a Christian pastoral/discipleship/study group as part of a rhythm of corporate prayer and Scripture reading. This may be a church ministry team meeting, or any setting in which Christians are gathering to worship God and to discern together how to live faithfully in response. The second case study examines how a church leadership team might use the model in the context of a particular pastoral problem that has arisen in their context which requires a decision to be taken. I show how the model can function in a comparable way to the pastoral cycle for addressing particular life situations but oriented around God's word as primary source for reflection. The third case study shows how the model can be used for personal reflection and devotion in a non-ecclesial context. The fourth case study illustrates how the model might be used in a faith explorers' group for catechesis and discipleship.

Case Study 1: A pastoral group theological reflection

Context

This case study involves a pastoral group of 12 theology students who meet weekly for theological reflection, discipleship and support as part of their formation for ministry. Some are sponsored to train for authorized ministry and others are studying theology independent of church sponsorship in order to be formed as Christians. The group begin in prayer, offering thanks to God and praying for God's presence and guidance through the time of reflection. They then turn to the Church of England lectionary readings for the day and decide on the Old Testament reading, which is Isaiah 40.21—41.10. The passage is read aloud twice to the group, with pauses and silences to ponder the words.

Scripture

As the group contemplate the question, 'What does the passage tell us about God and ourselves?', the discussion quickly focuses on the context and meaning of the text for the first recipients. Who is the 'victor from the east'? (41.2); why does Israel complain about their 'way being hidden'? (40.27); who are 'the coastlands'? (41.1, 5); why are Israel 'afraid'? (41.10). Two members of the group have studied the book of Isaiah recently and so they are invited to offer some thoughts on these questions based on their studies. They explain the critical-historical perspective on second Isaiah (chapters 40—55), which sees these chapters as addressed to exiles in Babylon around 540 BC during the rise of the Persian empire. It is Cyrus, the Persian 'victor from the east', who overthrows the Babylonians and ultimately allows the Israelites to return to the promised land. Another student describes a canonical perspective which resists the strict division of Isaiah into three separate books and sees rather that Isaiah can be read as a literary unity with common themes running through the whole book, such as judgement for sin, Babylon as an agent of judgement, and God's forgiveness and promise.

The group focus on the theme of exile and the experience of those who were displaced from Jerusalem to live in a foreign land and who now hear God's promise of restoration. The rhetorical questions of 40.21 – 'Have you not known? Have you not heard?' – are read as chides from God to those who have forgotten who their God is, followed by a reminder of God's unsurpassable greatness in relation to all other powers and gods. However, despite this glorious declaration of God's strength, a few members of the group are struck by the pain behind the question in 40.27: 'My way is hidden from the Lord, and my right is disregarded by my God'. They make links with the gap of many years that exists between

Isaiah 39.8 and 40.1, and begin to explore imaginatively the experience of God's silence and the difficulty of living faithfully when God seems absent. Another group member, who has been browsing a commentary for additional insight into the historical context, shares Brueggemann's (1998) interpretation of 41.1–7, that it is a courtroom summons in which Yahweh presents evidence of Yahweh's sovereignty above all other gods and Yahweh's claim for allegiance from listening Israel. Brueggemann highlights the political significance of this whole passage in that Yahweh is proclaiming Yahweh's active involvement in 'bringing princes to naught' (40.23) and 'rousing a victor from the east' (41.2). Thus, while God might appear silent, God has been actively directing world events, affirming that Israel have not in fact been disregarded.

The facilitator returns to the guiding question of this stage: 'What does the passage tell us about God and ourselves?' The group variously offer responses around the theme of the felt absence of God.

Testimony

The facilitator initiates a time of silence for the group prayerfully to listen for which life situation the Holy Spirit is bringing to their attention. The group are then invited to share their stories. One member of the group offers a testimony about resonating with the experience of exile and God's absence through her experience of being at college, which she has found to be a spiritually dry and difficult time. She strongly identifies with the liminal, dislocated feelings and a sense of being forgotten by God heard in 40.27. Other testimonies include situations of uncertainty about future options, questions about what God is doing within a particular life circumstance, and experiences of doubt over God's power and presence in a painful situation of family illness. At least two other group members explicitly testify to an exile-like experience through being at college, and so the group decide to focus together on this testimony.

Discernment

The group talk further about the experience of college. For some, college has been a place they felt they had been sent to, away from their home and where they were presently experiencing isolation and frustration at not being able to engage more fully in their sense of call to church ministry. Others share testimonies of experiencing college as a place of abundance and thriving, more like a homecoming than an exile, but they resonate with the experience of being left behind by students who had left college the previous year. There is a temptation for those feeling at home at college to jump quickly to an application from the Isaiah passage of God's faithfulness to the exiles in the midst of their isolation, or of the assurance of God's activity in their lives even if it is not apparent. However, the facilitator encourages the group to hold those thoughts but also to probe more deeply their encounters with God through the passage, before jumping to participation.

As the group think more about college as exile, they begin to complexify their understanding through a discussion of agency, and the differences between a situation being freely chosen and one forced upon someone. For many of the group members, they have chosen to be at the college because they recognize the overall benefits it will bring to their formation, even if there are difficulties within that choice. However, for other group members, they feel that they did not have such a choice of where to train from their sponsoring church, and this is influencing their perspective on their time in college. A group member who is at college in a self-funding capacity rather than being sponsored by a church admits to finding it difficult to hear people seeming to complain about their time in college when he sees it as a privilege to be here and when he is incurring considerable costs to have this experience. This leads into a discussion about access to education in terms of economics and class. The group make links back to the situation of the Israelite exiles, contrasting those exiles who wept in the strange land (Psalm 137) with those who built houses and took wives in Babylon (Jeremiah 29.5–6) and those who achieved favour and influence (Daniel 1). Thus, the group recognize that Isaiah 40.27 does not represent the entirety of the Israelite experience and so their reading of Scripture is diversified as they become aware of the different ways in which the various groups would have encountered God's activity.

The group consider those who were 'left behind' in the land during the Israelite exile as the elite were carried off, and wonder whether God's pronouncement of the return of the exiles would have been experienced as good news by those who remained in the land. Likewise, the 'host' nation might not rejoice that their Israelite friends/neighbours were being 'rescued' – and nor might the Israelites who were happily settled in the exile country. The group think about the churches and places they have left behind and how those people encounter God through their 'exile' to college. They also reflect on the places they would be going on to after college, many into church ministry, and they discuss whether their 'glorious' arrival in a new context might be a source of resentment for those people they could potentially be displacing from particular roles. The group begin to interrogate their church practices by thinking particularly about their host placement churches during their time at college, and the cost to those churches of continually welcoming new students and saying goodbye to them, although they also acknowledge the joy for the churches of receiving God's ministry through the students. These explorations highlight situations where practices might need to be reviewed, such as the support given for placement congregations and how students prepare to move on from college into their new church roles.

As the group reflect on the question, 'How do we reflexively discern an encounter with Christ through the passage and in our lives?' they are drawn to the interrelationship between transience and permanence within a context. They reread the Isaiah passage in light of this theme. They notice the creation references in the passage, which they had previously missed: 'beginning ... foundations of the earth' (40.21); 'stretches out the heavens' (40.22); 'Who created these ... calling them all by name' (40.26); 'Creator of the ends of the earth' (40.28). They notice the contrast between the steadfastness of God as Creator and the transient events of turbulent world politics (40.23–24) and also between a God who does not grow weary or faint and young people in need of strength (40.28–31). From this perspective, the passage is seen as less about a distinction between exiles and settled people and more about the distinction between God's utter steadfastness and the transience of all other powers and situations.

Encounter

The group move into another time of silence, listening to the Holy Spirit to reflect on the question, 'How are we encountering Christ's ministry?' A number of different things emerge from this, but a common theme seems to be about feelings of dislocation and isolation, not being linked only to a particular season of life but being a reality of the human condition. While there are times when this might be felt more acutely – and corresponding specific things that can be done to lessen the painful feelings – life is understood as transient whereas God is steadfast and the only trustworthy foundation upon which to find a sense of 'home'. The group discern an encounter with Christ's ministry as that of reassurance about God's steadfastness in the midst of transience and of Christ's presence, peace and provision for all those 'left behind'.

Participation

The group attend to the question of how God is inviting them to participate in Christ's ministry of reassurance, presence, peace and provision. There is a variety of responses. For some group members, they feel that their participation in Christ's ministry of peace involves praying for God to transform their attitude towards their time at college in order to focus on being rooted in God rather than craving for permanence in a particular place. For them, the participation with God involves ongoing prayer, accountability and spiritual direction to embed this changed perspective. For others, they have a strong sense that the college community could be a more hospitable place to support people working through experiences of dislocation and they discern an invitation to participate with God through engaging with the various college structures to suggest appropriate changes to the community life in order to participate with Christ's ministry of reassurance and peace. Another group member feels convicted about the way he had viewed his context church negatively, and has a new appreciation of the cost his training has had upon the church. His participation with God is through repentance and renewed engagement in the context, seeking to minister Christ's peace and healing to those negatively affected by hosting transient students. Another group member has begun to think about her community placement in a refugee drop-in centre and the significant experiences of transience and dislocation that they have experienced. She decides to engage in a further reflection about how her participation with Christ in ministering his peace and reassurance can be further extended in that context. As the group pray together to conclude, there is a renewed sense of faith and hope in their shared identity as transient people, united in their need to be more deeply rooted in God's steadfastness. They encourage one another to wait upon God for God's strengthening power, whatever their circumstances, and experience a renewed sense of mission to live in a way that enables others also to find their home in God.

Case Study 2: A ministry team with a problem

Context

An inner-city parish with a history of social action is currently feeling despondent in relation to a food bank they run for those in need in their community. It used to be very popular and in high demand, but of late, there seem to be fewer users and the volunteers are discouraged. Their disappointment is compounded by the fact that the users never end up coming to church. Some volunteers feel very strongly that the food bank must continue and all they need is more advertising and training, while others think it is not worth the effort and it would be best for the church to invest their limited resources in other outreach activities. The church minister has some awareness of the various complexities, history and power dynamics at work within the situation and the wider context, but is unclear about the way forward for this parish. She has tried to stall making a final decision in the hope that a consensus might emerge among the team. Things come to a head when two volunteers attempt to leave a quiet session early, before the published finishing time, which results in a heated argument. The parish ministry team schedule a meeting to discuss how to respond.

Scripture

The minister begins the meeting by asking for the guidance of the Holy Spirit and leads the group into a time of silent waiting. She has not chosen a Bible passage in advance for fear that the team might interpret her choice as manipulative. She asks the group if, during the time of silence, the Holy Spirit has highlighted a Bible passage they might read together to start their meeting. The Good Samaritan is suggested by two group members because this was the passage that the previous minister drew on to initiate the food bank ministry in the first place. The minister facilitates the reading of Luke 10.25–37 a couple of times, from different translations, and asks the group to try to hear the familiar story afresh. She then encourages the group to ask inquisitive questions of the story to examine its strangeness. Initially, the group are resentful about this activity because they just want to get on with the business of solving the food bank problem. But eventually they enter into the task and ask questions such as, 'Who is the man?', 'Where was he going?', 'Why did the priest pass by?', 'What did the innkeeper think about being left to care for the man?', 'Why didn't God prevent the robbery?' These questions are collected, and the group are encouraged to imagine some answers. One group member immediately makes links with the food bank, presenting the story as the obvious justification to continue the ministry, even if only for the sake of one person in need. To this, the minister responds by asking, 'What does the passage tell us about who we are?' Initially, nearly everyone agrees that Christians are to be the Good Samaritan for those in need, but one group member says that he feels like the beaten-up man.

Testimony

The minister invites the man to tell his story as to why he identifies with the beaten-up man in the story. He recalls a time of experiencing food poverty himself several years ago following a missed payment from a client and he testifies to feelings of shame and powerlessness. It was through a food bank that he got help and encountered God's love through that provision. This experience has been one of the main motivating factors for the man now volunteering in the food bank, to ensure that others get the support from which he once benefited and for them to be able to encounter God's provision and love through the food bank. Moved by this testimony, the minister suggests that they take some time to invite the Holy Spirit to highlight a relevant time in each of their lives when they too have felt like the beaten-up man, and they share their experiences in pairs and then with the wider group.

a time when I felt judged by my gender

Discernment

The minister suggests that the Holy Spirit might be inviting them into an encounter with Christ through the man's testimony of using a food bank by discerning together how it relates to the parable. A group member observes that, like the man's testimony and others that were shared, the Good Samaritan is a story of someone who experiences an occasion of bad luck and is abandoned by the priest and Levite, but experiences God's love through the Samaritan. The church therefore must be the Good Samaritan, to show God's love to those in need; this is how others will encounter Christ for themselves. Another group member complexifies the man's testimony through concepts of power and powerlessness within the situation, which the man mentioned. They discuss the shifting power dynamics from financial security to temporary poverty and back to financial security, and the empowerment – and consequent encounter with God's love – that came particularly from being able to choose which food to receive. One group member contrasts this with the ongoing powerlessness of the beaten-up man in the parable, as it is the innkeeper and the Samaritan who liaise over the practicalities and costs of his care and thus he remains powerless and lacking choice as the recipient of help. The group variously discuss the sense of an ongoing lack of power among the clients of the food bank because of their circumstances of poverty and the way the food bank gives them a choice of food and consequently some power. As they think about diversifying this experience, someone suggests that it might be helpful to do some interviews with clients to bring their experiences into the discussion and to test the assumptions the group are making – that the clients feel powerless and abandoned in their circumstances but are empowered through the provision and choice of food and that this is an occasion for encountering God's love. The group decide to pause the meeting to do further research – one person agrees to conduct interviews with some clients; another person volunteers to do some wider research on social demographics and processes relating to food bank users in the wider community to see if reduced food bank use is a general trend; and another agrees to read up about different interpretations of the Good Samaritan.

The group meet again the following week, bringing the fruits of their research. Two group members are keen to share what they have found out from speaking with the clients. The clients did have a sense of powerlessness about their situation, which sometimes brought a sense of feeling abandoned. However, significantly, they felt that their experience of the food bank further added to their sense of powerlessness and isolation because although the volunteers were polite and helpful, they kept the clients at a distance. The interviewees did not experience the provision of food as an encounter with God's love, but rather as further exclusion because of the way the volunteers seemed to see them only through the lens of their need, and they felt judged as a result. They also felt judged by the volunteers in their exercise of choice, for example when they chose certain unhealthy foods over other healthier options. The group members who had carried out the social demographics research corroborate that the problem of food poverty is much more widespread within their community than the current client numbers indicate. It seems that in recent years users have tended to frequent the school-run food bank in the community, because the church had a reputation for making people feel judged and labelled as 'poor' and 'needy'.

The group begin to get rather defensive about this and argue that the Samaritan did not become friends with the needy man but was commended for helping him in his time of need. Indeed, he went on his way, leaving the man in the care of the innkeeper, having 'done his bit'. At this point, the minister invites the group member who undertook the research of reading further about the passage to share their findings. The group member describes Rah's (2009) perspective on the Good Samaritan which argues that Western theological interpretations of the parable have tended to focus on a Christian ethic to do good to those in need. However, a postcolonial perspective challenges the paternalism and superiority to which this interpretation can lead. Instead, Rah sees that Jesus' answer to the question 'Who is my neighbour?' is that your neighbour is the one who helps you rather than the person you help. The story should cause us to identify ourselves with the beaten-up man – 'Which of these ... was a neighbour to the man?' (Luke 10.36) – rather than with the Good Samaritan, and thus we are enabled to understand neighbourliness as encountering Christ through the other who serves me. The group begin to question whether in the command to love our neighbour there is perhaps less a focus on helping the neighbour in need and more a focus on learning to recognize the capacity of 'the other' to bring mercy to us. The group find this difficult to understand, given that they have spent so long assuming that Jesus' command to 'Go and do likewise' (10.37) means to be the Good Samaritan to others. They begin to imagine what it might mean in their situation to 'go and receive mercy from others' rather than to 'go and give'.

Encounter

The group feel rather discouraged and upset by the research findings, but as they think about how they have encountered Christ through the passage they begin to see hope for how things might change. The group sense that the Holy Spirit may be inviting them into an encounter with Christ's ministry of reconciliation and empowerment of the marginalized. They wonder about inviting clients to their meeting to talk more about their experiences of the food bank and the church. In this way, the group hope they themselves might further encounter Christ's ministry of reconciliation and empowerment through the clients. One member asks if, in the spirit of 'go and receive', they might involve some people from the food bank to come and read the story of the Good Samaritan with the group to help the group better understand what the passage might mean for this community. This leads them to notice a fear and vulnerability they share about bringing 'outsiders' into their meeting, which supports the research findings. This reflexive thinking, exposed by the inclusion of wider research, enables the group to see other occasions in the life of the church where the same small group of 'capable' people organize church life on behalf of the whole congregation. This arrangement had been ostensibly about serving others and showing God's love, but they now begin to see that it might also be a way of 'maintaining the gap' between their position of power and those in need. They wonder if the Holy Spirit is inviting them into an encounter with Christ's ministry of weakness and humility, as well as reconciliation and empowerment.

Participation

The group realize that this will be an ongoing process and that not all of them are quite on the same page about embracing the idea of the church as vulnerable recipient rather than secure giver. They agree that they might participate in God's ministry by asking some of the clients from the food bank whether they would consider coming to help the group read and understand the story of the Good Samaritan. In doing so, they recognize that this will initiate a whole new theological reflection process. They agree to review the method by which church rotas and events are currently organized and look at involving a wider group of people in that review process. They see this interrogation of their church practices as participation with God's ministry of empowering others. Some also wonder about whether corporate confession and repentance might be appropriate responses to what the Holy Spirit seems to have revealed about Christ's ministry of weakness, and so they commit to a period of intercession to explore this further. The group decide to suspend the church's involvement in the food bank for the time being, as an expression of their weakness. They hope that the ways in which they have determined to participate with God's ministry might lead them, eventually, through a process of re-establishing the food bank in due course, but perhaps in partnership with members of the local community. However, the group are open to the fact that the process of participation with Christ might lead them in a different direction, as they seek ways to recognize neighbourliness in the 'other' and receive from them. They conclude their meeting by praying together and are particularly moved by a prayer that expresses Christ as their servant rather than them being servants of Christ, something that they recognize has not been prominent in their theology. They agree to spend time in personal prayer in the coming weeks, meditating on the story of Jesus washing the disciples' feet in John 13, to consider what it means to encounter Christ's ministry of servanthood.

Case Study 3: Personal devotions

Context

Sarah has a regular rhythm of personal reading of the Bible where she journals her thoughts and reflections. She decides to use the scriptural cycle model during a quiet hour as a way to deepen her engagement with the psalm she is reading and to structure her reflections.

Scripture

The psalm for the day is Psalm 23. Sarah spends some time in quiet prayer and then attempts to read the psalm through slowly a few times. Initially it is hard for her to get past her familiarity with the psalm and her knowledge that the psalm is about trusting in God's goodness and provision. She currently recognizes God's goodness and provision in her life and uses this as an opportunity to pray prayers of thanksgiving and praise. She decides to read the psalm in other translations to help her to hear it afresh. In one particular printed version she notices that verses 1–3 are grouped together, and also verses 5–6, leaving verse 4 on its own in the middle. On this layout, she observes a difference between the activity of God in verses 1–3 and 5–6 contrasted with the activity of the psalmist in verse 4. The psalmist has been the recipient of God's active, shepherding care in verses 1–3 and 5–6, but it is the psalmist who is active in verse 4: walking and not fearing. Sarah begins to journal about whether it is significant that the only active responsibility that the sheep/psalmist has in the psalm is to walk in dark valleys unafraid. She meditates on where the 'darkest valleys' might be in her life, in which she is afraid to walk.

Testimony

As she writes, she finds herself thinking about her engagement with public social media as the place she is currently afraid to 'walk'. A situation happened last week where she shared something that caused a number of people to respond with negative and hurtful comments and so she has given up social media for the time being, only engaging in closed chat groups. As she prays, she becomes more aware of the hurt, pain and isolation she felt as a result of the public shaming, something she can often feel through social media use, and she wonders where Christ was in that experience. She strongly resonates with 23.5, desiring to label as 'enemies' those people who wrote the negative comments. She wonders what God's provision and protection looks like in the sometimes cruel world of public social media and whether it is legitimate to call this a 'valley of death'.

Discernment

Sarah decides to do some reading and study to understand the psalm further. She discovers a general consensus among commentators that the context of the psalm is hard to determine from the language used, and thus it can be open to different interpretations. Some commentators wish to divide the psalm into different verses with distinct themes, such as the shepherd (verses 1–3), the guide (verse 4) and the host (verses 5–6), and this reading might support Sarah seeing something different in verse 4. Jacobson focuses on the changes between third-person and first-person references to God and divides the psalm according to 'speech about the Lord (vv.1–4b), speech to the Lord (vv. 4c–5), speech about the Lord (v.6)' (2014, p. 239), so that 'you are with me' is seen as the centre of the psalm. Sarah discovers that although various commentators present different structural accounts of Psalm 23, none do so on the basis of the passivity/activity/passivity of the psalmist, and so she decides to rethink this reading.

In arguing for the unity of the psalm through the theological significance of the shepherd metaphor, a number of commentators highlight the strong resonances between the psalm and the exodus (Wilcock 2001; Mays 1994; Craigie and Tate 2004). Therefore, the story of Israel's salvation is understood to be the basis for the psalmist's confidence in the Lord's faithfulness. God provided for Israel all that they needed such that they lacked nothing (Deuteronomy 2.7) and God brought them safely through the wilderness into the abundance of the promised land. Through this lens, Sarah re-approaches the psalm as a powerful declaration of confidence in God's provision in the midst of struggle. Thus, the focus is not about avoiding the painful valley but about encountering God in the midst of it. She wonders if it is perhaps a bit dramatic to associate social media use with walking 'in the shadow of death', until she recalls the news reports about suicides among young people that have been linked with social media use. Thus, social media can indeed be a 'wilderness', 'crisis', and even the fear of death for some people who feel that they are navigating a dangerous social space. To further complexify her experience, Sarah reads some of the news stories of young people's suicides in relation to social media use and finds some medical and sociological research about social media usage and mental health which informs her understanding. Sarah also reflects on all the times that she has encountered God positively through social media and experienced the social connections to be times of God's abundant 'green pastures'. She recalls the ways in which her friends have been significantly helped by online networks they have been part of, and thus seeks to diversify what could otherwise become an overly negative understanding of social media.

According to the psalm, it is God's presence that helps the psalmist to navigate the place of the darkest valley. Goldingay (2006) argues that God's presence is not just a feeling but is also action, evidenced through the rod and staff which are used by shepherds to fight off enemies and keep the sheep on the right path. Sarah is unsure how God might be seen 'fighting enemies' on social media; however, she is encouraged by the fact that it is God who holds the rod and therefore takes the initiative, thus freeing the sheep from the need to engage in retributive action or combative responses. Sarah can see more positive allusions in relation to the staff providing support and nudges in the right direction. For example, times when she might feel prompted to pray, or not post something, or to share something of her faith online could be seen as 'nudges' or encounters with the Holy Spirit and evidence of God's presence with her as she 'walks' through the online space. She is amazed that she has never thought of her social media engagement in spiritual terms before. She reads how Jacobson (2014) translates 'comfort' in verse 4 as less about emotional support and more about 'courage', and is further prompted to reflect on times when she has encountered God's 'nudges' guiding her into courageous engagement online.

Sarah begins to think about engaging more courageously with social media in ways that will enable her to share with others about the abundance of God's provision in her life. She thus begins to conceive of rejoining social media in a positive way. However, as she prays, she feels a sense of conviction about the times in the past when she has used social media as a platform for showcasing God's blessings, often justifying it as 'for the sake of glorifying God'. However, as she thinks about the research on social media's negative impact on mental health, she wonders about the times when her rejoicing has seemed like boasting and may have contributed to others' sense of inadequacy and isolation. She sees how it is God who prepares the table for us (Psalm 23.5), rather than we who lay it ourselves.

Encounter

As Sarah turns her attention to articulating Christ's ministry within this encounter with God through the psalm and in the context of social media use, she focuses on the terms 'hospitality', 'guidance' and 'empowerment'. She sees in the banquet imagery the possibility that the sometimes hostile space of social media can be a setting for God's ministry of hospitality, for herself and for others, even and especially when social media feels like 'the darkest valley'. The 'nudges' that she sometimes experiences when engaging in social media resonate for her with the shepherd's rod and staff and are seen as Christ's ministry of guiding her into those hospitable places. This guidance is a comfort to her but also an empowerment as Christ ministers courage to her to be both kind and bold when the valley feels dark. However, she also encounters Christ's ministry of hospitality and empowerment when social media has brought blessings and encouragement through connections with other people and the resources they have shared, and thus she can see that engaging with social media can be a participation in Christ's ministry of guidance, hospitality and empowerment for others.

Participation

Sarah spends some time in repentance for her own misuse of social media and prays about whether there is anyone to whom she specifically needs to apologize. She decides to use the psalm as a spiritual template for engaging with social media in the future. She prints a copy of the psalm to put next to her computer. She commits to not going on a public social media forum until she has spent a short time giving thanks for God's good provision and praying that she might encounter and participate in God's ministry of hospitality and guidance through her online engagement. She decides to talk to some friends about how they might work together to create an online environment among their peers that might help others to encounter God's hospitality and empowerment, perhaps through the sharing of their testimonies of God at work in their lives, in ways that avoid boasting. As she continues in these renewed spiritual practices, she feels prompted to raise the question of social media use within her church and wonders whether she could do a retreat/training day around the spirituality of engaging with social media, using the psalm as a template.

Case Study 4: A faith explorers' group

Context

Mike, an entrepreneur and licensed lay minister, ran an Alpha course for people he knew in the local community and with whom he had built up relationships over a number of years. After the course finished, the group wanted to continue to meet together to discuss their growing Christian faith. The participants include: Sue, a local teacher who grew up as a Catholic and has only recently returned to church; Claire, a local business owner who is still exploring faith; John, a civil servant working for the local council in the area of housing who is new to the Christian faith; and Jan, a multi-faith chaplain at the local hospital looking for collegiality and mutual support.

Scripture

Mike has chosen 1 Corinthians 12.12–26 as their passage, because the previous week the group were asking questions about the place and purpose of the Church within the Christian faith. Mike suggests that they try a *lectio divina* exercise in order to give space to discern how the Holy Spirit might be speaking to them. The passage is read slowly and prayerfully a few times, and the group are asked to pay attention to which word or phrase particularly stands out to them during the reading. They share as follows without wider explanation: Jan – 'I have no need of you', 12.21; John – 'all suffer together', 12.26; Sue – 'I do not belong', 12.15; Claire – 'greater respect', 12.23; and Mike – 'no dissension', 12.25. After a further time of silence, the passage is read again. Mike then asks the group to think about why their particular word/

phrase might have been significant; what is going on in their lives that means that the Holy Spirit might have highlighted that phrase to them? The group are invited to share their responses in the form of a testimony.

Testimony

Sue shares that her phrase 'I do not belong' resonates with a situation in her school where there is a challenging member of staff who regularly has emotional outbursts because he feels that others are not including him in the team. Sue is often required to smooth things over and she has been praying recently about how to handle this in a better way. Claire is perplexed by verse 23 – 'our less respectable members are treated with greater respect' – as she is currently having to put an unpopular staff member on a competency procedure because of poor performance. She has been trying to pray to God for guidance about what to do and wonders whether 'give her greater honour' might be God's answer. John is struck by 'all suffer together' in verse 26. He works with a lot of deprived tenants on a housing estate and he is wondering how his Christian faith should inform his work among them. What is his Christian responsibility in alleviating their suffering? Mike resonates with verse 25 – 'no dissension' – and he thinks about an argument in church last week when some parents in the congregation were complaining again that the older generation are intolerant of their young children in church. He just wishes they could all get along and stop arguing, as the passage says. Jan resonates with 'I have no need of you' in verse 21 as she is feeling a lot of pressure at her chaplaincy work because a tricky hospital manager is querying the purpose of chaplains in a climate of cutbacks. She feels attacked and wonders where God is in it all. As the group listen to one another's situations and resonances with the passage, they are unsure how far the passage can be considered to relate to their individual circumstances. They decide to explore this question further by returning to the passage.

Discernment

Mike draws on his preparatory reading about the passage to highlight that Paul is deliberately using a body metaphor because it would be familiar to his hearers; it was frequently used in civil life to reinforce political hierarchy between the greater and lesser 'organs' of society. However, Paul is subverting the metaphor to show that the Church as body is not hierarchical like society. While a physical body might be able to do without some lesser parts, such as a finger or an appendix, the body of Christ has been given by God and therefore cannot do without any of its members. No member can rule themselves out of the body – 'I do not belong' – nor can they rule others out – 'I have no need of you' – therefore the body is unique in being given and perpetually held together by God's Spirit. The members are given, one to another, as different – 'If the whole body were an eye, where would the hearing be?' – with necessarily different functions, but where the particular role/gift is unrelated to the person's worth – 'our less respectable members are treated with greater respect'. Paul's vision of the Church is as a body of mutual dependence with no 'master organ' which relies on the Spirit of Christ acting as a 'decentralized circulating nervous system' (Brock and Wannenwetsch 2018, p. 93) connecting all the different parts together. Through this summary, the group realize that Paul is writing specifically about the body of Christ, the Church, and his logic of mutual dependence and unity cannot simply be applied to any other organization or group of people. Therefore, Paul's vision of unity in diversity does not apply in the same way to Sue's colleague or Claire's staff member or John's tenants or Jan's managers. It is only the agency of the Holy Spirit within the context of Christ's body, the Church, that makes 'no dissension' and 'special honour' logical and possible.

However, the group observe that their experience of the Church is far from Paul's description. Sue comments, 'Yes, but it is not as if Christians are any easier to get along with, in fact, it is often harder.' They can each identify a fellow Christian about whom they have been tempted to think, 'I have no need of you', and they explore together, reflexively, some of the issues that have caused these feelings towards particular individuals. They focus particularly on Mike's testimony and the evident lack of understanding within the church situation of the mutual dependence on one another that comes with being Christ's body. The group realize how counter-cultural it is for Christians to commit to loving the diverse and often difficult people whom the Spirit has formed into the church. The group begin to imagine what it would look like to treat all other Christians as those given to them by God and united to them by the Holy Spirit, who brings gifts of grace that they need, for the good of the whole body. They come to appreciate their own identity as given members of the body, joined to the body and called to contribute their gifts for the sake of the whole – and also they recognize that they will be seen as 'difficult' members by others.

Jan queries the definition of 'Christian' because in her context of the hospital it is impossible to put clear boundaries around who is and who is not a member of Christ's body. She highlights the secular definitions of faith and spirituality that inform her professional work. This perspective begins to complexify the group's interpretation, as they question what it means to treat all people as a fellow member of Christ's body 'just in case' they happen to be so. They return to John's testimony to further explore the implications of this way of thinking. Through analysing John's situation, they conclude that Paul's vision of the Church as mutually dependent and jointly suffering, rejoicing, caring and honouring one another is not given as a pattern for John's interactions with all the tenants among whom he works. They see a difference between his professional service prescribed by his job for all the tenants, and his particular obligation of mutual dependence to the tenants who are 'baptized into one body' (12.13). While there are often very blurred lines between those who are 'in' and 'out' of the body, there are certainly some tenants that he can clearly identify as members of Christ's body and he sees these as the ones with whom he is particularly committed to suffer and to rejoice. The group name this distinction of relationship through the concept of mutuality, which is only manifested in the Church through the Holy Spirit and does not characterize his professional relationships with the other tenants. However, the fruits of the Spirit grown in John through being united with his tenant brothers and sisters in Christ spill over and extend out into his interactions with other tenants. Therefore, while John is called to show respect, value, care and love for all his tenants, there is a qualitative difference in the way this manifests between fellow Christians, because of the mutuality given by the Holy Spirit. It is this quality of mutual unity, dependence and honour between believers – John and the Christian tenants – that witnesses Christ's ministry of love and reconciliation to the world.

Encounter

John feels a sense of excitement about a vision of what the Church is and should be, and he discerns a possible invitation to encounter Christ through the recognition of a mutual dependence particularly between him and the Christian tenants with whom he works. He thinks about what it would mean to love and value them – and, crucially, receive from them – as brothers and sisters in ways that would witness Christ's love to his colleagues and the other tenants. Sue has been thinking that in spending so much time trying to help her challenging colleague she has neglected the possibility of fellowship with the other Christians who work in her school, whom she had dismissed as 'not my sort of Christian'. Sue discerns an encounter with Christ's ministry of encouragement through engaging more with the other Christians in her workplace. Claire has realized through the discussion that perhaps giving greater honour to her underperforming colleague is not what God is saying about her situation. However, she has been encouraged that the ways in which she is learning to love and value people who are different from her through the faith explorers group is forming her character and it is out of this growing habit of love and respect that she might be able to handle the workplace situation. Jan realizes that she has perhaps overemphasized the blurred boundaries of the body of Christ and that this has been to the detriment of feeling a part of a distinctive community of believers who can support her. She sees that this experience of isolation might be why her manager's questioning of her role feels like a personal attack. Jan senses the potential for encountering Christ's ministry of empowerment through closer association with her other chaplaincy colleague. Finally, Mike has been reminded of the counter-cultural nature of a diverse and united Church giving greater honour to its inferior members. He is not sure who the 'inferior members' are in his intergenerational church conflict – perhaps all groups in different and particular ways – and he senses that Christ's ministry of reconciliation will be found in walking towards that conflict in order to make peace rather than in ignoring it, as might be his natural inclination.

Participation

Sue discerns Christ's invitation to participate through focusing on the relationship with her Christian work colleagues and perhaps asking them if they would like to form a prayer group. She wonders if she should invite her challenging colleague to come as a way to help him feel included and valued. John discerns an invitation to participate with Christ through making contact with the tenants he knows who are Christian in the hope of beginning to build a friendship with them. He is anxious that his reaching out might be treated with suspicion or interpreted as patronizing, and he is unsure where it will lead, but he feels called to make that first move. Mike asks the others to pray for him to have courage to tackle the ongoing tensions that he has been ignoring in his church. He senses that participating with Christ in reconciliation will involve calling a meeting with the parties involved and doing some teaching about who they already are as the body of Christ. Claire has been inspired to use a strengths-based approach to the competency proceeding to give her employee a sense of value in the process. She also has a greater understanding of the importance of church in the life of faith and has committed to attending Mike's church this weekend. Finally, Jan has decided to reach out to her chaplaincy colleague from the Baptist Church to explore how they might provide mutual support to one another, and perhaps in the process together be able to articulate to the sceptical manager a distinctive contribution that Christian chaplaincy makes to the health service in which they work.

How to Lead the Scriptural Cycle: Step by Step

The outline of the model in Chapter 6 and the case studies in this chapter have aimed to give potential facilitators sufficient insight into the ways that a group might be led in a theological reflection using this model. As with all group reflections, good facilitation is essential to its successful and satisfying implementation. Here, I collate relevant questions and prompts for a potential facilitator to refer to in preparing to lead a group in theological reflection following the scriptural cycle.

Context

The model can be used within a variety of Christian groups and settings – study groups, home groups, discipleship/mentoring settings, ministry team meetings, supervision sessions, prayer groups, faith explorers' groups, PCC meetings, team away days, spiritual direction sessions. On most occasions, it will be helpful to inform the group in advance of the intention, rationale and method of the reflection to manage their expectations. However, there may be times when it is appropriate to begin a session with, 'Today, we are going to start with reading this passage from the Bible ...' and see where the Spirit leads. It is important for there to be a sufficient length of time for the group to discuss in depth. One and a half to two hours is often a suitable length of time for a reflection and a group of 5–12 people would seem to be the optimum size to enable enough diversity of voices and to allow everyone a chance to contribute. The space needs to be conducive for honest sharing and times of quiet reflection. It is important for the facilitator to prepare for the reflection, through prayer and through the selection and preparation of the Bible passage. The facilitator can do this preparation themselves, or they may choose to ask members of the group to do some preparation of the passage in advance, which may involve wider reading and consulting commentaries. I have advocated for the use of a lectionary or other reading plan to select the passage, so that the group are formed through reading a wide range of Scripture. However, it is also possible to choose a particular passage for a particular reason, in which case it is important that the facilitator is reflexive and honest with the group about their choice.

Scripture

What does this passage of Scripture reveal to us about God/ God's interaction with the world/God's story of who we are? Or: What does the passage tell us about God and ourselves?

The group begin in prayer and/or worship, acknowledging the presence of the Holy Spirit in their midst as co-agent in the process of reflection and affirming the Bible as the primary place through which the Holy Spirit speaks to God's people. The chosen passage is then read prayerfully, often more than once, and perhaps using different translations. The facilitator may ask the group to listen for a particular word or phrase that strikes them, to then be shared with the group. Or they might ask the group to identify puzzling aspects of the passage or questions it raises for them. Alternatively, the facilitator might initiate the discussion by asking the group to suggest what the passage reveals to them about God, or about God's interactions with the world, and/or God's story of who we are. These various questions, puzzles, ideas and thoughts might be collated in written form, and the group might want to identify one or two themes to explore in detail. It often helps to have commentaries available so that members of the group might refer to them in the search for specific answers to identified questions. It is helpful if at least one or two members of the group have done some preparatory work on the passage in order to be able to give responses to specific questions. The facilitator might encourage the group to explore the historical context of the passage or the literary structure in the joint quest for meaning. Through this, the group identify questions raised by the passage, and draw on available resources and prior learning to suggest answers. The focus of this section is not to answer all the questions raised, but to identify areas for further exploration later in the reflection. The guiding question can be used to structure the discussion and to keep the group on track. For a two-hour reflection, I suggest allowing 30 minutes for this stage.

Testimony

What particular life situation is the Holy Spirit bringing to our attention through the passage within which we might give testimony to Christ's present ministry? Or: Which part of our lives does the Holy Spirit bring to mind to share as testimony?

As this is a dynamic process, testimonies may have already begun to emerge in the exploration of the biblical passage, and the facilitator might encourage the group to hold onto these thoughts or note them down to be shared in more detail at this point. Alternatively, they may want to allow stages 1 and 2 to merge so as not to disrupt the flow. It is often appropriate to have a time of silent prayer following the asking of this question, to enable group members to listen to the promptings of the Holy Spirit, even if they have already begun to share their connections. 'Life situation' is intentionally very broad and might be a personal circumstance, a specific event in the wider community or an issue in public life. It might be a question or theme that they have been pondering in their times of prayer or something they have read or seen in the news. But in each case, the group are encouraged to focus on the life situation as testimony, or potential testimony, of an encounter with Christ. If group members are struggling to notice just what has been brought to their attention, the facilitator might ask, 'Why do you think the passage raised the initial questions/ resonances that it did for you?' Alternatively, if the group seem to be telling 'random' stories, the facilitator might focus them by asking, 'Where do you think you might have encountered Christ in that story?' Or, 'Where do you experience Christ at work in that situation?' These questions might be unfamiliar for a group and initially difficult to answer. This is the reason why the model is a process for formation, nurturing participants' familiarity with the concept of encountering Christ and forming the necessary habits of discernment. Therefore, it is a process that needs to be practised together over time. It is important to allow everyone the opportunity to share, which depending on group size might happen better in pairs or smaller groups, before getting each pair to summarize their discussions to the whole group. As facilitator, you are trying to discern from the different testimonies a particular focus for more in-depth exploration. It may be that people have shared similar experiences and a consensus naturally emerges around a particular testimony. On other occasions, there may be a variety of testimonies and you will need to choose one, either through asking the group prayerfully to vote or by exercising your discernment as facilitator. A guiding principle in choosing a particular testimony would be: what would seem to be most relevant and potentially transformative for this group to explore at this time for the purpose of ongoing participation in Christ's ministry? For a two-hour reflection, I suggest allowing 15 minutes for this section.

Discernment

Where do we discern the Holy Spirit inviting us into an encounter with Christ's ministry through the passage and the identified testimony, and how might this need to be complexified, diversified or interrogated? Or: How do we reflexively discern an encounter with Christ through the passage and in our lives?

The process of discernment will depend significantly upon the identified passage and chosen testimony. The focus is upon exploring the interrelationships between the passage and the testimony, with an awareness of the need to complexify, diversify or interrogate practices, in order to discern and encounter Christ's present ministry. The discussion therefore will be fairly free-flowing as the group ask questions of one another, exploring together the one Christ encountered in these different 'locations' of Scripture and testimony, mediated by the Holy Spirit. However, for the more structurally minded, the list of questions below can be used to guide the discussion. It is not anticipated that the group must cover all the questions in detail; it will be for the facilitator to focus the questions as seems appropriate.

- How do we discern an encounter with God in Christ, through the Spirit, in this passage?
- How do we discern an encounter with God in Christ, through the Spirit, in the testimony?
- How do these mutually inform one another?
- How might other disciplines/testimonies complexify our interpretation of the testimony?
- How might other disciplines/testimonies diversify our reading of the passage?
- Do we need to interrogate our church practices in light of the anticipated encounter?

For a two-hour reflection, I suggest allowing 45 minutes for this section.

Encounter

How is Christ ministering in and through the Holy Spirit's invitation to encounter through Scripture and testimony? Or: How are we encountering Christ's ministry?

The group have been discussing and discerning their encounter with Christ through the passage and the testimony through the previous stage. However, there will come a point when the facilitator needs to draw the threads together by focusing the group to articulate what they discern Christ is doing, through the Spirit, in the particular situation, or how they are encountering Christ's ministry through the passage and the testimony. The group should be encouraged to be specific at this stage, if they can, to name the particular ways in which they discern and encounter Christ's ministry. Of course, this is not to say that this is the only thing Christ is doing, but the focusing helps with discerning participation in the next stage. Again, time for silent listening and prayer is often helpful and appropriate to enable the discernment and articulation process. Sometimes there will be a clear and shared answer to the question; at other times individuals may each have an answer for themselves and it can be more challenging to come to a group consensus. This will depend on the nature of the testimony. One of the benefits of the model is that even when one particular testimony is chosen for deeper exploration, all members of the group are expectant that the Holy Spirit will be speaking to them about their own testimonies through the discussion, and it is the role of the facilitator to draw these out. As with the other stages of the process, it may be appropriate to invite people to share their thoughts in pairs or smaller groups before summarizing their thoughts for the whole group. For a two-hour reflection, I suggest allowing 15 minutes for this section.

Participation

In light of where we discern an encounter with Christ's ministry, how does the Holy Spirit invite us to participate? Or: How is God inviting us to participate?

Often, members will have begun to articulate their responses in the previous stage as part of their exploration of the encounter with Christ's ministry, in which case an explicit fifth stage may not be required, but may be merged with stage 4. However, this stage does give the opportunity for clarifying and committing to particular Holy Spirit-inspired responses. The participation may be to identify specific actions, individual or corporate. It may be to come to God in intercession, asking God to act in and through the situation before we do anything. It might involve rereading the passage to check if the discerned ways of participating with Christ are congruent with the group's reading of the text. It may be that returning to the passage exposes the idea that the discerned present ministry of Christ among the group challenges a dominant interpretation of the passage and prompts fresh exegesis to critique the traditional readings. It is nearly always appropriate to conclude with some form of intercession, corporately, silently or in pairs, with people praying for one another in light of the identified participation. This way, the group can give thanks to God for guiding their reflection and commit their ongoing participation to God's gracious initiative and guidance. For a two-hour reflection, I suggest allowing 15 minutes for this section.

Summary

Within this chapter, I have given specific examples of how the model might work in different contexts. I have deliberately refrained from giving an analysis of each reflection so that readers can develop their own critical perspective. However, readers might like to return to the 'Potential Criticisms of the Model' section at the end of Chapter 6, which gives a framework for possible critiques of the case studies and my responses to those critiques. The chapter has concluded with guidance for group facilitators on how best to lead others through this model. The guidance given here is also applicable to self-facilitation in the case of the model being used in personal reflection.

A tool I regret not being able to provide in this chapter is a step-by-step guide for students in how to write an academic theological reflection using this model. This is because assessment criteria differ between institutions, and many of those assessment criteria can assume a particular experience-based method of theological reflection that conforms to the pastoral cycle. It is therefore incumbent upon teachers of practical theology to help students translate assessment criteria to be applicable for different models and methods to avoid the present domination of a particular approach. I hope I have given sufficient material to show how this model can be as academically rigorous and reflexive as other approaches. Students and assessors may find it problematic to account for the active agency of the Holy Spirit within an assignment in a sufficiently 'academic' way. However, if this problem becomes a prohibiting factor to the model's use, we must ask whether 'academic' forms of teaching and assessment are the most appropriate tools for structuring the formation of Christian disciples for ministry.

positivism - empirical
a posteriori facts derived by
reason and logic from sensory
'imposed on the mind by experience' *experience'*

Assessing the Project: A Conclusion

Summarizing the Argument

This book has sought to challenge the prevailing wisdom in theological education that methods of theological reflection such as the pastoral cycle and critical correlation are appropriate and even primary ways of forming Christians for ministry, whether lay, ordained, authorized or voluntary. I have argued that these methods have their own particular histories and epistemologies which make their use in Christian formation at best questionable and at worst potentially harmful. This is because these methods privilege experience, the present, critical incidents, other disciplines, and Enlightenment thinking, and consequently disadvantage the distinctively Christian sources of the Bible, Christian religious experience and God's agency through the Holy Spirit. Therefore, an alternative method for theological reflection is needed if it is to form Christians for Christian ministry.

Methods for forming and nurturing Christians as ministers with Christ must start from Scripture as God's authoritative story revealing Christ. The Bible is the primary means by which we discern and testify to Christ's present ministry and is therefore the essential starting point if our goal is to participate with Christ. I have drawn on a narrative, cultural-linguistic model of theology to explain and justify this faith conviction of the authority of the Bible. Starting theological reflection from Scripture does not mean that experience is irrelevant, or that theology is necessarily applied to life from outside, nor is it a positivist assumption of objectively 'pure' starting points. Rather, starting from Scripture is the enactment of faith which affirms that God knows best about Godself, creation, and our place within it, and that this grand narrative is revealed in Scripture due to God's election and sanctification of the Bible as trustworthy witness to that all-encompassing story. Given the manifold oppressive ways in which this grand story has been told and used, we must read the Bible in humility, as a whole, with other Christians, through the Holy Spirit, for transformation.

Likewise, methods of theological reflection for formation must have a more developed pneumatology as the grounds for which theology from experience makes sense theologically. Many of the contemporary practical theologians shaping the discipline have not attended to the agency of God in their methods, and thus have restricted their field of study to human moral reasoning or human practices as the primary horizon for theological reflection. However, the Holy Spirit mediates the risen Christ to us as an objective fact beyond ourselves that we can know and encounter through faith as an agent in our lives. Christians encounter and participate with the risen Christ through the Holy Spirit and this is the reason why theology is necessarily practical; human experience is the 'location' of encounter with Christ's ongoing ministry to the world. I have employed a pentecostal epistemology of encounter with Christ via the mediation of the Holy Spirit to theorize and explain the particularly Christopraxic shape of all theology as necessarily practical.

Furthermore, theological reflection for formation must attend to the ways Christians already experience and live out their faith if it is to be useful and meaningful for Christians training for ministry. Following on from the discussion about pneumatology, it is the Holy Spirit's mediation of Christ in our lives that justifies human experience as a source for theology. Therefore, experience must be understood as testimony of encounter with Christ if it is to generate theological insight. I have described how the sources of Scripture and testimony are mutually enlightening of one another, in an asymmetrical way, with logical priority given to Scripture as the cultural-linguistic framework that provides the worldview for us to recognize our testimonies of Christ-encounters. The Holy Spirit works to unite the Christ revealed in Scripture with the Christ we encounter in our daily lives and to which we give testimony. Thus, theological reflection for participation in Christ's ministry must primarily and necessarily attend to the revelation of Christ's ministry in our midst through Scripture and testimony. Such an approach foregrounds Christian spiritual disciplines as the ways in which Christians encounter and discern Christ's ministry in their lives. However, other disciplines are important resources for theological reflection because they can bring the necessary reflexivity and accountability to our reflections – particularly through complexity, diversity and the interrogation of practices. This prevents our theology from being exclusive and marginalizing, and enables our participation in Christ's ministry to the world to be expansive and all-embracing.

I have described this method as particularly reflective of an evangelical, charismatic approach to theological reflection. However, I have argued that Christians who do not identify with these labels or their corresponding theological convictions might still find the model better suited to formation for Christian ministry than the models presently in use. This is because, as I have sought to demonstrate, the other methods were not primarily intended for the formation of socio-economically privileged Christians for ministry. Training for Christian ministry is training to participate with Christ in his ministry to the world through the Church. Such training requires methods whose primary purpose and focus is the discerning of Christ's ministry, and this is what the scriptural cycle has advocated through the five stages of Scripture, Testimony, Discernment, Encounter and Participation. One of my particular aims was to suggest a simple, diagrammatic model of the stated method so that students would have a framework to aid implementation and which might enable theological educators more easily to teach it. Doubtless, there will be other models one could devise to implement the stated method, and my hope is that through the use of the model, and the formation of habits for discernment, encounter and participation, students and users might devise other models that further develop their use of the method in their contexts.

Responding to Critics

In the conclusion of Chapter 6, I outlined a number of criticisms I anticipate being made against the proposed model, with my responses. Particularly, I anticipate criticisms in regard to what might be perceived as a church-centric, echo-chamber method and model, where the scriptural cycle is accused of being unable to nurture engagement in the world beyond the Church. Because of the focus on Scripture, the Holy Spirit and Christ's ministry, the scriptural cycle may be seen as not suitable for use in secular contexts, multi-faith contexts, or public forums. Such critics would argue that the Church must make it a priority to form and train ministers who can engage in public theology given our post-Christendom context, and that the methods I criticized in Chapter 2 are actually best suited for that goal. I wholeheartedly agree that Christians must engage in public theology, but that they do so primarily as Christians – those who discern Christ's present ministry in order to participate and in so doing witness to Christ. It is increasingly popular to talk about our calling to join in with God's mission to the world, and to understand that mission in very broad and holistic terms. Again, I do not disagree with this, but God's mission is to reconcile and redeem the whole of creation under the Lordship of Christ. Christians who constitute the Church join in with God's mission in a thousand different loving and practical ways, but in order to witness to God's mission of redemption and reconciliation in Christ. We participate in the Holy Spirit's ministry to witness to Christ and proclaim his victory over evil and death, and his promised return when all will be made new. Therefore, when Christians participate in public theology, or multi-faith contexts, they do so as Christians with a testimony and a story to share, and with a unique vocation to witness to Christ through participation in Christ's ministry. Of course, they must do this in sensitive, caring and serving ways, but also in distinctively and unapologetically Christ-shaped ways that witness to Christ. As Bonhoeffer argued:

The church does not have a twofold word, the one general, rational, and grounded in natural law and the other Christian – that is, it does not have one word for unbelievers and another for believers ... Instead, its commandment is the *one* commandment revealed in Jesus Christ, which it proclaims to the whole world. (2009, p. 399)

It is my conviction that the scriptural cycle is better able to form and nurture Christians to witness to this one word: to develop the necessary prophetic imagination and confidence in the Christian story that frees the Church to be the Church. It is a method that better equips Christians to engage in any forum as those who, distinctively and primarily, participate with and witness to Christ for the sake of the world. Furthermore, my articulation of the role of other disciplines within theological reflection means that the model is not advocating a naive and simplistic fundamentalism but recognizes the vital role other disciplines have to play as resources for holding the Church to account and developing humble reflexivity. Christians engage in public forums eager to learn how their story might need to be complexified or diversified by the dialogue and willing to interrogate their church practices to expose occasions and situations where their presumed participation with Christ has been inconsistent with their proclamation. Yet they recognize, as Christ-followers, that these insights of other disciplines may themselves need to be challenged and transformed in light of God's story, which has logical priority in telling us who we are.

Critics may argue that this account of other disciplines is insufficient because if the Bible always has priority in the process of discernment, then the complexifying and diversifying role of other disciplines may be easily rejected. Thus, the model may be seen to obstruct the necessary liberation and transformation of a patriarchal text and tradition. However, such a criticism fails to account for the active agency of God, in Christ, through the Holy Spirit. As reflectors engage with the whole, self-subverting story of the Bible, which resists closure, reading it with other Christians through time and space, in a worshipping and praying community, in humility, desirous of transformation, expectant of encountering Christ's ministry, then in this way the Holy Spirit is desirous and able to lead the reflectors into all truth. The Holy Spirit as agent in the reflection process exposes and transforms oppressive beliefs and practices by mediating the reign of Christ, who is ultimate liberator and redeemer. The use of other disciplines is therefore only one tool that Christians possess to assist in the renewal and critique their practices. The Holy Spirit is the primary active agent in the process of renewal, critique and transformation which enables the necessary judgement upon and liberation from excluding practices.

Likewise, God's story challenges and interrogates accounts of what the world thinks liberation, inclusion and freedom look like. For Christians, liberation and freedom involve confessing sin and being obedient to God in Christ, testifying to the freedom, peace, joy and hope that come through forgiveness and reconciliation with Christ. Such an account is seriously challenging to contemporary dogmas of choice, self-determination and freedom of expression, and thus very likely to be deeply unpopular and strongly resisted. However, those familiar with the Christian story know that it was ever thus: generations of martyrs testify that this was always a dangerous occupation. The Church is called to witness to Christ in every age, regardless of the opposition it faces, and to do so in ways that witness to the world its rebellion and sin, and also its created goodness, redemption and promised renewal in Christ. Likewise, the Church is also called to be renewed by that same testimony, confessing its own rebellion and sin and looking to the Holy Spirit's renewal and transformation as part of its witness to the world.

Stating the Implications

The scriptural cycle seeks to form Christians who are able to inhabit and testify to God's story of the world as revealed in Scripture in ways that enable the Church to fulfil its vocation to participate in Christ's ministry for the world. Such an approach to Christian formation for ministry has much wider implications than just particular theological reflection methods. I suggest that the whole enterprise of Christian theological education may need to be reconsidered in light of the arguments of this book. I state five potential implications of taking this starting from Scripture method seriously.

First, starting from Scripture requires formation in community to nurture the necessary habits of discernment and scriptural interpretation. Diverse community is vital for formation because it is only together that we can discern and participate in Christ's ministry. As the body of Christ, joined by the Holy Spirit, and nurtured by word and sacrament, we encounter Christ with and through others, and we participate in Christ's ministry to and for others. Such a community shapes, challenges, encourages and teaches one another through studying and worshipping, eating and serving, praying and celebrating, mourning and questioning. Such a model is not a retreat from the world, nor a cosy 'bubble', but rather an intensification of formation for the sake of the world. Theological education for ministerial formation should be characterized by intentionally and deeply journeying with diverse others on the same path of training, learning and forming in order more effectively to shape habits of witness and participation with Christ for the world. As ever new dispersed and online pathways emerge for training increasingly diverse Christian ministers, it is vital that the Church retains a vision of formation in community, if it is fruitfully to train people to discern, encounter and participate in Christ's ministry.

Second, the proposed focus on Scripture may require a differently structured curriculum. While Christians training for ministry (as in participation with Christ rather than any particular authorized form of 'ministry') need training in topics such as mission, pastoral care, leadership, spirituality, worship and liturgy, these topics could come to squeeze out quantity and quality of time for studying the Scriptures. Of course, many of these topics are often taught with a strong biblical and doctrinal basis, but there is a danger of making them the focus of our scriptural engagement: what does the Bible tell us about mission, pastoral care, identity, gender, creation, family, worship? Thus, we perpetuate a habit of approaching the Bible on our terms with our questions. Skills of exegesis and hermeneutics of Scripture are essential for forming Christians who can confidently inhabit the world of the Bible and interpret our lives in its terms. Likewise, a deep grounding in the doctrines of the Church as the reading rules of Scripture are vital for Christians to interpret what they read in Scripture. We do not always know what is relevant or necessary for our formation, ministry or lives. Neither do we know what the world of the future looks like in order to prepare ministers for it. Therefore, forming Christians who can discern Christ's present ministry in whatever age, through reading Scripture and discerning the Holy Spirit, requires primarily a good academic grounding in the Bible. This is not to advocate for an applied theology paradigm – the focus on testimony and encounter ensures that we must pay close attention to our contemporary lives and particularly to our encounters with Christ for mutual, asymmetrical interrogation of encounter, text and tradition. It may be that the scriptural cycle is a model for teaching all theological sub-disciplines, not just theological reflection. Imagine a curriculum structured entirely around the Bible, rather than topics. In this way, the pertinent leadership, mission, pastoral care, worship, spirituality and anthropology insights might be discerned through the prayerful, communal, exegetical study of Genesis, Daniel, Luke or Romans.

Third, the focus on encounter, participation and testimony, alongside Scripture, has the potential to break down the persistent theory/practice divide that characterizes so much of theology and academia. Frequently, we talk about theological training in the classroom and practical training in the Church as if the two are distinct, and then we engage in endless discussions about their relative importance. Such a divide can often be perpetuated by critical correlation and pastoral cycle methods of theological reflection which distinguish the theory from the praxis in order to unite them! Consequently, it has become popular to extol the virtues of contextual training, which is marketed as combining both theological and practical. This is usually in opposition to a somewhat stereotyped concept of exclusively theoretical, 'ivory tower' academia. Increasingly, I perceive this tension particularly between 'residential' training stereotyped as focusing on the academic and 'mixed mode' training highlighting the practical. Such a dichotomy informs discussions about learning in community – whether it should be in college or context – and also informs curriculum designs – how to relate and balance theory and practice. However, a focus on everything as encounter and participation with Christ begins to break down these false dichotomies. For example, I might discern an encounter with Christ in the library through reading for an essay on Isaiah that gives unexpected wisdom for a present pastoral situation in my family. Or I might encounter Christ in praying the Lord's prayer in worship and feel convicted to extend forgiveness to my next-door neighbour with whom I have had conflict. Or I might encounter Christ with others on a march for climate change and engage anew with my sermon preparation on Genesis 1. Or I might encounter Christ while doing a school assembly on the Christmas story, which causes me to reframe my exegesis of the passage for a dissertation. Or we might encounter Christ together through reading Acts in our home group and feel called to participate with Christ through reaching out to our ecumenical partners in the town. Or we might encounter Christ in the lecture room through a discussion on mission and this informs how I approach the supermarket queue on my way home. When seen as encounter and participation, all is life and faith, theory and praxis: library, church, world and work fuels our theology and our theology inevitably informs our day-to-day living. Full-time theological study in the library and the classroom is the 'real' world just as waiting at the school gate can be a theological interpretation of Jesus' great commission. Scripture, testimony, encounter and participation is a model that has the potential to break down the theory/practice divide that can be so damaging for course and curriculum design.

Fourth, theological training and reflection for formation is necessarily confessional and Christian, which is at odds with the priorities and expectations of secular universities accrediting ministerial training programmes. As I have argued, formation of Christians for ministry is oriented towards discerning the guidance of the Holy Spirit and participating with Christ. This aim requires Christian methods of prayer, worship, meditation, silence, Eucharist, giving, in order to discern the Holy Spirit in our midst. Also, such a method for training and formation needs to be rooted in the Church, as the body of Christ on earth, joined by the Spirit with the risen Christ participating in his ongoing ministry. Therefore, it might be time to revisit afresh the rationale for all theological training for ministry being accredited by secular universities. Of course, I am committed to the importance of rigour, critical thinking, assessment, evaluation and rational judgement uniquely offered by the higher education setting. However, it is problematic that these become the defining paradigms for assessing the 'success' of participating in Christ's present ministry. Not only does such a system devalue various forms of knowledge essential to theological reflection for formation – intuition, emotion, testimony, embodiment – and not only does it rule out mysticism, the supernatural and the agency of God, but its focus is entirely upon the rational individual. I have already highlighted the fundamental importance of community for formation. It is therefore a cause of significant dissonance that our higher education paradigm has very limited scope for facilitating and assessing collaboration, corporate discernment or community ministry. It is entirely legitimate to ask whether the benefits of higher education training really do outweigh the costs when it comes to forming Christians for participation in Christ's ministry. It might be time to reconsider our enthralment to the academy and bring theological training and education back into the heart of the Church as a confessional, rigorous, spiritual discipline in community.

Fifth, if the scriptural cycle were to be taken seriously as a method for forming Christians for ministry, this would have significant implications for the life of the Church. Theological training would be seen as essential for all Christians, not just authorized ministers, so that all Christians, whether in the workplace, at home or at the gym, could be more effective in discerning and participating in the ministry of Christ. Small group Bible study attendance, rather than just church attendance, might be seen as at the heart of a life of Christian faith. Of course, Christians must regularly gather together as the Church to worship, celebrate, pray, hear God's word and receive the sacrament, but the scope for personal discernment of one's particular day-to-day vocation and participation with Christ is limited in such a setting. Smaller study groups are desirable for all Christians as the way to discern Christ's ministry and participate with it in one's own context, supported and enabled by the community of believers. Ongoing theological education and ministerial development might move away from additional skills-based training and focus more on ongoing Bible study. Lifelong learning for authorized ministers might look less like only doing the latest course on mental health or internet safety – important as these are – and more like doing a refresher course on 2 Samuel or Hebrews, just for fun and for the love of God. The 'relevance' of such study may not be immediately obvious, but we trust in the agency of the Holy Spirit to bring revelation through God's word, highlighting our testimonies of encounter with Christ's present ministry for our ongoing participation. This is what makes all Bible study 'relevant' and life-giving, not just for us as students but for the congregations and communities we serve.

Suggesting Next Steps

I stated in Chapter 1 that I imagine my primary audience to be theological students training for ministry – either in authorized roles or Christians wishing to engage in theological study to equip them in their Christian faith as lived out in the world. I particularly have a focus on evangelical, charismatic students who might already be finding the present models of theological reflection taught on their courses to be somewhat in tension with their theological convictions and spiritual practices. For such students, I advocate a testing and a trying of the model and a study of the underpinning method in order

to see for themselves the types of habits, dispositions, outcomes or insights it facilitates. The model is only one way of
implementing the method, and students may feel encouraged
to develop other models from having engaged with the scriptural cycle. For those readers who do not identify with the
charismatic, evangelical convictions of this book, and remain
unconvinced, similarly I advocate for them to try the model
and see. However, almost more importantly, I hope this book
has encouraged all students to think about how they think,
and to pay more attention to the implicit theological and epistemological assumptions of any model or method they have
been taught. No method is neutral, and if nothing else I hope
this book and the scriptural cycle model has exposed that. How
we go about thinking about something dictates what we think.
Methods matter, even if they appear to be overly theoretical
and dry, and this book is an encouragement for students to
pay more attention to methods in all their theological classes.

For theological educators – in many ways the gateway to
my student readers – I hope this book has given you sufficient
material to consider adding the scriptural cycle to your reper-
toire of theological reflection methods. A typical learning
outcome for theological reflection courses is to assess and evaluate different methods. The scriptural cycle might be sufficiently
different from the pastoral cycle for you to compare and contrast them in your classes, and in so doing enable students to
develop their critical engagement with different methods. More
than this, you might have come to recognize through this book
some of the challenges with the other methods, particularly for
use in the formation of Christians for ministry, and to consider
introducing the scriptural cycle model in your formation training. As I have said, the scriptural cycle is only one proposed
model for implementing the method, and I am sure you might
be able to adapt it or develop it to better suit your context. I
am not advocating the particular model so much as a method
that prioritizes the Bible, and Christian encounters with God
for the purpose of discerning Christ's present ministry in the
world in order that we might participate, through the Holy
Spirit's gracious invitation. This is what it is to be a Chris-

tian ministering in the world, and our confessional theological students need methods that nurture and form these habits of spiritual and theological discernment.

For the Academic Guild of Practical Theology, I anticipate that my method might be rejected as not practical enough, or too theoretical, or not sufficiently theorized, or too applied, or too Christian. I have tried to give sufficient justification to substantiate my method as necessarily practical *and* theological. My aim is to see greater engagement within the discipline over the role of the Bible, the Holy Spirit and Christian experience, and I hope to engage in further discussions about theological reflection for the formation of Christians for ministry as a primary task of the discipline. Now that the turn to the practical, the lived and the experiential has gained significant traction in systematics and biblical studies, the distinctive role of practical theology is less clear. Practical theology has significantly tried to move away from the exclusive clergy-training niche it once occupied. However, I think this turn to the experiential in all of theology is a significant moment for practical theology to reclaim and redefine its heritage. No longer focusing on clergy training or skills-for-ministry acquisition, practical theology is well placed to contribute distinctively to the formation of all Christians for participation in Christ's ministry, to attend to the encounter with Christ's present ministry and to witness to that for the sake of the world. Practical theology has the potential to lead the way for all other theological sub-disciplines about why and how the experiential matters – because of our encounters with the person and ministry of Christ. I hope it is not too idealistic to situate practical theology as that which might facilitate the abolition of the theory/practice divide, the transformation of the theological curriculum, the restoration of theology to the heart of the Church for the formation of Christians in community for ministry; and the inspiration of a renewed ecclesiology shaped around discipleship, community, theological education and participation in Christ's ministry. I recognize that were this vision to be realized, practical theology as a sub-discipline would become redundant – as indeed would all other sub-disciplines as separate silos.

Finally, for Christian practitioners – all those who recognize their vocation to participate with Christ's ongoing ministry, including the students and academics addressed above – perhaps this book has been an affirmation of some of the things you are already doing in your ministry practice, and/or an inspiration to try a different way of thinking about and practising your life of Christian faith in the world. Maybe you are already in a small group or ministry team or similar context where you could introduce this model and journey together into forming habits of discernment and encounter for participation, through Scripture and testimony. Alternatively, you may have been challenged to think about forming or gathering such a group in order to embark on that journey together. Wherever you are and whatever you are doing, as a follower of Jesus and member of his body on earth, you have a vocation to testify to and participate in Christ's present ministry. Maybe you already have a clear sense of what your vocation to participation looks like, but might benefit from the rigour and reflexivity provided by the scriptural cycle to nurture the habits of spiritual and theological discernment to live out your vocation day by day. Maybe you have little sense of what encounter, testimony and participation mean for your (individual and corporate) situation. Practising the scriptural cycle with other Christians as part of a habit of discipleship might be an important tool for developing your discernment in this regard, and I hope the book has given you sufficient guidance and help in implementing the method.

Whether this book sparks a re-envisioning of all theological education for formation or simply provides yet one more theological reflection method for students to critique alongside the others, my hope is that readers might have found something thought-provoking and life-giving through engaging with the proposed model and method. My prayer is that, through using this and other similar models of reflective discernment, the Church of Christ might receive renewed confidence and passion to witness to its story in order to discern Christ at work and participate with Christ's ministry for the sake of the world and for God's glory.

Bibliography

Anderson, Ray S. (2001) *The Shape of Practical Theology: Empowering Ministry with Theological Praxis* (Downers Grove, IL: InterVarsity Press).

Bacote, Vincent, Laura C. Miguelez and Dennis L. Okholm (eds) (2004) *Evangelicals and Scripture: Tradition, Authority and Hermeneutics* (Downers Grove, IL: InterVarsity Press).

Ballard, Paul (2000) 'The Emergence of Pastoral and Practical Theology in Britain' in James Woodward and Stephen Pattison (eds) *The Blackwell Reader in Pastoral and Practical Theology* (Oxford: Blackwell), pp. 59–70.

Ballard, Paul and John Pritchard (2006) *Practical Theology in Action*, 2nd edn (London: SPCK).

Barth, Karl (2009a) *Church Dogmatics: I.1 The Doctrine of the Word of God § 1–7*, Study Edition, eds G. W. Bromiley and T. F. Torrance, (London: T & T Clark).

Barth, Karl (2009b) *Church Dogmatics: I.2 The Doctrine of the Word of God § 19–21*, Study Edition, eds G. W. Bromiley and T. F. Torrance, (London: T & T Clark).

Bauckham, Richard (2003) 'Reading Scripture as a Coherent Story' in Ellen F. Davis and Richard B. Hays (eds) *The Art of Reading Scripture* (Grand Rapids, MI: Eerdmans), pp. 38–53.

Bebbington, David W. (1989) *Evangelicalism in Modern Britain: A History From the 1730s to the 1980s* (London: Unwin Hyman).

Biggs, John and Catherine Tang (2011) *Teaching for Quality Learning at University*, 4th edn (Maidenhead: McGraw-Hill).

Bonhoeffer, Dietrich (2009) *Ethics: Dietrich Bonhoeffer Works, Volume 6*, trans. Reinhard Krauss, Charles C. West and Douglas W. Scott (Minneapolis, MN: Fortress Press).

Bonhoeffer, Dietrich (2015) *Life Together*, trans. D. W. Bloesch (Minneapolis, MN: Fortress Press).

Bonnington, Mark (2007) *Patterns in Charismatic Spirituality*, Grove Renewal Series 28 (Cambridge: Grove Books).

Brittain, Christopher Craig (2014) 'Why Ecclesiology Cannot Live By Doctrine Alone: A Reply to John Webster's "In the Society of God"' in *Ecclesial Practices* 1: 5–30.

Brock, Brian and Bernd Wannenwetsch (2018) *The Therapy of the Christian Body: A Theological Exposition of Paul's First Letter to the Corinthians, Volume 2* (Eugene, OR: Cascade Books).

Browning, Don (1996) *A Fundamental Practical Theology: Descriptive and Strategic Approaches* (Minneapolis, MN: Fortress Press).

Brueggemann, Walter (1978) *The Prophetic Imagination* (Minneapolis, MN: Fortress Press).

Brueggemann, Walter (1993) *The Bible and Postmodern Imagination: Texts Under Negotiation* (London: SCM Press).

Brueggemann, Walter (1998) *Westminster Bible Companion: Isaiah 40–66* (Louisville, KY: Westminster John Knox Press).

Buchanan, Colin (1977) *Encountering Charismatic Worship*, Grove Worship Series 51 (Nottingham: Grove Books).

Cameron, Helen, Philip Richter, Douglas Davies and Frances Ward (eds) (2005) *Studying Local Churches: A Handbook* (London: SCM Press).

Cameron, Helen, Deborah Bhatti, Catherine Duce, James Sweeney and Clare Watkins (2010) *Talking About God in Practice: Theological Action Research and Practical Theology* (London: SCM Press).

Cameron, Helen, John Reader, Victoria Slater with Chris Rowland (2012) *Theological Reflection for Human Flourishing: Pastoral Practice and Public Theology* (London: SCM Press).

Cameron, Helen and Catherine Duce (2013) *Researching Practice in Mission and Ministry: A Companion* (London: SCM Press).

Cartledge, Mark J. (2003) *Practical Theology: Charismatic and Empirical Perspectives* (London: Paternoster Press).

Cartledge, Mark J. (2006) *Encountering the Spirit: The Charismatic Tradition* (London: Darton, Longman and Todd).

Cartledge, Mark J. (2015) *The Mediation of the Spirit* (Grand Rapids, MI: Eerdmans).

Cartledge, Mark. J. (2017) *Testimony in the Spirit: Rescripting Ordinary Pentecostal Theology* (London: Routledge).

Chopp, Rebecca (2009) 'Practical Theology and Liberation' in Lewis S. Mudge and James N. Poling (eds) *Formation and Reflection: The Promise of Practical Theology* (Minneapolis, MN: Fortress Press), pp. 120–38.

Church of England (1981) *The Charismatic Movement in the Church of England* (London: CIO Publishing).

Clark, David. K. (2003) *To Know and Love God: Foundations of Evangelical Theology* (Wheaton, IL: Crossway Books).

Collins, Helen (2018) 'Weaving a Web: Developing a Feminist Practical Theology Methodology from a Charismatic Perspective' in Nicola Slee, Fran Porter and Anne Phillips (eds) *Researching Female Faith* (Oxford: Taylor & Francis), pp. 54–69.

Cox, Harvey (1995) *Fire From Heaven: The Rise of Pentecostal Spirituality and Reshaping of Religion in the Twenty First Century* (Cambridge, MA: Da Capo Press).

Craigie, Peter C. and Marvin E. Tate (2004) *Psalms 1–50: Word Biblical Commentary 19*, 2nd edn (Nashville, TN: Thomas Nelson).

Daly, Mary (1973) *Beyond God the Father: Toward a Philosophy of Women's Liberation* (Boston, MA: Beacon Press).

DeVries, Dawn (2006) '"Ever to be Reformed According to the Word of God": Can the Scripture Principle be Redeemed for Feminist Theology?' in Amy Plantinga Pauw and Serene Jones (eds) *Feminist and Womanist Essays in Reformed Dogmatics* (Louisville, KY: Westminster John Knox Press), pp. 40–57.

Drake, Nick J. (2014) *A Deeper Note: The 'Informal' Theology of Contemporary Sung Worship*, Grove Worship Series 218 (Cambridge: Grove Books).

Farley, Edward (1983) *Theologia: The Fragmentation and Unity of Theological Education* (Philadelphia, PA: Fortress Press).

Fiorenza, Elisabeth Schüssler (1984) *Bread Not Stone: The Challenge of Feminist Biblical Interpretation* (Boston, MA: Beacon Press).

Fowler, James W. (1983) 'Practical Theology and the Shaping of Christian Lives' in Don Browning (ed.) *Practical Theology: The Emerging Field in Theology, Church, and World* (New York, NY: Harper & Row), pp. 148–66.

Fowler, James W. (1985) 'Practical Theology and Theological Education: Some Models and Questions' in *Theology Today* 42.1: 43–58.

Frei, Hans W. (1974) *The Eclipse of Biblical Narrative: A Study in Eighteenth and Nineteenth Century Hermeneutics* (New Haven, CT: Yale University Press).

Freire, Paulo (2017) *Pedagogy of the Oppressed*, trans. Myra Bergman Ramos (London: Penguin Classics).

Fulkerson, Mary McClintock (2007) *Places of Redemption: Theology for a Worldly Church* (Oxford: Oxford University Press).

Gilligan, Carol (1982) *In a Different Voice: Psychological Theory and Women's Development* (Cambridge, MA: Harvard University Press).

Goldingay, John (1996) 'Charismatic Spirituality: Some Theological Reflections' in *Theology*, 99 (789): 178–87.

Goldingay, John (2006) *Psalms, Volume 1: Psalms 1–41, Baker Commentary on the Old Testament Wisdom and Psalms* (Grand Rapids, MI: Baker Academic).

Gooder, Paula (ed.) (2008) *Searching for Meaning: An Introduction to Interpreting the New Testament* (London: SPCK).

Graham, Elaine (2002) *Transforming Practice: Pastoral Theology in an Age of Uncertainty* (Eugene, OR: Wipf and Stock).

Graham, Elaine (2013) 'Is Practical Theology a Form of Action Research?' in *International Journal of Practical Theology* 17.1: 148–78.

Graham, Elaine, Heather Walton and Frances Ward (eds) (2005) *Theological Reflection: Methods* (London: SCM Press).

Graham, Elaine, Heather Walton and Frances Ward (eds) (2007) *Theological Reflection: Sources* (London: SCM Press).

Green, Laurie (2012) *Let's Do Theology: Resources for Contextual Theology*, new edn (London: Bloomsbury Academic).

Grenz, Stanley J. (2004) 'Nurturing the Soul, Informing the Mind: The Genesis of the Evangelical Scriptural Principle' in Vincent Bacote, Laura C. Miguelez and Dennis L. Okholm (eds) *Evangelicals and Scripture: Tradition, Authority and Hermeneutics* (Downers Grove, IL: InterVarsity Press), pp. 21–41.

Groome, Thomas H. (1980) *Christian Religious Education: Sharing Our Stories and Vision* (New York, NY: Harper & Row).

Gutierrez, Gustavo (1988) *A Theology of Liberation*, revised edn (London: SCM Press).

Hastings, Thomas John (2007) *Practical Theology and the One Body of Christ: Towards a Missional-Ecumenical Model* (Grand Rapids, MI: Eerdmans).

Heyer, Kristin E. (2004) 'How does Theology go Public? Rethinking the Debate Between David Tracy and George Lindbeck' in *Political Theology* 5.3: 307–27.

Hocken, Peter D. (2002) 'Charismatic Movement' in Stanley M. Burgess and Eduard M. van der Maas (eds) *The New International Dictionary of Pentecostal and Charismatic Movements* (Grand Rapids, MI: Zondervan), pp. 477–519.

Hudson, D. Neil (1998) 'Worship: Singing a New Song in a Strange Land' in Keith Warrington (ed.) *Pentecostal Perspectives* (Carlisle: Paternoster Press), pp. 177–203.

Hunsinger, Deborah van Deusen (1995) *Theology and Pastoral Counseling: A New Interdisciplinary Approach* (Grand Rapids, MI: Eerdmans).

Jacobson, Rolf A. (2014) 'Psalm 23: You are With Me' in Nancy de Claisse-Walford, Rolf A. Jacobson and Beth LaNeel Tanner, *The Book of Psalms: The New International Commentary on the Old Testament* (Grand Rapids, MI: Eerdmans), pp. 238–46.

Jagessar, Michael N. and Stephen Burns (2014) *Christian Worship: Postcolonial Perspectives* (London: Routledge).

Johns, Cheryl Bridges (1998) *Pentecostal Formation: A Pedagogy Among the Oppressed* (Eugene, OR: Wipf & Stock).

Jones, Serene (2019) *Trauma and Grace: Theology in a Ruptured World*, 2nd edn (Louisville, KY: Westminster John Knox Press).

BIBLIOGRAPHY

Killen, Patricia O'Connell and John de Beer (2002) *The Art of Theological Reflection* (New York, NY: Crossroad).

Kim, Kirsteen (2008) *The Holy Spirit in the World: A Global Conversation* (London: SPCK).

Kings, Graham (2003) 'Canal, River and Rapids: Contemporary Evangelicalism in the Church of England' in *Anvil* 20.3: 167–84.

Kolb, Daniel (1984) *Experiential Learning: Experience as the Source of Learning and Development* (Upper Saddle River, NJ: Prentice Hall).

Land, Steven J. (2010) *Pentecostal Spirituality: A Passion for the Kingdom* (Cleveland, TN: CPT Press).

Lartey, Emmanuel (2000) 'Practical Theology as a Theological Form' in James Woodward and Stephen Pattison (eds) *The Blackwell Reader in Pastoral and Practical Theology* (Oxford: Blackwell), pp. 128–34.

Lewis, Hannah (2007) *Deaf Liberation Theology* (Aldershot: Ashgate).

Lindbeck, George A. (2002) *The Church in a Postliberal Age*, ed. James J. Buckley (London: SCM Press).

Lindbeck, George A. (2009) *The Nature of Doctrine: Religion and Theology in a Postliberal Age*, 25th anniversary edn (London: SPCK).

Loder, James (1999) 'Normativity and Context in Practical Theology: The Interdisciplinary Issue' in Fredrich Schweitzer and J. A. Van der Ven (eds) *Practical Theology: International Perspectives* (New York, NY: Peter Lang), pp. 359–81.

Loughlin, Gerard (1996) *Telling God's Story: Bible, Church and Narrative Theology* (Cambridge: Cambridge University Press).

McGrath, Alister (2000) *Christian Theology: An Introduction*, 2nd edn (Oxford: Blackwell).

McLeish, Tom (2014) *Faith and Wisdom in Science* (Oxford: Oxford University Press).

Mays, James L. (1994) *Psalms: Interpretation – A Bible Commentary for Teaching and Preaching* (Louisville, KY: John Knox Press).

Metz, Johann Baptist (1980) *Faith in History and Society: Toward a Practical Fundamental Theology* (New York, NY: Seabury-Crossroad).

Miller-McLemore, Bonnie J. (1994) *Also a Mother: Work and Family as Theological Dilemma* (Nashville, TN: Abingdon Press).

Miller-McLemore, Bonnie J. (ed.) (2014) *The Wiley Blackwell Companion to Practical Theology* (Chichester: Wiley Blackwell).

Moschella, Mary Clark (2008) *Ethnography as Pastoral Practice: An Introduction* (Clevedon, OH: The Pilgrim Press).

Mudge, Lewis S. and James N. Poling (eds) (2009) *Formation and Reflection: The Promise of Practical Theology* (Minneapolis, MN: Fortress Press).

O'Neill, Gary and Liz Shercliff (2018) *Straw for the Bricks: Theological Reflection in Practice* (London: SCM Press).

Osmer, Richard R. (2008) *Practical Theology: An Introduction* (Grand Rapids, MI: Eerdmans).

Pattison, Stephen (1989) 'Some Straw for the Bricks: A Basic Introduction to Theological Reflection' in *Contact* 99: 2–9.

Pattison, Stephen, Judith Thompson and John Green (2003) 'Theological Reflection for the Real World: Time to Think Again' in *British Journal of Theological Education* 13.2: 119–31.

Purves, Andrew (2004) *Reconstructing Pastoral Theology: A Christological Foundation* (Louisville, KY: Westminster John Knox Press).

Rah, Soong-Chan (2009) *The Next Evangelicalism: Releasing the Church from Western Cultural Captivity* (Downers Grove, IL: InterVarsity Press).

Root, Andrew (2014) *Christopraxis: A Practical Theology of the Cross* (Minneapolis, MN: Fortress Press).

Ruether, Rosemary R. (1983) *Sexism and God-Talk: Towards a Feminist Theology* (London: SCM Press).

Scharen, Christian (2004) *Public Worship and Public Work: Character and Commitment in Local Congregational Life* (Collegeville, MN: Liturgical Press).

Schipani, Daniel S. (1984) *Conscientization and Creativity: Paulo Freire and Christian Education* (Lanham, MD: University Press of America).

Schleiermacher, Fredrich (2011 [1830]) *Brief Outline on the Study of Theology*, 3rd edn (Louisville, KY: Westminster John Knox Press).

Schon, Donald A. (1991) *The Reflective Practitioner: How Professionals Think in Action* (Aldershot: Ashgate).

Scotland, Nigel (2000) *Charismatics and the New Millennium: The Impact of Charismatic Christianity from 1960 to the New Millennium* (Surrey: Eagle Inter Publishing Service).

Segundo, Juan-Luis (1982) *The Liberation of Theology* (Maryknoll, NY: Orbis).

Smail, Thomas A., Andrew Walker and Nigel Wright (1995) *Charismatic Renewal: The Search for a Theology* (London: SPCK).

Smith, James K. A. (2010) *Thinking in Tongues: Pentecostal Contributions to Christian Philosophy* (Grand Rapids, MI: Eerdmans).

Steven, James (2002) *Worship in the Spirit: Charismatic Worship in the Church of England* (Carlisle: Paternoster Press).

Stoddart, Eric (2014) *Advancing Practical Theology: Critical Discipleship for Disturbing Times* (London: SCM Press).

Stratis, Justin (2016) 'Widening the Frame on Redemptive History: A Response to Michael Goheen' in Jason S. Sexten and Paul Weston (eds) *The End of Theology: Shaping Theology for the Sake of Mission* (Minneapolis, MN: Fortress Press), pp. 21–34.

Suurmond, Jean-Jacques (1994) *Word and Spirit at Play: Towards a Charismatic Theology* (London: SCM Press).

Swinton, John (2012) *Dementia: Living the Memories of God* (Grand Rapids, MI: Eerdmans).

Swinton, John and Harriet Mowat (2006) *Practical Theology and Qualitative Research* (London: SCM Press).

Tate, W. Randolph (2008) *Biblical Interpretation: An Integrated Approach*, 3rd edn (Grand Rapids, MI: BakerAcademic).

Thompson, Judith, with Stephen Pattison and Ross Thompson (2019) *SCM Studyguide to Theological Reflection*, 2nd edn (London: SCM Press).

Tillich, Paul (1953) *Systematic Theology, Volume 1* (Welwyn, Herts: James Nisbet).

Tomlin, Graham (2011) *The Prodigal Spirit: The Trinity, the Church and the Future of the World* (London: Alpha International).

Tracy, David (1983) 'The Foundations of Practical Theology' in Don Browning (ed.) *Practical Theology: The Emerging Field in Theology, Church, and World* (New York, NY: Harper & Row), pp. 61–82.

Tracy, David (1989) 'The Uneasy Alliance Reconceived: Catholic Theological Method, Modernity, and Postmodernity' in *Theological Studies* 50: 548–70.

Tracy, David (1990) 'On Reading the Scriptures Theologically' in B. Marshall (ed.), *Essays in Conversation with George Lindbeck* (Notre Dame, IN: Notre Dame University Press), pp. 35–68.

Tracy, David (1996) *Blessed Rage for Order: The New Pluralism in Theology* (Chicago, IL: The University of Chicago Press).

Trible, Phyllis (1984) *Texts of Terror: Literary-Feminist Readings of Biblical Narratives* (Philadelphia, PA: Fortress Press).

Village, Andrew (2007) *The Bible and Lay People: An Empirical Approach to Ordinary Hermeneutics* (Aldershot: Ashgate).

Volf, Miroslav (2010) *Captive to the Word of God: Engaging the Scriptures from Contemporary Theological Reflection* (Grand Rapids, MI: Eerdmans).

Walton, Heather (1993) 'Breaking Open the Bible' in Elaine Graham and Margaret Halsey (eds) *Life Cycles: Women and Pastoral Care* (London: SPCK), pp. 192–9.

Ward, Frances (2005) *Lifelong Learning: Theological Education and Supervision* (London: SCM Press).

Ward, Pete (2005) *Selling Worship: How What We Sing has Changed the Church* (Milton Keynes: Paternoster Press).

Ward, Pete (2008) *Participation and Mediation: A Practical Theology for the Liquid Church* (London: SCM Press).

Ward, Pete (2017) *Introducing Practical Theology: Mission, Ministry and the Life of the Church* (Grand Rapids, MI: Baker Academic).

Warrington, Keith (2008) *Pentecostal Theology: A Theology of Encounter* (London: T & T Clark).

Webber, Robert E. (2002) *The Younger Evangelicals: Facing the Challenges of the New World* (Grand Rapids, MI: Baker Books).

Webster, John (2003) *Holy Scripture: A Dogmatic Sketch* (Cambridge: Cambridge University Press).

Webster, John (2012) '"In the Society of God": Some Principles of Ecclesiology' in Pete Ward (ed.) *Perspectives of Ecclesiology and Ethnography* (Grand Rapids, MI: Eerdmans), pp. 200–22.

Whitehead, James D. and Evelyn Eaton Whitehead (1995) *Method in Ministry: Theological Reflection and Christian Ministry*, revised edn (Lanham, MD: Sheed & Ward).

Wilcock, Michael (2001) *The Message of Psalms 1–72: The Bible Speaks Today* (Nottingham: Inter-Varsity Press).

Wiles, Maurice (1987) 'Scriptural Authority and Theological Construction: The Limitations of Narrative Interpretation' in Garrett Green (ed.) *Scriptural Authority and Narrative Interpretation* (Philadelphia, PA: Fortress Press), pp. 42–58.

Williams, Rowan (1999) *On Christian Theology: Challenges in Contemporary Theology* (Oxford: Blackwell).

Woodward, James and Stephen Pattison (eds) (2000) *The Blackwell Reader in Pastoral and Practical Theology* (Oxford: Blackwell).

Wright, Nicholas Thomas (1992) *The New Testament and the People of God* (London: SPCK).

Wright, Nicholas Thomas (2005) *Scripture and the Authority of God* (London: SPCK).

Yong, Amos (2017) *The Hermeneutical Spirit: Theological Interpretation and Scriptural Imagination for the 21st Century* (Eugene, OR: Cascade Books)

Index